THE COMPLETE IDIOT'S GUIDE® TO

Playing
Bass Guitar

THE **COMPLETE**
IDIOT'S
GUIDE® TO

Playing

Bass Guitar

by David Hodge

ALPHA

A member of Penguin Group (USA) Inc.

This book is dedicated to the memory of my parents, Margaret and Donald, who showed me the joys of music and playing with others, the importance of teaching and sharing, and the necessity of being at peace with life.

ALPHA BOOKS

Published by Penguin Group (USA) Inc.

Penguin Group (USA) Inc., 375 Hudson Street, New York, New York 10014, USA • Penguin Group (Canada), 90 Eglinton Avenue East, Suite 700, Toronto, Ontario M4P 2Y3, Canada (a division of Pearson Penguin Canada Inc.) • Penguin Books Ltd., 80 Strand, London WC2R 0RL, England • Penguin Ireland, 25 St. Stephen's Green, Dublin 2, Ireland (a division of Penguin Books Ltd.) • Penguin Group (Australia), 250 Camberwell Road, Camberwell, Victoria 3124, Australia (a division of Pearson Australia Group Pty. Ltd.) • Penguin Books India Pvt. Ltd., 11 Community Centre, Panchsheel Park, New Delhi—110 017, India • Penguin Group (NZ), 67 Apollo Drive, Rosedale, North Shore, Auckland 1311, New Zealand (a division of Pearson New Zealand Ltd.) • Penguin Books (South Africa) (Pty.) Ltd., 24 Sturdee Avenue, Rosebank, Johannesburg 2196, South Africa • Penguin Books Ltd., Registered Offices: 80 Strand, London WC2R 0RL, England

International Standard Book Number: 978-1-59257-311-0
Library of Congress Catalog Card Number: 2006924209

15   10 9

Interpretation of the printing code: The rightmost number of the first series of numbers is the year of the book's printing; the rightmost number of the second series of numbers is the number of the book's printing. For example, a printing code of 06-1 shows that the first printing occurred in 2006.

Printed in the United States of America

Publisher: *Marie Butler-Knight*

Editorial Director: *Mike Sanders*

Managing Editor: *Billy Fields*

Acquisitions Editor: *Michele Wells*

Senior Development Editor: *Phil Kitchel*

Production Editors: *Billy Fields, Kayla Dugger*

Copy Editor: *Amy Borrelli*

Cartoonist: *Richard King*

Book Designers: *Trina Wurst/Kurt Owens*

Cover Designer: *Bill Thomas*

Indexer: *Julie Bess*

Layout: *Brian Massey*

Proofreader: *Aaron Black*

Contents at a Glance

Contents

Introduction

It takes a special person to play the bass guitar. He or she must be able to make ordinary things (such as keeping time and establishing harmony) interesting, while making exceptional things (such as imaginative arpeggios, beautiful bass lines, and lightning-quick runs of notes) seem like just another part of a song. And he or she has to do this in a supportive role, without being the slightest bit concerned with having the spotlight on them.

A good bassist can help every member of a band be better because, in essence, the bass player *is* every member of the band. He or she punches out the beat like a drummer, creates rhythmic and chordal patterns like the rhythm guitarist, and adds elegant embellishments like a lead guitarist, keyboard player, or other soloist.

That's a lot to ask of a person, isn't it? But the bass player loves what his or her instrument can do and understands that each song calls out for the bassist to fill a specific role (sometimes multiple roles) and rises to the occasion each time.

Why This Book Is for You

The Complete Idiot's Guide to Playing Bass Guitar is a step-by-step guide designed to get you started, and to get you well on your way to becoming a bass player. You will learn the basics of bass guitar, and you will also learn the basics of music, which are essential to becoming a good bassist.

Just as important, this book is meant to help you *think* like a bass player. No matter what type of music you like and want to play, the bassist's approach has to be concerned with holding things together—with making the song the focus. The skills you learn in this book will allow you to play bass on *any* song, in *any* style. You will also learn that you can transfer musical ideas from one style to another, creating something new and unique in your playing.

I tend to have the "teach a man to fish" philosophy about things. In music, and especially where the bass guitar is concerned, being able to think, and think on your feet, will make you a better musician. Even if you just want to play some songs with your friends, you will find that the more you can put into your playing, the happier you will be. And this book will get you there. Where you end up is, of course, totally up to you—but I hope you will find yourself playing bass guitar and enjoying music for the rest of your life.

The Evolution of a Bass Player

As you'll read in the first chapter, most people come to the bass either because they were "born" bassists or "converted" to the ways of the bass guitar. Either way is good, and, not surprisingly, both ways tend to follow the same evolutionary path. People start out with the basics (learning the notes and where they are on the bass) and gradually fan out from there, learning how to find the roots of chords, what notes make up chords, how to progress naturally from one chord to another by means of arpeggios and scales, and how to use all this knowledge to come up with bass lines, riffs, and solos. The bass player incorporates each new skill, each new bit of knowledge, into his or her playing, becoming better and more confident with each step. From arpeggios to jazz-style walking bass lines, from playing hammer-ons to creating and improvising your own bass lines, you will find everything here to get you off to a great start as a bass player.

This book deliberately follows this natural evolutionary path, taking care to let you learn at your own pace. If you already know some things about playing, you can skip ahead to sections of unfamiliar material. If you feel like you need a bit of a refresher on some aspects of music or playing, then take a step back a chapter or two. You determine what you learn and how quickly. Think of this book as a personal guide, always at your beck and call.

What You'll Find in This Book

The Complete Idiot's Guide to Playing Bass Guitar is composed of 28 chapters in 6 parts. They are:

Part 1, "Meet Your New Bass," introduces you to the bass guitar and to the role of the bass player. You will learn about the parts of your new instrument, how to go about shopping for one, how to tune your new bass, and how to start producing music.

Part 2, "Facing the Music," will teach you about reading both bass guitar tablature and music notation. You don't need to know how to read music to play the bass; if you choose, you can get through this entire book without learning to do so, but it is an incredibly easy skill to acquire and will help you a lot should you decide to become a professional bass player. It will also help you a lot if you just plan to play with some friends!

Part 3, "The Great Leap Forward," shows you how to form the major scale and chord arpeggios for just about every chord you'll ever encounter. This section will provide you with a strong foundation for becoming a solid bass player, as well as give you skills you'll use in soloing and improvising.

Part 4, "Movin' and Groovin'," takes you from being a "static" bass player to one who creates interesting, moving bass lines. You'll also learn about key signatures and chord progressions in this section.

Part 5, "Moving On Up," raises your playing up a notch or two by introducing you to some easy-to-learn advanced playing techniques and to playing all over the neck of your bass guitar.

Part 6, "Playing for Life," explores some more advanced techniques and looks at the bass player's role in almost every musical genre. Whether you want to play rock, country, blues, jazz, or funk, you'll find tips and examples of each style here.

At the end of the book you will find helpful appendices, listing sources, books, and recordings, to help you grow as a bass player.

Using the CD

Throughout this book, you will find an icon that looks like this:

This indicates that the example in question is on the audio CD included in this book. In addition to a tuning track and some exercises and audio examples of various scales, arpeggios, and riffs, you will also find a good number of "play-along" or "jam-along" tracks. Because playing bass usually involves being in a band, we've taken the liberty of providing you with one! These jam-along tracks often will not have a bass part, so it will be up to you to be the bassist for the band.

To best utilize these jam-along tracks, simply cue up the track you want and then hit the Repeat function on your CD player (or your computer's CD player). This way, you can work on a specific song to your heart's content.

I'd like to thank Todd Mack and Will Curtiss (another wonderful bass player!) of Off The Beat-n-Track Studio, Southfield, Massachusetts, for their invaluable assistance in recording, engineering, mixing, and mastering the CD.

And it would also be good to thank "The Complete Idiots Guide to Playing Bass Guitar Band" for the time and energy and fun they provided: Karen Berger, piano; Jeff Brownstein and Greg Nease, guitars; and Anne O'Neil, drums. And each one of them plays bass, too!

Other Features

In addition to the text, music examples, and audio examples, you will also find numerous *sidebars*—each offering definitions or containing tips or other information that you will find useful in your studies. These are the four types of sidebars that occur in this book:

Rock Bottom

These contain little bits and pieces of information that can help you to understand more about music and your bass.

Basso Profondo

These take questions that most beginning bass players have and give you answers straight from professional bass players and bass manufacturers.

Covering the Basses

These offer tips and advice on numerous subjects from deciding on playing left- or right-handed to laying down some funky bass lines.

def•i•ni•tion

These provide definitions and details about specific musical terms and bass-playing techniques.

Acknowledgments

I'd like to thank my agent, Marilyn Allen, and all the people at Alpha Books, including but not limited to Marie Butler-Knight, Mike Sanders, Billy Fields, Kayla Dugger, Michele Wells, Phil Kitchel, Amy Borelli, Trina Wurst, Tom Stephens, and Renee Wilmeth for giving me the opportunity to work on this project and for their hard work on turning my manuscript into the book you now hold. Thank you to Kenn Smith for taking part in this project, as well as to Helena Bouchez for her many contacts in the bassists' community. I'd also like to thank Paul Hackett, creator and owner of the Guitar Noise website (www.guitarnoise.com), for introducing my music lessons to people all over the world.

To my students I'd also like to offer thanks for all the things you've taught me. I hope I continue to grow as a teacher.

No acknowledgements on my part could ever be complete without a thank you to Laura Pager and Greg Nease for a lifetime of friendship and support (musical and otherwise), and to Karen Berger, for her assistance, patience, and insights into almost all things concerning writing and music.

Finally, I'd like to thank all the great bass players I've been lucky enough to know, to play with, and to learn from, especially Pauline Blackwood, Dan Lasley, Pete Mazzeri, Tony Nuccio, and Joe Nuccio.

And an extra special thank you to Roy Wogelius, whose bass playing has been my inspiration (and measuring stick) for more than 30 years now.

Special Thanks To The Technical Editor

I would like to give a very special thank you to Dan Lakin, owner of Lakland Bass in Chicago, for serving as technical editor on *The Complete Idiot's Guide to Learning Bass Guitar*. Dan spent a lot of time answering my questions and making certain that this book gives you the best possible instruction, and I am indebted to him and his staff for their participation in this project.

Let Me Know What You Think

Teachers and writers, like other people, can't live in a vacuum. Your thoughts and opinions are not only appreciated, they are usually quite helpful. Please feel free to write me anytime at dhodgeguitar@aol.com. I try to answer each e-mail (an impossible task sometimes!), but I read and appreciate them all. I look forward to hearing from you and to hearing how things are going with your bass playing!

Don't Forget!

Becoming a good bass player involves many things. Knowledge is important, but so is putting that knowledge to practical use. Practicing the skills you learn is essential to becoming a better bassist. So no matter how much you enjoy reading this book and no matter how much you are learning from reading it, please do me a favor and put the book down from time to time and *play your bass!*

Trademarks

All terms mentioned in this book that are known to be or are suspected of being trademarks or service marks have been appropriately capitalized. Alpha Books and Penguin Group (USA) Inc. cannot attest to the accuracy of this information. Use of a term in this book should not be regarded as affecting the validity of any trademark or service mark.

Part 1

Meet Your New Bass

Welcome to the wonderful world of the bass guitar! You are about to take the first step on a lifelong journey of creating music. To make certain that your trip gets off to the best possible start, let's take a moment and check our gear. We'll take a quick look at the bass guitar, its history, and its anatomy, and then explore your options on purchasing your first bass. We'll also discuss the other equipment you'll need, such as an amplifier.

Once you have an instrument, you'll learn how to tune it and how to best position your hands to produce good clean notes. And you'll also get to sit in and play your bass guitar on a couple of jam-along songs!

The Bass and the Bassist

In This Chapter

♦ The roles (and character) of the bass guitarist

♦ A brief history of the bass guitar

♦ Bass guitar anatomy

♦ The "electric" parts

♦ Choices of strings

There's something special about you. Why else would you be interested in playing bass guitar? You could be drawn to the deep and majestic tones of the instrument. Perhaps its hypnotic, driving rhythms grab your imagination. Or maybe you're intrigued by the role of the bass player—providing the band's pulse while also serving up harmonies and the occasional lead line. The bass player does it all, usually leaving the glory to others.

The bass guitarist understands his instrument as well as the role of the bassist in the band. To get you started on the right path, this chapter will focus on both the bass and the bassist. We'll look at what makes each one tick and help you make some decisions about your bass before you even hold one in your hands.

The Role of the Bassist

It's no accident that the bassist and drummer, not just the drummer, are called the band's "rhythm section." Keeping the rhythm tight and steady should be every bass player's top priority. If a band can't hold the tempo of a song together, everyone notices.

But in addition to establishing and maintaining the beat, the bass player also provides harmonic support. The notes that he plays add to, and often define, the tonal textures of the music you hear. The bass player also often provides melodic "fills," short phrases of notes that give songs "hooks" or memorable qualities. Put on a copy of The Beatles' "Come Together" and you can hear for yourself. The right bass line can make an average song exciting and a great song unforgettable. Good bass lines also move a song along, providing musical links from one chord to another.

Keeping things steady, keeping things moving, keeping things musical, and keeping things interesting—these all fall under the care of the bassist.

Who Plays Bass?

Mention The Beatles, and everyone will say "Paul McCartney." Jazz lovers may immediately think of bassists Stanley Clarke or Jaco Pastorius. There's Sting, of course, with or without The Police.

But these bassists are the exception to the rule. Chances are that unless you are either into a particular band or truly into good bass playing, you think of the bassist as just "one of the guys in the group." But take a look around a music store or a bookstore or anyplace that sells CDs and recorded music. See all those CDs? Someone's playing bass on them! On many of them you might even find two or three bass players.

And there are many more bass players out there who you don't ever get to hear on the radio or the stereo. That middle-aged gentleman you met at a picnic last year who told the funniest stories? He plays bass! The young woman who runs the horse-riding program at summer camp? She's a bassist, too. The teenage boy who mows lawns for the older folks in the neighborhood? You guessed it. Likewise with the mom whose daughter plays piano in the high school jazz band. And the soft-spoken geology professor at the prestigious college? He might be the best of the bunch!

And let's not forget—you play bass! Or you will be playing one very soon.

The "Born" Bassist

Some people are simply born to play the bass guitar. Say what you want about the music of the '60s and the '70s, but for many it was a time when the bass guitar was the coolest instrument around. Anyone growing up listening to the bass players of this time couldn't help but want to play.

From the Motown grooves of James Jamerson to the thunderous, rocking bass lines of The Who's John Entwhisle; from the intricate, soulful R&B sounds of Chuck Rainey to the slapping, popping funk of Larry Graham; there was no end of idols for the aspiring bass player.

Those born to play the bass have got rhythm to spare. They could easily be drummers but want to also add melodies and harmonies to their music.

Almost everyone at some point takes a stab at playing a musical instrument of some sort, and the electric bass guitar is possibly one of the easiest instruments to start out on. If you've got a musical ear and a feel for rhythm, you can begin making music almost immediately and be jamming along with other people in next to no time. Unlike other instruments, such as the drums or guitar or piano, even the simplest bass lines sound *right* in a song. As a bassist, you have the luxury of learning as you go along.

The "Converted" Bassist

Many people don't start life as bass players. Some pick up the bass as a second instrument. Quite often a guitar player will take up the bass because there are too many guitarists in his band and, well, *someone* has to play bass!

"Converts" from the guitar often find playing the bass quite exhilarating. While many of the same techniques are used by both guitarists and bassists, the mindset of the bass player tends to be more "group oriented" than that of the guitar player. The song has to take precedence over the solo.

Pianists find the bass fun to play because it provides them with an ideal test of their knowledge of chords and music theory. Drummers get to expand their rhythmic skills. People who play "soloing" instruments such as the trumpet or the saxophone find the best of both worlds, being both group player and occasional soloist.

Whether you are a convert or someone who was destined to play bass, the instrument offers unlimited fun and plenty of challenges.

> **Rock Bottom**
>
> Most of the elder statesmen of the bass guitar are converts who didn't start out on the instrument. Carol Kaye, Robbie Shakespeare, Jack Casady, Joe Osborn, even Paul McCartney were guitarists who ended up with basses in their hands. Phil Lesh of the Grateful Dead is a trumpet player. But because of their playing, many people today have the chance to become "born bassists."

Low Notes Through the Ages

As far as musical instruments go, the bass guitar is definitely one of the younger children. The first commercially successful bass guitar, the Fender Precision Bass, dates only back to 1951.

The immediate ancestor of the bass guitar, in spirit at least, has to be the double bass, also called the stand-up bass. You've no doubt seen them in orchestras, looming large in the background. Or perhaps you've caught a performance by a jazz combo whose bass player uses one.

Like the bass guitar, the *double bass* has four strings, and, again just like the bass guitar, these string are tuned to the notes E, A, D, and G. Unlike most bass guitars though, the double bass is a fretless instrument, which means that you have to be a pretty competent musician to play one.

The double bass may seem like a dinosaur to people now, even though it's still used in orchestras and is the instrument of choice for many jazz bass players. In its infancy, though, this instrument underwent many of the same growing pains as the bass guitar. In Europe during the 1600s, many bass players used five-string basses. Three-string basses were all the rage for awhile.

As more music came to be performed by smaller bands, the bass player tagged along. All the big bands had one. And as the big bands became smaller, the bass player still hung on. Other bandmates might have been out looking for work, but if you could play stand-up bass, chances were you could count on getting a job.

> **def•i•ni•tion**
>
> The "double" of **double bass** has multiple meanings. While touching upon the instrument's size, it also refers to its role in the orchestra. Before the nineteenth century, bass parts were usually the same as the cello, played an octave lower; "double" refers to both "double octave" and "doubling" a part. "Double" also means "lower," as in "double bassoon." The bass has other nicknames due to its size, such as "doghouse" bass.

The Discovery of Electricity

The idea of the electric bass, as opposed to the electric bass guitar, has been around for over 75 years. Throughout the 1930s, numerous instrument manufacturers produced what were, essentially, electric double basses.

In 1936, Paul Tutmarc built what is considered to be the first solid body electric bass guitar. His instruments didn't catch on, however, and the world had to wait another 15 years for Leo Fender and his Precision Bass.

Leo Fender had already made a name for himself by creating the Broadcaster (later renamed the Telecaster) electric guitar. His Precision Bass, the first line of mass-produced bass guitars, were simply larger Broadcasters. This made them much more portable than the huge acoustic double basses, which he called "doghouses." The name "Precision" referred to two things: the instrument being fretted gave the bass player more precise intonation than one would have playing the acoustic; and the Fender factory's machinery was considered more precise than the tools of a typical luthier of that time.

Bass Anatomy 101

Fender's design for his Precision Bass has been the basic blueprint for just about every electric bass built since 1951. You can find body shapes of all types, but the essentials are pretty much the same. The following illustration points out the main parts.

Head and Neck

Unless you own a very unusual bass, the headstock is where you'll find the tuning gears of your instrument. These are used to tighten and loosen the strings of your bass, thus raising or lowering the pitch of the string. You'll be learning how to tune your guitar in Chapter 3.

The headstock meets the neck at the nut, which is a slotted piece of plastic, graphite, wood, or metal that holds each string as it passes on down the neck.

The neck of the bass has two sides. The flat side (where you put your fingers) is called the fretboard or fingerboard. The small strips of metal embedded in the fingerboard are your frets. Usually the fingerboard is made of a different piece of wood than the neck and glued onto it, but there are basses whose neck and fingerboard are made of the same piece of wood. Often, the neck will be maple while the fingerboard is rosewood, ebony, or a different piece of maple.

Necks can be attached to the body in one of three ways—they are glued on, bolted on, or are already part of the same piece of wood that makes up the body. The latter is what is called a "neck-through."

Inside the neck is a metal rod to maintain the curvature of the neck and keep the tension of the strings from causing your neck to warp. It's called the *truss rod* and it has a nut on one end that you can use to adjust the neck's tension and bowing. From time to time the truss rod will need some attention. We'll cover that in Chapter 27.

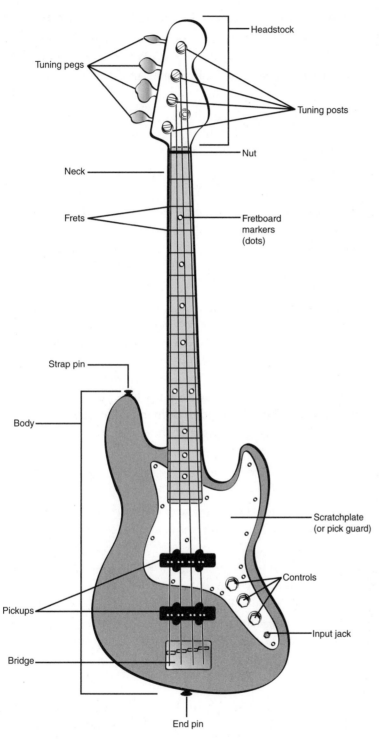

Anatomy of the bass guitar.

Body and Soul

The body of the electric bass guitar is usually solid wood (often ash, maple, or alder). There are also many hollow body and semi-hollow body basses available, which some players prefer since they sound a little more like the old acoustic double basses.

To protect the body from most minor mishaps, most new basses have polyurethane finishes. Lacquer is also still used, often to beautiful effect, on the bass's body.

Many basses will also have a pick guard, or scratchplate. This is to protect the wood of the guitar from getting scarred by the use of a pick. Most bass players use their fingers to play instead of a pick, so don't be too concerned if your bass doesn't have a scratchplate.

The bridge holds the end of each string to the body of the bass guitar.

Your bass will also have two pins where you can attach the ends of a guitar strap, so you don't have to worry about dropping your instrument. The end pin is at the base of the body while the second strap pin, depending on the size and shape of the body, is usually located somewhere on the body close to the neck.

There will be a set of control knobs on the body of your bass. The number and purpose of the control knobs varies from manufacturer to manufacturer and even model to model. Usually you will have a volume control and a tone control. Sometimes there will be one set for each pickup and sometimes there will be one volume control and two tone controls. The volume adjusts the loudness of the bass while the tone adjusts the balance between the treble and bass tones by trimming the highs.

There will also be an input jack where you connect one end of your cable. The other end will go into the amplifier.

The Inner Self

There's a lot more going on inside your bass than you'd suspect. Cavities have been routed out and covered with plates, and this is where you find many of what I call the "mystery parts."

The pickups contain magnets and are responsible for turning the vibration of your strings into the sounds you hear from your amplifier. Depending on your bass guitar, the pickups may be arranged in different ways. A lot of thought (and engineering) goes into the placement of the pickups on the guitar. Trying out different types will help you to find the sound that's best for you.

Active Electronics

Most bass guitars work without supplying the bass with additional power. This means that your pickups work when you connect your bass to the amplifier.

Some basses have active electronics, which are separate controls for treble and bass tones, much like the controls of a car stereo. Some offer a control of midrange as well. If your bass has active electronics, there will be a cavity for the battery or batteries.

Some active-electronic bass guitars have a bypass switch so that you can turn them into passive-electronic instruments in case of the batteries going dead at the wrong time. But it's still smart to keep extra batteries in your case.

Although active electronics offer a player more options, many bassists prefer the simpler traditional set-up of "passive electronics."

Strings

Think of your strings as part of your bass. The type of strings you choose for your instrument can vary greatly in tone. Some people prefer the jangle of roundwound strings while others like the mellow, almost acoustic sound of the flatwound.

The invention of the overwound string, way back in the 1600s, was a blessing for bass players. Before this, gut, woven into a big cord like strands of a rope, was the standard string material. But to get the deep, low notes of a bass, you needed one really thick piece of gut! When they started winding metal wire around the outside of a gut core string, they got thinner strings that sounded better than the pure gut ones.

Flatwounds

Because the double bass is often played with a bow, the optimal string surface is a smooth one. This is accomplished, for the strings of most double basses, by giving the wound string a final wrap of flat metal tape.

The early electric basses used the same string type as their acoustic upright counterparts. While most basses these days come from the shop with roundwound strings, flatwounds are still the choice of many bass players. They offer a "warm," or mellow, sound that fits most styles of music. Some people like them because they don't wear the frets of the bass (or your fingertips!) as much as roundwounds can. Bassists who own fretless basses prefer them as well.

Roundwounds

Roundwound strings were invented by James How, a British string maker, in the early 1960s. Round nickel wire, used in place of the final flat metal tape, gives roundwound strings a sharp, aggressive sound. "Bright" or "trebly" would be most people's description. They certainly propel the bass into the limelight, giving it a clear, crisp sound. If you're into what I call the "loud stuff," roundwound strings might be the choice for you.

You can see that you've got a whole bunch of choices ahead of you—not only concerning strings, but also dealing with bodies and necks and all sorts of things. That's okay because it's a good place to be. And you're in good company with your fellow bass players!

Basso Profondo

Q: Do the type of strings I use make a big difference in my sound or style of play?

A: Yes and no. A good player can use most types of commercially available strings and play whatever style of music the situation calls for and sound just fine. However, there are particular types of strings that go together with certain eras of pop music. For example, there were no roundwound strings before the early '70s, so any of the Motown or Beatles hits from the '60s were recorded with flatwounds, the only string type then available. Consequently, when you use a bass with roundwounds to play any of those tunes, it sounds fine, but it's not quite "perfect" unless you put on a set of flatwounds.

The two main types of strings—roundwound and flatwound—each have different qualities. Roundwounds are brighter while flats are warmer. One needs to try both and decide. Flats are easier on the fingers and frets of the bass, but are not good for some styles of playing, such as popping and slapping.

The Least You Need to Know

◆ Bass players are special people!

◆ The bassist is responsible for keeping the rhythm and providing harmonic and melodic support to the band.

◆ It's good to be familiar with the basic parts of your instrument.

◆ Different types of strings can give your bass a different sound.

Shopping

In This Chapter

- Do you play right- or left-handed?
- Researching before you buy
- A visit to your local music store
- Other places to shop
- Deciding on an amplifier
- Other items you'll need

To be a bass guitar player, you need a bass guitar. You can't just stay at home and continually drop hints to your family and friends that there's something *really* special you'd like for Christmas or your next birthday. Chances are they'd get one in the wrong color—at best!

The prospect of a trip to the music store, though, might give you some anxiety. Perhaps more than a bit. After all, you don't want to look like a nerd. There's all those cool dudes hanging out at the guitar store, and all sorts of things about the bass guitar you don't know yet.

The key word here is "yet." With a little thought and planning, you can learn enough to get started. By taking notes and doing research, you can learn what you need to know to bring a bass home. The first steps begin with some honest questions, but also one very basic one.

Right-Handed or Left?

Since most people are right-handed, most people play the bass right-handed. Their right hand strikes or picks the strings while the left hand frets the notes on the neck. Playing the bass left-handed means your left hand strikes the strings while your right hand frets the notes.

Even many left-handed people play the bass right-handed. If you feel comfortable doing so, it's certainly worth considering—you'll have an easier time finding an instrument since they don't make all that many lefty bass guitars, although companies manufacture more left-handed basses now than they used to.

But deciding which way to play should be a matter of comfort, first, not of instrument availability. Many left-handed people, myself included, have an awkward time keeping rhythm with their right hands, so it's better for us to play left-handed. And keeping the rhythm has to be your first priority.

In this book I use the terms "right hand" and "left hand" as I would when talking with a right-handed bass player. If you play left-handed, then simply reverse the terms while reading. Being left-handed, I already know you're smart enough to do that!

How Much Can You Spend?

One of your first questions should be, "What is my budget?" immediately followed by, "Is that just for the bass guitar or is it for the entire package, namely a bass, an amp, a case, and all the accessories?"

You also need to ask yourself, "How serious am I about this?" because that can help answer your question about the budget. Over and over again you'll hear, "Buy the best bass your money can get you," but if you're just playing with friends every other weekend, you don't need to spend a couple thousand dollars on a bass, even if you can afford to.

What you need from a bass is very simple:

◆ You need the bass to fit you, physically and philosophically.

◆ You need your bass to sound good.

How Does It *Feel?*

Even if you've never held a bass before, you have to understand the importance of the feel of the instrument. When you play, you have to be comfortable with the bass—comfortable standing, and we're talking about standing for long periods of time, and comfortable sitting down. Picking an instrument with an exotic shape may mean never playing it while sitting.

The fingers of both hands should feel like they belong to the instrument. The index finger of your right hand will be plucking the strings to sound the notes. It should be able to reach all the strings with relative ease. You should be able to fret the strings while in a relaxed position and move your hand smoothly up and down the neck. There should be no sharp fret edges along the top or bottom of the neck.

You should be able to press the strings onto the neck fairly easily. The distance of the strings from the neck is called the guitar's *action*. If the action is too high, it will be difficult—and quickly very painful—for your fingers to press the strings and fret the notes. If the action is too low, you may get a lot of buzzing from the strings making unwanted contact with the frets. Be sure to check the action of each string all the way up and down the neck.

As far as sound goes, anyone can sound *loud*. How loud your bass is depends on your amplification. How clean and clear the sound is usually depends on your instrument. When trying out an instrument, play it at different volumes and in different styles (with a pick, with your fingers) and try to get a feel for the instrument's response to your touch. Your bass should fit your music and personality. Most of the time this isn't even an issue because the bass guitar is such a versatile instrument. The instrument you use to play country music this afternoon can play death metal tonight and Broadway show tunes tomorrow.

We'll cover more test-driving tips in a moment. What you need to know now is that buying your bass guitar requires patience and honesty. Even if you're just taking up the bass as a hobby, it's important to get as good an instrument as possible. Not all that long ago, cheap basses were just that—cheaply and poorly made. Trying to learn on an instrument that is difficult to fret or won't stay in tune is a waste of your time, not to mention your money.

Don't Skip the Research

Saving time and money begins by learning a few things. Which music stores are in your area? Even if you're planning on buying something through a catalog or making an online purchase, you should hold an instrument in your hands before you do.

You can go online, find some music store websites, and take notes of brands and prices. Ask your musician friends about the professionalism of the sales staff and the quality of service at local stores. Don't be put off by one negative review. That can be the result of someone (on the staff, or possibly your friend) having a bad day. But if you get a number of complaints, you might want to avoid the store in question.

Your research should be an ongoing process. As you visit stores and take notes on manufacturers and models, you can come home and visit websites that post reviews of instruments. Keep comparing prices. Once you know what you're looking for you might find a better price somewhere else, but keep in mind that a lower price might not be a bargain.

Service is an important aspect to keep in mind. If your dream bass costs a little more at the local store, but they have a great reputation for service and repair, then it may certainly be worth the extra dollars.

While you're at the music store, pick up some bass guitar magazines and learn more about the instrument you want to bring home. If the store has any manufacturer's literature, get some. Become as much of an expert about the bass guitar as you can.

Buying your bass should take some time. You might find the right instrument immediately, and that's terrific. Most people, though, will need to try out several instruments and do research and comparison shopping. Unless you've got a gig coming up in a few days (not likely for most beginners), you owe it to yourself to find the best bass you can, regardless of how long it takes.

Four-String, Five-String, Six-String, More?

It used to be that bass players had a choice of four-string basses and … other four-string basses. Nowadays, there are five-string basses, six-strings basses, and

def•i•ni•tion

Most basses have a 34-inch scale length. A bass guitar's **scale length** is the distance between the nut and the bridge of the guitar. The longer the scale length, the greater the spacing of the frets will be. If you have small hands or short arms, a shorter scale length, such as 30 or 32 inches, may feel more comfortable.

Covering the Basses

The body of an electric bass guitar is usually made of two or three pieces of solid wood laminated together. "Acoustic" bass guitars are basically large acoustic guitars with longer necks and bass strings. Acoustic basses aren't very loud (some can be overpowered by a zealously strummed acoustic guitar); in fact, many acoustic basses have built-in electronics, so you can plug them into an amplifier. These "electric/acoustic" basses can be great for someone who wants to play with and without amplification, but they do tend to create feedback when played at loud volumes.

Covering the Basses

Taking and keeping notes is about the smartest thing anyone can do when buying a bass guitar. Start out with your own checklist and carry a small spiral-bound notepad in your pocket (take a pen!) to jot down things like manufacturers' names, model numbers, and your own impressions. The more notes you take, the more successful your research is likely to be.

more. Six-string basses have an extra high note and an extra low note. On five-string basses, the extra string is usually lower.

Any bass with more than four strings is going to have a longer and wider neck, so take that into account when shopping. If you have small hands to begin with, you may have difficulties fretting notes on a wider neck.

If you're planning on doing a lot of jazz playing and soloing, then a six string or "high five" might fit your desires. The "low five" is terrific for dance, hip-hop, metal, and other genres that get into the low, deep tones of the bass.

In *The Complete Idiot's Guide to Playing Bass Guitar*, all of our examples will be written out for the four-string bass, but you can still play all the material in this book with a five- or six-string bass.

The Hands-On Approach

In order to know if a bass guitar fits you and feels good, you're going to have to try some out. Don't worry about making a fool of yourself at the music store. Most people working there deal with first-time musicians on a regular basis. But it's important to not do silly things like walk in and ask what kind of discount you can get before you've even said hello.

Try out as many basses as catch your eye. Don't even look at price tags. What you want to do is to hold them and feel them. Is it too heavy? Too awkward? You might need a lighter guitar. Or one with a lighter neck. Or a thinner (or thicker) neck.

Give a prospective bass a good looking over. Check the body for cracks, dings, and dents. Speaking of which, handle each instrument with care. Don't wear jewelry that could scratch the finish and either don't wear a belt with a huge buckle or wear something over it so that you don't scar the back of the instrument.

Can your fingers reach the frets furthest away from you? You may need a bass with a shorter scale length (the distance from the bridge to the nut). Thirty-four inches is the norm, but you can find bass guitars with shorter (30 or 32 inches) scale lengths. There are some longer ones as well.

Be sure to test the bass guitar. Plug it into an amplifier and play a few notes. It doesn't matter if you don't know how to play; you want to hear how it sounds. If you have a friend who plays bass, bring her along and sit back while she plays the selected bass. If you don't have someone to tag along with you, ask a salesperson to play the instrument for you. But make sure whoever plays the bass guitar plays something very simple—fancy playing will make any bass sound great. You need to know what it's going to sound like while you're learning to play! After you get a good feel for that, then let your friend or the salesperson show you what the bass will sound like when you've been playing a little while.

Where (and What) to Buy

Buying at a local music store offers more than just a chance to test out a prospective instrument in person. You also get to meet the people who will take care of you and your bass should the need arise. When you talk with the salespeople at your local store, be sure to talk with them about repair work and other store policies, such as returns and loaners. This is probably more important if you don't buy your bass locally, but rather purchase it via mail order or the Internet. Knowing that someone close at hand can take care of any problems will take some of your worries away.

Something Old, Something New

In all likelihood, you'll probably purchase a new bass guitar. But while you're at the store, check out whether or not they have any used basses. Sometimes you can find what would normally be a more expensive bass sitting smack within your budget, simply because it is used. Depending upon where you live, there might be stores that sell only used equipment. These are always worth checking out, if not to buy an instrument, then to do research.

With used equipment, be certain to ask about what kind of limited warranties might be available. Try to make certain that everything about the instrument is otherwise good. Scratches in the finish can be dealt with or ignored, but stay away from fundamental problems like a warped neck or an inability to stay in tune.

Buying a musical instrument online, or from an offline catalog supplier, requires a bit of faith that not everyone has. You can test out the exact make and model of a bass guitar at your local shop, then find one and order it, only to find the instrument you've gotten doesn't feel anything like the one you tried at the store. Often, any bass in question will be very close, or close enough that you may not notice the differences. But you do run that risk, so it's very important to know exactly what the return policies of the online or offline catalog entail.

Sometimes people find and buy musical instruments through online auctions, such as eBay. Like shopping at used instrument stores or pawnshops, you may occasionally find a great deal, but don't abandon your research. With the stock-market mentality that pervades many people's thinking, there are quite a number of folks who use these auction sites simply to make a profit. They'll buy an instrument at a low price simply to sell it again a week later at a higher price. They truly aren't interested in the instrument or anything about it. Just because you bought something online doesn't mean that you got a great deal or a great price. The very opposite may be the truth.

And don't forget to look at the for-sale ads in your local paper. You never know when and where the right instrument will turn up.

Going Through Customs

If you have the money, a custom-made bass guitar is certainly worth considering. There are many fine *luthiers*, people who build guitars, who will craft an instrument to your personal taste and needs. Custom basses will cost more and may take some time to acquire, but if playing bass is your life's calling, having a unique instrument may be just what you need. People who go the custom bass route, as a rule, have played for quite a few years and have tried out enough basses to know exactly what they want and require from their instrument.

def•i•ni•tion

A **luthier** is a professional guitar builder. You might be surprised, but there are many of them and the art of crafting guitars is experiencing a bit of a boom. Many luthiers specialize in acoustic guitars but a growing number devote their skills to creating electric guitars and electric bass guitars.

Basso Profondo

Q: If I'm just a beginner, how much power do I need for a bass amp?

A: If you're just practicing alone in your living room, not much at all. Practice amps can be as small as 25 watts and be just fine for a beginner. But if you're playing with a band and a drummer, that's a different story. You'll want to get an amp rated at least at 300 watts. Just as important, you'll want a decent-sized, quality speaker cabinet with at least a single 15-inch speaker or a couple of 10- or 12-inch speakers. For gigs, you want to have as much power as you can afford and speakers to match. A typical pro rig will have a minimum of 400 watts and either a 4×10-inch, 1×15-inch, or 2×12-inch speaker configuration.

Amplifiers and Accessories

Unless you already have one, you're going to need a bass amplifier, or amp. Notice I specified *bass* amp. You don't want a guitar amplifier, and you *don't* want to try to play your bass guitar through the speakers of your stereo system. You need an amplifier specifically designed to handle the sounds of the bass guitar.

Everyone wants to get the biggest, loudest amp possible. But if you're just starting out and/or have no intentions beyond playing with some friends and having fun, then you don't need a huge amp. If you're going to be in a band and playing gigs, you will need something that can be heard over the drums and maybe be powerful enough to use in small clubs.

It's also useful to note that your first bass amp is likely to be just that, the *first* of other choices. When you're just beginning on the bass guitar, try to put as much of your budget into your instrument as you can. Later, when you know your instrument and also know just where and what you want to play, you can make a more permanent choice in regard to your amplifier.

Also remember that you are very likely to find more amp for your dollar by shopping around for used equipment. Perfectly good amps are traded in on a regular basis by people looking for more power. Do your research, and you're very likely to find a great deal on your bass amplifier.

What Makes an Amp Work

The bass amp takes the electronic signal from your bass and boosts it to a sufficient voltage level to have the speakers convert it to sound. Bass amps are generally more powerful than guitar amps because the low sounds of the bass require more power to generate. Bass "practice" amps, which you might consider to start out with or to have when playing by yourself, generally start out between 20 to 30 watts.

You can think of your amp as being two separate parts: the amp, which receives, processes, amplifies, and sends the signal on to the speakers; and the speakers, which produce the sound you hear. You can buy amps either in their separate components or together as a single unit known as the combo amp.

Combo Amps

Beginners generally start with a combo amp. Both the amp and speakers come in the same, single unit. They can be large or small, light or heavy—usually depending upon how many speakers are in the combo amp. A single 12- or 15-inch speaker (respectively called a 1×12-inch or 1×15-inch configuration) is the norm. You might find other speaker configurations as well, such as two 10-inch speakers (a 2×10-inch). Small practice amps will have smaller speakers and will sound distorted at high volumes.

Separate Speakers?

Buying the amplifier and speakers separate means that you can upgrade either part as desired and even add additional speakers as you see fit. But remember that it's also more equipment to lug around. And it's bulky. It used to be that the bass players rode all by themselves to gigs because they had to carry around that old stand-up bass. Nowadays it's often because the bass amp and speaker setup is the only thing that will fit in their cars!

The Case for a Case

Any instrument gets dinged. But a lot of dings happen "in transit," when taking your bass from your house to wherever it's going to be played. Having a good case will give your bass a longer life.

Often, but not always, the case is included in the price of a bass guitar. Make certain before you buy your instrument. Hard-shell cases are terrific if your bass will be doing a lot of traveling with other gear. It will protect your bass if it ends up on the bottom of a pile of bags, drums, and gear.

Gig bags are soft-sided cases, which are lighter, and great for carrying around when you're not worrying about your bass banging into (or getting banged around by) things like other instruments or people. They are also usually less expensive.

Cords, Straps, Etc.

A cord, or cable, connects your instrument to the bass amplifier. They come in all sorts of lengths, so consider whether you'll be wandering all over a stage or sitting next to your amp in your bedroom. Aside from your strings, the cable gets more wear and tear than almost any other part of your bass. Doing research on the various makes of cables is not a bad idea, since you want one that will hold up under a lot of use.

Whether you're sitting or standing, you'll want a strap for your bass. Straps could be considered the fashion accessory of the bass guitar, since they come in all sizes, colors, and patterns. Just as with your instrument, fit and comfort should be your first concern. Have a strap that supports your bass without digging into your shoulder. Some people like wider straps or padded straps for this reason.

Think about buying a music stand and an instrument stand. Having a safe place to put your instrument is especially nice when you're playing a lot and don't want to put it into the case for just a few minutes. Music stands will enable you to read your music and books while playing. Be sure to get an adjustable one so you can use it sitting or standing.

Tuners and Timers

A tuner is certainly worth considering, especially if you intend to play in clubs or other places where the noise level will make it harder to tune your bass. Be sure to carry extra batteries in your case.

Basso Profondo

Q: Are effects necessary? What ones are typically used by bass players?

A: No effects are needed. Bass players have been known to use the same effects as guitar players to alter their sound, but, as a rule, bassists use far fewer effects than guitarists. Some common ones include distortion, compression, or an envelope filter. Most tonal differences on a bass come from the physical technique one plays with. You can get lots of different tones with different picking (fingers or pick or thumb) and placing the right hand in different places. Effects often get in the way of that solid round tone that needs to sonically synch with the drummer to make a song sound good.

Depending on your sense of timing, you might want to consider adding a metronome to your shopping cart. A metronome counts off the beat of a tempo for you. They can be electronic or battery powered. Some merely click, while others flash a little light in time with the music. Most musicians, and most bass players, consider it an essential piece of gear.

For those of you who like to be practical, there are combination tuner/metronome devices out on the market these days.

Cause and Effects

Your bass guitar is an electric instrument, and as such it's easy to alter its sound by means of effects boxes, which take the signal of the instrument and alter it in some fashion before sending it on to the amplifier. Some amplifiers come with effects built in.

While electric guitarists will rarely play without some sort of effects, the bassist tends to prefer a clean sound. But it doesn't hurt to check out your options. You might look into a volume-control pedal, which allows you to control the volume of your instrument while playing (so you don't have to fiddle with the control knobs on either your bass or your amp).

The Setup

Finally, you should have your new bass "set up" before it leaves the store. A setup is like the tune-up a car gets before going home with its new owner. The strings get a final adjustment (new strings might be included—something to ask about!), as well as the nut, neck, and bridge of the instrument. Your bass is once again inspected and cleaned and you get to start playing your bass once you get it home.

Most stores will do this for you, offering the setup as part of the cost of the instrument. Ask first, though! Better to make certain than to assume.

The Least You Need to Know

- Whenever possible, personally try out as many basses as you can.
- Research manufactures and models, either through magazine reviews or via the Internet.
- You need to have a bass amplifier, not a regular guitar amplifier.
- Be sure to get a case, a cable, and a strap for your new bass.

Chapter 3

Getting Acquainted With Your New Friend

In This Chapter

◆ Position, posture, practice, persistence, and patience

◆ The names of your strings

◆ How to tune your bass

◆ Playing and fretting the strings

◆ The importance of string muting

◆ Your first play-along songs

Now that you have your bass (or new bass) in hand, it's time to make some sounds with it. Maybe even learn a simple song or play a little blues tune.

The Five Ps

It's important at this stage to make note of some habits that will help you play better in the future. It's never too early to develop good habits.

Too often, beginners start with poor posture or positioning and then wonder why they cannot fret notes or make a note sound clean. Frustration sets in and the mindset becomes "I can't do this," and the instrument is set aside, never to be played again.

You can avoid this by taking the time at the start of your adventure in bass playing to pay attention to the little things that may cause trouble down the road. It doesn't involve much more than common sense, and it will help you be happy with your playing right from the start.

Proper Positioning (Part 1)

When you perform live, you will probably play your bass standing up. Some people practice standing as well, but that's very much a matter of personal preference. If you're going to be playing for hours, sitting is good. It's good to be able to play either way and it's important to have good positioning for both standing and sitting.

If you're sitting, try to use a stool or a firm, but comfortable, tall chair without arms. The ideal musical chair allows you to sit up straight and doesn't encourage you to slouch. The body of the instrument should be right at your waist. The fingers of your right hand should be able to reach each string without difficulty.

The neck should be at an angle so that if someone were looking at you, they'd say it was pointing at two o'clock. Your fretting hand should be about chest high and have comfortable access to the entire neck, up and down.

Proper Posture

Comfort, as we mentioned in Chapter 2, is a key word. And comfort comes from good posture. Tension often starts in big places and works itself down to the little ones. If your back and shoulders are uncomfortable holding the bass, that tension will soon make its way to the wrists and fingers of both hands. That's not good.

Sitting and standing straight help immensely. Even before you strap on your bass, take a few minutes to loosen up and unwind. Roll your shoulders back and forth to relax them. Stretch out your fingers, even flap your arms if you're so inclined. The point is to make yourself comfortable.

If you're sitting, you might want to have your right leg raised slightly to give the body of your bass a little more support. Some people use little footstools (the same type used by classical guitarists) for this purpose. Others simply cross their legs!

Proper Practice

Now I have to tell you some bad news: your bass won't play itself. And simply strapping it on and plucking out some notes won't make you a bass player. You do have to practice.

When you start out, your hands and fingers may not always be up to the task. You're not used to pressing down the strings or plucking the notes, and, in not too much time, your fingers may start to hurt. When that happens, stop playing. No, not forever! Just take a break. If you play for 10 minutes and can't take it anymore, do something else for an hour and then come back to it. You probably will get in another 10 minutes. That's okay. That's 20 minutes of practice that you wouldn't have had otherwise.

Fueled by the enthusiasm of a new instrument, you will probably find yourself doing a lot of practicing at first. Then your fingers will begin to hurt, and you'll start taking your practice time in little doses. This happens to everyone, so don't let it worry you. Before you know it, your fingers will get used to playing, and you'll be able to play for a half-hour, an hour, two hours, and more.

It's also important to practice intelligently. If you're having difficulty with part of a song, don't just practice the song over and over from beginning to end—work on the part that's giving you trouble. Break it up into little pieces that you can manage and then put them back together again. Then go back to the whole song.

Covering the Basses

Remember to use your strap, even while sitting, as it will help keep the bass from sliding around. It will also help keep the neck at a good angle while sitting. Too often, and this is especially true of guitar players for some reason, beginners tend to use their left leg as an arm rest (I suppose "wrist rest" would be a more accurate term), which can be detrimental when trying to finger notes on the fingerboard.

Covering the Basses

Throughout the rest of this book you'll find numerous practice tips. One thing you might want to do from the start is to keep a practice diary or "practice journal." As people progress it's sometimes hard for them to realize just how far they have come from their beginning days. A log of your practice sessions will help you to keep track of what you've learned as well as to remind you of all the work you've put into your instrument.

Persistence and Patience

Like practice, persistence is also often taken for granted. You probably can't remember when you learned to walk, but it's a good bet that you fell down on many attempts. Each time you play your instrument, your fingers are compiling muscle memory. Something that may seem impossible right now may simply happen "by magic" one day. But magic had nothing to do with it. It was all the practice that did the trick.

Patience walks hand in hand with persistence. None of this will happen overnight. When you hear a musician you really like playing effortlessly, it's easy to ignore the fact that, at some point in his life, he was going through this same beginning phase you are now. It's hard to imagine your idol not being able to put together three notes at a time, isn't it?

Getting in Tune

Tuning your bass should always be the first thing you check when getting ready to practice or play. Basses don't tend to go out of tune, or very far out of tune, on a regular basis, so it usually won't take but a moment of your time.

You tune your bass by turning the tuning gears on the headstock of your bass guitar. There will be one for each string on your bass. Turning the tuning gear in one direction will tighten the string, thus raising the tone. Turning the gear in the opposite direction will loosen the string and lower its tone.

You should take a moment and check which direction is which. Not all basses are set up the same, and it's a good thing to know before you set about tuning your instrument. You won't need to turn any of the tuning heads very far in order to find out.

There are lots of ways to get your bass into what's called "standard tuning," but before you do, it might be a good idea to know what notes you want to tune each string to! So let's take care of that right now ....

Name That String

One way to get a head start on learning your notes is to learn the names of your strings. After all, when you play an open string, you're playing a note!

Notes, as you will learn in our next chapter, use the letters A through G for their names.

When your bass is tuned to standard tuning, your strings will be tuned to specific notes. Your thickest string, the one closest to the ceiling, will be E, the next one will be A, the next D, and the one closest to the floor will be G.

Now that you know the names of the notes, how do you get your bass in tune? Well, to make your life easier, we've included a tuning track on the CD.

⊙ It's the very first one, so put the CD in your computer or the CD player of your choice and come along and tune up.

Rock Bottom
Standard tuning, with the strings tuned to E, A, D, and G, is the way most bass guitars are tuned. There are all sorts of other tuning options. We'll look at some of the more common ones in Chapter 22.

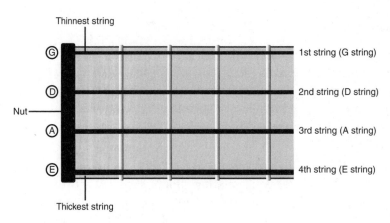

The string names of the bass guitar.

Using a Tuner

Spending the $15 to $25 for a tuner won't seem like much after you own it. It should last you a lifetime and will make tuning your bass a breeze. Be sure to get one that is designed for a bass or guitar (most guitar tuners these days do both), as you want something that will pick up the low vibrations of your instrument.

Most tuners will allow you to plug the bass directly into it, just as you would plug it into an amplifier. There are many different makes of tuners, but most of them work the same way. Pluck the string and the name of a note should appear somewhere on the tuner's screen. It will also indicate if you are higher or lower than the desired pitch, usually by means of an arrow or colored lights (or both). Adjust the tuning head so that you've got the correct pitch and then move on to the next string.

> **Covering the Basses**
>
> When tuning, it's better to tune *up* to a note than down to it, because the string has less chance to slip if you're tightening it and not loosening it. If the string you're tuning is higher than what you want, turn it lower than the target note then tighten it back up to the desired pitch.

Owning this type of tuner will be good if you intend to play someplace outside the home, like at a noisy club or party. Being able to *read* whether or not you're in tune is very handy when you can't *hear* if you're in tune.

Tuning to a Keyboard

If you own a piano, you can always tune your bass to it. The following is an illustration of how the notes of the open strings of your bass compare to the piano.

The tricky part of tuning your bass to a piano is that you want to hear the notes at the same time, and that's not always easy if you don't have someone there to help. You can strike the piano key with one hand and the open string of the bass with the other. Most pianos also have pedals that allow the piano's notes to sustain.

Once you get the E string in tune with the piano, you can then tune the rest of the strings without outside help, simply using your own instrument.

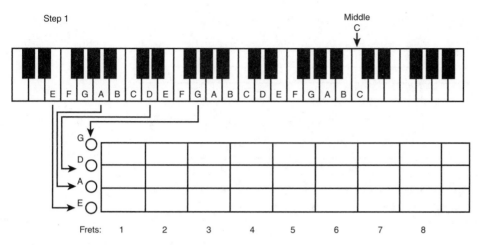

Tuning your bass to a piano or keyboard.

Tuning to Yourself

With the exception of the notes found on the first four frets of your E string and the last few frets of your G string, every other note you can play on your bass can be found in multiple places on the fretboard. Play the open A string. While it is ringing, finger the fifth fret of your E string with your left hand and pluck that string with your right. If they are in tune, the two notes will sound the same. When your strings are not in tune, not only will they sound different, but you'll also hear a slight wavering sound. This wavering sound is more clearly heard when you tune with harmonics, which we'll cover next.

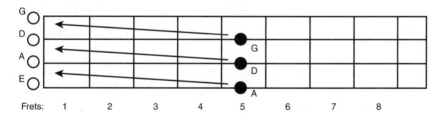

Tuning your bass to itself.

As you turn the tuning gear, the wavering sound will actually slow down as you get the two notes closer in pitch. If you eliminate that fluctuation, then you've successfully gotten those two strings in tune with each other.

Now you need to repeat this procedure, using the fifth fret of the A string to match against the open D string, and then matching the fifth fret of the D to the open G string. When you've gotten the G string in tune, you're in tune!

Harmonic Tuning

Harmonics are higher pitched tones that occur when you lightly fret your strings at certain points and then sound the string as you normally would. You can create harmonics at many points on your fingerboard, but the easiest places to locate them are the twelfth, seventh, and fifth frets.

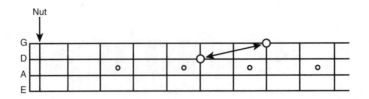

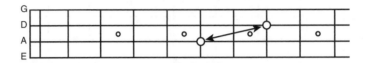

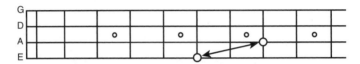

Tuning with harmonics.

Place the index finger of your left hand on the fifth fret of your E string. Unlike fretting a note, you want your finger to be over the metal of the fret, not the space between. Make your touch as light as possible. Now strike the string with your right hand. You should hear a clear, ringing, almost bell-like tone. That is a harmonic, specifically the fifth-fret E harmonic.

Repeat this using the pinky or ring finger of your left hand on the seventh fret of the A string. These two ringing harmonics should sound the same if your bass is in tune. Otherwise, the wavering sound should be quite distinct, and you can adjust accordingly.

Like before, you'll need to do this with the remaining strings, matching the fifth fret A harmonic to the seventh fret D harmonic, and then finally matching the fifth fret D harmonic to the seventh fret G.

🔘 So you can get a good idea of what this sounds like, Track #2 on the CD demonstrates tuning by harmonics.

Sounding the Strings

All right, then! Your bass is tuned, and you've got it plugged into your amp. Let's make some noise! Ultimately, you're going to need both hands to play the bass, but for now let's concentrate on the right hand.

Proper Positioning (Part Two)

Begin by being relaxed. Shake out your hand a little bit and take a deep breath. Place your right hand on your bass as shown in the following illustration.

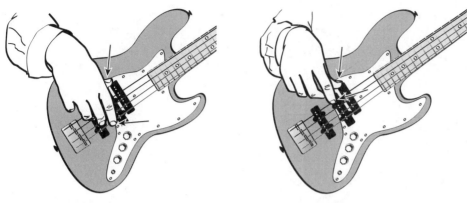

Right hand position.

Many basses have a thumb rest, a short bar of wood, metal, or plastic where the thumb can be anchored when playing. You can also let your thumb sit on the top edge of a pickup. Your right elbow should sit at your side. Most bass players prefer to have the forearm and elbow run parallel to the body of the bass while some let the elbow sit slightly behind, which means draping the forearm over the top of your instrument. More often than not, this is a matter of how long your arm is and how comfortable you feel.

Be sure that your index finger can reach each string with relative ease. Your thumb will scrunch up a little when you reach for the G string and straighten somewhat when you reach for the E string. That is normal.

Using Your Finger

Most bassists use either their index finger or middle finger to strike the strings. The sound or tone of a note can vary greatly, depending on how you go about striking it. When we use our finger, we have three basic options: plucking the finger *up* on the string, much like a classical guitarist; strumming the finger *across* the string; and striking the string *down* into the bass.

Each of these methods produces a different quality of sound. Most bass players prefer the third method, striking the string down and into the bass, as it gives the note a full and round tone.

Strike the G string with your index finger. You will find, especially if you use the downward strike, that your finger naturally comes to rest on the D string. This is good as it will help mute that string, keeping it from giving off any unwanted noise.

Continue striking the other strings. When you play the E string, your index finger will come to rest against your thumb.

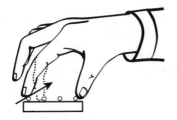
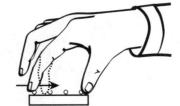
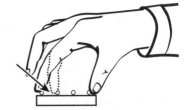

Striking the strings.

Using Your Fingers

Once you're comfortable using one finger, it's time to get another one involved. Using two fingers instead of one will bring more speed and accuracy to your playing.

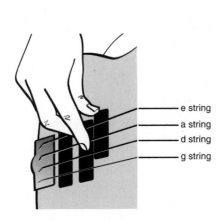
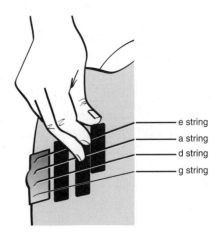

Striking the strings with two fingers.

Again, start very simply and slowly. First, strike the open A string using your index finger. Then strike it again using your middle finger. Then speed up slightly while continuing to alter your striking fingers.

As you do this, try to strike the string evenly, having each finger give the note close to equal volume. Then give the index finger more emphasis, accenting that strike, if you will. Then give the middle finger strikes more emphasis. Don't go overboard! Let the accented notes be only slightly more punctuated. You are learning to let your bass "speak," to give your music phrasing. Repeat this exercise with each string.

Now start switching strings when you switch fingers. Begin with the E string, striking it with the index finger, and then strike the A string with your middle finger, the D string with the index, and finally the G with the middle finger. This is known as *string crossing* and is another terrific warm-up exercise. Do this again starting with the E string and the middle finger (you'll use the index on the A, the middle finger again on the D, and finally the index on the G). Then reverse string direction—begin with the G string, using your index finger.

Playing the bass involves both hands, but many beginners focus so much on their left hand fretting the proper notes that they neglect the importance of the right hand. Good technique with the picking hand will help to provide good, clean tones and strong, steady rhythm. As you practice and develop, make certain to spend time with your right hand and not concentrate solely on the left.

Using a Pick

Back in the early days of the electric bass, many bass players were "converts," guitar players who didn't want to be out of work. As guitarists, they tended to use picks when they played and, when converted, they brought those picks over to the bass. For some, such as "bass greats" Carol Kaye and Joe Osbourne, playing with a pick produced a sound singular enough for record producers to seek them out.

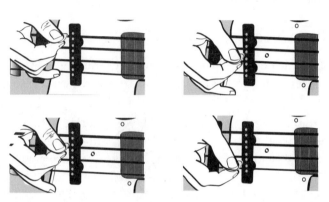

Using a pick.

Picks (also called plectrums) come in all shapes and sizes and are made from many different types of materials. They also come in different thicknesses, usually designated as heavy, medium, or thin. Thick, or heavy, picks are usually best for playing the bass, but don't let that stop you from trying out different types. Each has its own sound, and you might find something you really like.

You want to grip the pick firmly, but not so tightly that you make your hand all tense. Being relaxed will make your picking a lot smoother.

If you've never played with a pick before, start out by holding it with just enough of the tip exposed to strike the string and try to strike the string at a right angle with the pick. As you get more comfortable using a pick, you will find all sorts of ways to subtly change the angle of the strike.

Being able to use a pick will give you a sharper attack on the strings. It can also give the fingers of your right hand a break if they are getting sore!

Using Your Thumb

Playing the strings with your thumb is another option. You'll learn about the technique of "slapping" with the thumb in Chapter 21. In addition to slapping, some bassists use their thumbs to strike the strings in much the same manner as using one's fingers.

> **Covering the Basses**
>
> When using a pick, try to make your strikes short and not stray too far from the strings. A common mistake among beginners is to use the whole forearm to pick, generating all the motion at the elbow. Let your wrist do the work.

> **Basso Profondo**
>
> *Q: Is it better to play with a pick or with my fingers? What about picking with my thumb?*
>
> A: Certain songs and styles of music call for certain right hand techniques— a pick, your fingers, or slapping and popping the strings with your thumb and middle finger. However, it's never a bad thing to be able to get through a song or gig with just your fingers—in case you've dropped or forgotten your picks! Experiment with other styles and see which technique best suits your style(s) of music.

You may wonder which of these ways of sounding the strings is right for you. The best thing to do is to try each and see what feels most comfortable. Each method has its own sound and there may come a time when that particular sound is exactly what you're looking for.

Most people (especially beginners) start out with the two-finger approach, but be versatile and able to adapt. Some of the great innovations in bass playing have come from people trying out new things.

Getting Your (Other) Hand On

Now we need some other notes to play besides those of the open strings. This is where the left hand comes into play. As I mentioned earlier this chapter, try to keep your left hand about chest-high in order to give it the freedom and leverage it will need to finger the notes properly.

Proper Positioning (Part Three)

Once again, begin by relaxing. It doesn't do you or your hands much good to be all tensed up. Place your left hand on the neck of your bass as shown in the following illustration.

First and foremost, don't grab the neck of your bass with your thumb! When you do, you pull your fingers down toward the floor, and this will limit their reach and flexibility. The bass should just rest upon the thumb. Concern yourself with the fingers and, for most of you, the thumb will take care of itself. It will naturally seek the most comfortable (and usually proper!) place, namely the center of the back of the neck, usually opposite the index and middle fingers.

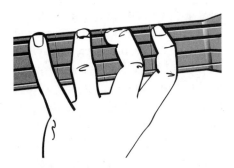

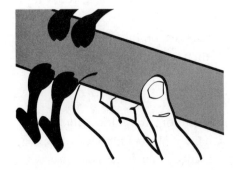

Left hand position.

Ideally, you want to have your fingers set so that each covers one fret. That will not be easy at first, most certainly not at the far end of the fingerboard. If this is the case with you, position your hand further up the neck (closer to the bridge), where the frets are closer together. Practice the exercise in the following section up there and move down one fret at a time. This will allow your hands to acclimate to the neck of your bass.

Fretting

When you fret a note, you want to use the tip of your finger, placing it as shown in the following illustration.

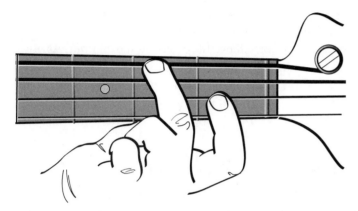

Fretting a note.

As you begin to play notes on your bass, take the time to listen to what you're doing. The notes should ring clean and clear. If they don't, then adjust your finger position in the fret. Spending time on this simple thing now will ensure that you get good, clean notes later on and will also help you to feel comfortable and confident in your playing.

Start by fretting a note with your index finger. Which note on which fret is not important at this point. When you have a good, clean tone with that note, lift your index finger off the neck and place your middle finger in the next fret *up*. Again, make certain you have a note free of buzzing, one that rings out clearly. Repeat this using your ring finger on the next fret up the neck and then finally your pinky. Then come back *down* the way you went up, starting with the pinky, switching to the ring finger, on to the middle finger and then ending with the index finger.

Once more, I'd like to stress the importance of being able to get good, clean tones. A simple exercise such as this sets the groundwork, and settling for sloppy fingering now might mean relearning it later on. "Relearning," by the way, usually involves "unlearning," and that's often the most difficult thing to do.

In Appendix D, you will find some exercises written out for you in bass guitar tablature and notation, which will help you to warm up and exercise both your hands. After you learn how to read either (preferably both) TAB or notation, you should use this appendix to limber up your fingers anytime you want to play your instrument.

def•i•ni•tion

In this book, and with most musicians you'll meet, the terms **up** and **down** refer to tones. Going *up* a fret or up the neck means moving in a direction from the head-stock to the body of the bass. As you move in this direction, the pitch of the notes gets higher. Consequently, this is *up. Down* is the opposite direction, moving from the body of the bass toward the head-stock. If you are moving down a fret or two, you're moving your fingers closer toward the headstock.

Likewise, moving *up* a string means moving to the next string higher in pitch. That's the next thinner string, which means you're actually going closer to the floor! Moving *down* a string means to move to the next thicker string, which is lower in tone.

Not Sounding the Strings

You may have noticed that there are other things going on when you fret and play a note. Perhaps one of the strings you're not playing is vibrating and causing a little ruckus. Part of the challenge of playing bass is controlling the unwanted notes and sounds caused by things like sympathetic vibrations. Not to mention simply deadening a note after you're done with it!

There are two obvious ways of handling this: using the free fingers of your left hand to lightly touch the strings you're not fretting or using the free fingers of your right hand to lightly touch the stings that you're not striking. Usually it's a combination of both.

It probably doesn't seem fair to have to deal with this on top of everything else. But becoming aware of unwanted string noise and vibrations is a good first step. And this gives you another reason for taking things slowly starting out. As you get better at fretting and sounding the notes, you'll get better at dampening the notes and sounds you don't want. The more you play and practice, the more things like striking notes, fretting notes, and muting unwanted sounds will become second nature to you.

> **Covering the Basses**
>
> Get into the habit of keeping the fingers of your left hand on the strings even when not fretting a note. Staying close allows you to easily dampen any strings that may be causing unwanted noise.

Playing Around and Playing Along

Since your bass is in tune and you've learned the names of your strings, why don't we play a couple of songs? You might not think you have the ability to do that at this stage, but you do. We're going to play two very basic pieces, a blues number and then a little bit of rock and roll, and both will involve playing only the open strings.

Open-String Blues

● But that doesn't mean that there won't be a little bit of work to do. First, listen to the song, "Open-String Blues," on the CD.

The song starts with four clicks, which sets the beat. You are going to play your open strings at that pace. Start with the A string, playing it four times.

Then play the D string four times and then the A string again, eight hits this time. Now play the D again eight times and then eight more on the A string.

Finally, play the E string four times, then go back to the D string for four strikes and then end with five hits on the A, letting the last one ring out.

What you are doing here (and you'll be learning this in Section 2) is playing the root notes of the chords in quarter notes, one beat at a time.

I've included the bass part for the first pass at this song. The second time around, there is no bass. That's because you get to play it all by yourself. Don't worry about making mistakes. Everyone does when he or she first starts out playing. The important thing is not to lose your place. If you do, wait for a change of chord to cue you in.

Open-String Rock

Our second song, "Open-String Rock," will be faster but less work in terms of the pattern of striking the strings. Give it a listen.

Our playing pattern for this song will be two picks of the open A string, followed by two on the open D. Then play the open G string twice and then return to the open D string for two more hits. This pattern repeats over and over again until the song ends with a single long note on the open A string.

The band will play through this change of four chords a total of twelve times, the first six with the bass and then six more times without. And again, the whole point of this is to get you used to playing your bass in general, as well as to get you accustomed to playing in a group setting.

It's important, with both of these songs, to pay attention to keeping the beat. Remember that the bass is a rhythm instrument, and it's up to you to not speed up or slow down.

Congratulations on playing your first two songs! At the end of sections 2 and 3 (as well as further on in the book), you will find more play-along pieces designed to help you with the specific material covered in those sections, as well as to help you make huge steps toward improving as a bass player.

The Least You Need to Know

- Position, Posture, Practice, Patience, and Persistence
- The strings of the bass guitar are tuned: E, A, D, G.
- Tuning with a tuner is best, but other ways will work.
- Keep your fingers loose and relaxed while playing.

Part 2

Facing the Music

The bass guitar player is responsible for two essential elements of music: rhythm and harmonic tone. So it goes without saying that the bassist needs to know as much as possible about these building blocks of music.

In this section you'll start by learning to read musical notes, both in bass guitar tablature and in standard notation. Then you'll discover rhythms and how they are written out in music notation. Some old familiar melodies will help you understand the beat values of different notes.

Finally, you'll learn about the "root notes" of chords, which will provide you with a solid foundation as a beginning bass player. This knowledge will give you the tools to play alternating bass lines, your first big step toward sitting in with any band.

Chapter 4

Reading the Directions

In This Chapter

- Reading bass guitar tablature
- Learning the names of notes
- How to read music notation
- All about accidentals
- Your first position notes
- Why reading both notation and tablature is best

You've got your bass, and you're making sounds with it. Now it's time to learn what those sounds are. Since most music involves more than simply playing open strings (you knew that, right?), you have to learn the names of the notes you're playing.

Fortunately, there are two very easy ways to do this. Let's look at both methods—tablature and notation.

Bass by Numbers

Bass guitar *tablature* is a system of reading and writing music using four lines and numbers. As you might imagine, this is a very popular format, especially because it makes it easy to write out music using a computer.

Many converts from the guitar may already be familiar with tablature, or "TAB," for short. If you've never worked with TAB before, relax. It is an incredibly easy-to-learn visual system that makes reading music even less painless. Let's look at a typical example of TAB.

Tablature is a system for reading and writing music using four lines, which represent the four strings of the bass guitar. Numbers placed on the lines indicate which fret to finger in order to produce the desired note.

def•i•ni•tion

Standard tuning (often written as "EADG") means tuning the strings of your bass, from lowest to highest, to the notes E, A, D, and G, as we did in Chapter 3. When you tune your strings to different notes, it is called an **alternate tuning**. You'll see a few examples of alternate tuning in Chapter 22.

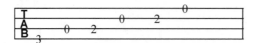

Sample of bass guitar tablature.

Reading the Lines

As you can see, we're dealing with a set of four horizontal lines. On the left, you'll usually see the word "TAB" or perhaps "Bass TAB," depending on the software used to create it. Believe it or not, this is so you won't confuse tablature with notation, which is written on a staff of five lines. Bass tablature usually has four lines (as in the example).

These lines represent the four strings of your bass guitar. The bottom line is your lowest string, the E string. Second line from the bottom is the A string, the next to the top line is the D string, and your G string is the top line.

If you were looking at tablature for a five-string bass, the TAB would have five lines. Six lines would represent TAB written for a six-string bass. But the same principle would apply—the bottom line is always your lowest string.

If for some reason the music calls for a tuning that is different from standard (EADG), the string names would either appear on the left side or there would be some kind of note to tell you what the new tuning is.

On these lines you will see numbers, which can range anywhere from 0 to 24. These are your notes.

Pick a Number, Any Number at All …

In tablature, whether for bass, guitar, or any other fretted instrument, the numbers on the lines are fret numbers. In our last example, for instance, you see a "3" on the bottom line. This means to place a finger on the third fret of the E string and to play the string. A "0" indicates to play an open string—think of it as the "zero fret." Again, in our last example, the note at the third fret of the E string is followed by the open A string, followed by the second fret of the A string, followed by the open D, the second fret of the D, and finally the open G string.

Let's take a look at another example. These are the first two lines of the melody to the song, "Twinkle, Twinkle," written out in bass tablature:

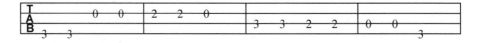

"Twinkle, Twinkle."

To play "Twinkle, Twinkle," just follow along with the numbers as they move from string to string. For the first phrase, play the note on the third fret of the E string twice, then the open A string followed by the third fret of the E string once again. Finally play the note on the third fret of the A string followed by the note at the second fret. You've just made it through the first phrase of "Twinkle, Twinkle"!

The second phrase starts out exactly like the first one. The only difference is that your last two notes are going to be the open D string and the note at the third fret of the A string.

You can see that learning to read music with TAB is pretty easy. But it's not foolproof.

What Tablature Rarely Bothers to Tell You

Take another look at our TAB of the first few notes of "Twinkle, Twinkle." If I hadn't told you it was "Twinkle, Twinkle," would you have known it? How would you have known how long to hold each note?

Most tablature—and it doesn't matter whether we're talking about bass or guitar tablature—doesn't tell you a thing about timing. Unless you already know the song in question, or have it handy to listen to, tablature will simply show you a group of notes run together, and you won't have a clue as to how they are supposed to be played in terms of timing. And since being a bass player is all about rhythm and timing, knowing the rhythm of the notes is pretty vital information.

Another problem with tablature is that you may know where the note you want to play is, but you don't know what that note is. That, too, is pretty vital information.

Learning to Read a New Language

Music is possibly the easiest language of all to learn. If you can recite the first third of the alphabet or if you're capable of counting to 12 (and occasionally to 13), then you can learn to read music.

Easy as A, B, C

When we read music, we are actually reading "notes," the sound that you make when you pluck a single string. Whether you play an open string or whether you've got a finger on a particular fret, you're playing a note. All notes have names. And their names correspond to a letter in the alphabet. Fortunately for us, there are only seven letters to learn:

A–B–C–D–E–F–G

When you play notes in sequence, they cycle through these letters. In other words, when you come to G, the next note will be A and then B and so on.

I'm sure that most of you are familiar with "Do, Re, Mi" from *The Sound Of Music*. If you sing along with the song, you sing a scale, in this case a series of eight notes, which goes like this:

Do–Re–Mi–Fa–Sol–La–Ti–Do

Rock Bottom

Many people think of tablature as a relatively new invention, but in truth it is at least as old as the Middle Ages, when it was used primarily by lute players. Since the proliferation of home computers, tablature has had quite a resurgence owing to the fact that it's a lot easier to type numbers and dotted lines than it is to buy, learn, and use special notation software.

Basso Profondo

Q: Is it important for a bass player to be able to read music? Do I really need to know much about music theory?

A: The more you know, the more gigs will be open to you. Reading and theory are not requirements to play some types of music (most rock, for example), but reading music will help you learn things that your ear may give you trouble learning. The same goes for theory.

Covering the Basses

Don't be confused that different notes have the same name! If it helps, think of a calendar that covers several years. You know that January 2008, while it will have the same number of days, and probably the same general temperatures and weather, will not be the same January that occurs in 2021. Notes with the same name actually have similar sounds, even though they are eight notes (called an octave) apart. Again, think about how similar the low Do in "Do, Re, Mi" sounds to the high Do. You'll find out much more about this in Chapter 7.

Now suppose I told you that "Do" was the note named "C." And suppose I also told you that in this scale, all the notes follow each other in sequential order. You would then know that you could sing this scale with these notes:

C–D–E–F–G–A–B–C

Do–Re–Mi–Fa–Sol–La–Ti–Do

You also know from singing this song that, even though the two Do or C notes have the same name, they sound different. The last Do is higher in pitch than the first one.

So how, when you're reading music, do you tell the difference?

Meet the Staff

Written music is not a series of letters or numbers, but a set of symbols placed on what is called a staff, which looks like this:

The staff.

As you can see, the staff looks a lot like the lines of bass tablature. There are five horizontal lines instead of four. And there are four spaces, one space between each line. Don't laugh at how basic this seems! The spaces are important, as you'll discover shortly.

When we put notes on the staff, they look like this:

Various notes on a staff.

Where a note appears on the staff is important. The line or space that the note occupies tells you the name of the note. And when you have two notes with the same name, as in our "Do, Re, Mi" example, the placement of the notes on the staff tells you which one is which. This is because staffs are also visual guides in terms of pitch. The higher a note is on the staff, the higher its tone. Notes that appear lower on the staff sound lower.

And here's the real beauty of it all: these positions never change. The A note that you get by playing the open A string of your bass, for example, always occupies the same place on the staff. Once you know where it is, you will always know where it is.

The Bass Clef

There's always a catch though, isn't there? First you have to know which type of staff you're dealing with. All staffs are identified by a symbol that sits on their far left edge. This is called a clef.

Bass players generally read music in the Bass Clef, which is also called the "F clef." It looks like this:

The bass clef.

The bass, or F clef, is one of several different clefs. Most instruments use music in the treble, or G clef, which looks like this:

The treble clef.

For now, though, let's take a closer look at the F clef and learn something important. Do you see those two dots that surround the second line from the top? Guess what note is placed on that line?

Reading the Lines—and Between Them

Of course you know that it's F! And with this piece of information, we can easily start naming our other notes. Since F occupies the second line from the top, a note in the space immediately between F and the top line is G. A note on the very top line will be A, since A comes after G.

Going in the opposite direction, notes in the space immediately under F will be E, those on the middle line are D, and so on. Looking at all the notes within our staff, we have the following:

The notes of the bass clef.

Some people prefer to learn the notes by separating them into "line" notes and "space" notes. There are all sorts of mnemonic devices that lend themselves to learning in this fashion. Let's look at the notes again, this time separated into those on the lines and those that occupy the spaces.

"Line" notes and "space" notes.

Covering the Basses

Many people find it easier to remember note positions on the staff by coming up with their own mnemonic phrase. Instead of using "Good Boys Do Fine Always," try "Great Bassists Deserve Full Attention." I think my favorite one came from a friend of mine who is a big Buddy Holly fan: "Good Buddies Don't Fade Away."

"Good Boys Do Fine Always" and "All Cows Eat Grass" are far and away the most popular ways of remembering these notes. You can, of course, come up with all sorts of memory aids of your own.

Now that you know the names of our notes and where those notes are located on the staff, it's time to see exactly how to apply this knowledge to your bass guitar. Here are the notes for our open A, D, and G strings, in both notation and bass guitar tablature:

Notes of the open A, D, and G strings.

So far, so good! But where's the note for our open E string? In order to find it, we need to expand our staff a little.

Beyond the Bottom Line

The bottom line of our staff is G. The space below the bottom line, and by now you can say this with confidence, is F. And if we were to draw a line below that space, it would be E. This line beyond the staff is called a ledger line, and they can go both below and above the staff, as shown in the following example:

Notes on the ledger lines.

Unless you get into alternate tunings (more on that in Chapter 22), this E note is as low as you can go on your bass. And while you will occasionally play higher than the C note on the ledger line above the staff, most of the music you're likely to see as a bass player will consist of the 13 notes we've seen. Let's review them in the following chart, which once again shows both the notation and bass guitar tablature:

All 13 notes from E to C.

So you see that there's not a whole lot to learn here, just 13 total lines and spaces. If you can learn just one note position a day, then you'll be reading music in less than 2 weeks. And you'll know it for the rest of your life. What a deal!

Accidentals Will Happen

You'll need to know one more bit of information about notes. You've seen a piano, right? And you've seen how it has white keys and black keys? All the white keys are the notes we've covered so far, that is, A through G. The black keys are called flats and sharps, and these terms refer to raising or lowering a note by a half step.

In music notation, any symbol for sharp, flat, or natural is called an *accidental*.

Look Sharp!

Your bass guitar doesn't have keys like a piano; it has frets. Moving up the neck from fret to fret on the same string raises the tone of a string half a step from the note on the fret before it. Play the open A string. Now place a finger of your left hand on the first fret of the A string and play it again. Congratulations! You have just played the note A-sharp.

If you were to read this in music notation, it would look like the following:

A and A-sharp.

def•i•ni•tion

Accidentals are symbols, sharps, flats, or naturals, which signal a change in the pitch of a note, either raising or lowering it half a step—that is, by one fret.

See the symbol that looks like a pound sign (#) directly in front of the second note? That, in music notation, is the sharp sign. When you see that, it means to play the note immediately after it one fret higher than you normally would.

In addition to the notes you already know, there are five sharps to add to the list. So the 12 notes you will need to know are:

C–C#–D–D#–E–F–F#–G–G#–A–A#–B

Notice that there is no sharp between E and F, as well as no sharp between B and C. Why? This is simply the way Western music—"Western" meaning the Western Hemisphere and not songs by Roy Rogers—is written. It's like knowing that the world is round. We accept it for what it is.

Finding a Flat

Physics is an important part of music, particularly the part about "what goes up must come down!" If we can raise any note up half a step, then we should be able to lower any note half a step as well. The flat sign, which looks like a small, pointed "b," tells you to lower a note half a step.

Go back and play your open A string. In our last chapter, you also learned that this A note can be played on the fifth fret of the E string. Play that A on the E string now and then guess where A-flat is? That's right, on the fourth fret of the E string. In music notation, it would look like this:

A and A-flat.

Let's look at our 12 notes again. Remember, since there is no sharp between E and F or between B and C, there won't be any flat between those notes either. So our 12 notes will look like this:

C–Db–D–Eb–E–F–Gb–G–Ab–A–Bb–B

Seeing this may make a light bulb go off in your head. Db and C# occupy the same place in our chart. Could they be the same note? Indeed they are!

Naturals

Sometimes after a note has been marked as being flat or sharp, we might want to play it again in its regular form. A natural sign, which is shown in the example below, negates any flat or sharp sign.

A A# B A

Use of the natural symbol.

In this example, we start with A, the open A string, then play A# (the first fret), then B, (the second fret) and then end with the open A string once more, as notated by the natural sign. You won't run into these symbols often, but you will come across them often enough that it's a good idea to know what they are.

Notes in Open Position

Now that we know both notation and TAB, let's take a look at the notes in "open position," that is, the notes that occupy the open strings and first five frets of each string. You'll be seeing these a lot in the very near future, so now's a good time to get comfortable with them.

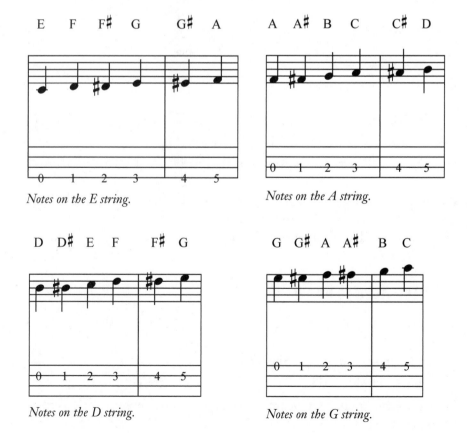

Notes on the E string.

Notes on the A string.

Notes on the D string.

Notes on the G string.

The Best of Both Worlds

Given the choice, most guitarists and bass players will read TAB rather than music notation. I'd like to suggest that, whenever possible, you try to use both these ways of reading music. And that, to many teachers, is possibly the best thing you could do to help yourself learn your instrument. We've mentioned that TAB usually can't do much for you in terms of timing. But it does have some very important things going for it.

Throughout the rest of this book, you will find all the musical examples written out in both music notation and bass guitar tablature. This way you'll be able to learn the notes, or not if you so choose. As your teacher, I highly recommend that you try to use both methods. In the long run, it will make you a much better musician. After all, the last thing most of us need is less knowledge!

Where Do You Put Your Fingers?

As you've already figured out, you can play one particular note in several different places on the neck of your bass. The note of the open G string, for instance, can also be found on the fifth fret of the D string, the tenth fret of the A string, and the fifteenth fret of the E string, as you can see in the following example:

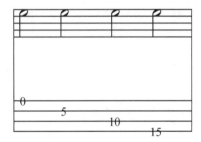

G on all four strings.

While music notation will always show this note as occupying the top space of the staff, TAB goes one better and can show you on which string and which fret to play it.

As you progress through the rest of this book, you will find many instances where you will learn a particular riff (a short musical phrase) at one particular position of the neck. TAB will make this process painless by telling you which string and fret to use.

The Least You Need to Know

- ◆ Knowing tablature allows you to read music without reading music notation.
- ◆ Most bass music is written in the bass clef.
- ◆ "Good Boys Do Fine Always" and "All Cows Eat Grass."
- ◆ Both music notation and tablature have good and bad points. Your best bet is to learn and use both.

Covering the Basses

While people can come up with lots of excuses for not being able to read music, no one ever says reading music is a bad thing. Being able to read notation will allow you to access songs throughout history and from all over the world. No other single skill will allow you to learn so much for so little effort. And remember, the more you practice reading, the easier it gets.

Fascinating Rhythm

In This Chapter

- Learning the timing of notes
- Understanding eighth notes, sixteenth notes, and triplets
- Reading time signatures
- Dealing with dotted notes and ties
- Learning rest notation
- The difference between timing and tempo
- Learning to dissect tricky timings

Thanks to notation and bass tablature, you now know the names of your notes and how to find them on your bass guitar. It's time to learn about timing, that is, knowing how long any given note is supposed to last. Being able to read rhythms will help you to get good at playing various patterns as well as creating your own.

Keeping time is one of the most important tasks for the bass player. Maintaining a steady rhythm keeps a song moving smoothly. In this chapter we will learn how to read the rhythm of notes and begin to work on becoming excellent timekeepers.

Measure for Measure, Note for Note

When you watch a band perform live, you'll often hear someone (usually the drummer) start a song by counting off the beat, "One, two, three, four." When you listen to music, you might keep the beat yourself by tapping your toe or clapping your hands or snapping your fingers.

Music is measured in beats. Most songs that we listen to fall into one of two categories—songs that the beats are counted in sets of four and those that are counted in sets of threes. In both music notation and bass tablature, the grouping of beats is done by measures. A measure is indicated by a vertical line, which cuts through the horizontal lines of either the staff or the TAB, such as in the following example.

Within any measure, you will find your notes. As mentioned in our last chapter, the symbols of music notation tell you two things: where the symbol appears on the staff determines the name of the note, and what the symbol looks like tells you the duration of the note.

Whole, Half, and Quarter Notes

Let's take a look at the basic types of notes:

Whole notes, like the one seen in the first measure, are four beats long.

A *half note*—you'll see two in the second measure of the above illustration—looks just like a whole note except it has a "stem," that vertical line on its edge. Stems can go either up or down from the note-head. As you might suspect from its name, a half note receives two beats, or half as many as a whole note.

The third measure contains four *quarter notes*. They also have stems, which again can go either up or down, and they look like half notes that someone has filled in. The quarter note gets a single beat.

Eighth and Sixteenth Notes

A lot of notes, particularly for the bass player, last less than one beat. These are eighth notes and sixteenth notes. Written in music notation, they look like quarter notes with little flags on the stems. The eighth note has one flag and the sixteenth note has two, as you can see in the following illustration:

As you can see, these notes can be written singly or grouped together. When in a group, the flags are often joined by a solid line (two solid lines for sixteenth notes).

One helpful way of learning the concept of note lengths, particularly when it comes to eighth and sixteenth notes, involves a little toe tapping and speaking. Start by tapping your foot in a slow steady pace. Each time your foot hits the floor, say "walk." You are counting quarter notes.

Now say "running" over and over again, but be sure to do it evenly. You should be saying the first syllable each time your foot hits the floor and the second syllable when your foot comes up. Your foot is still counting quarter notes but you are speaking in eighth notes.

Finally, and while your foot is still keeping the same steady beat, say "running faster" with each tap. Keep the pace of the foot tapping the same, so that you're squeezing four syllables into each foot tap. You should be saying "running" when your foot hits the floor and "faster" when it comes up. You are now speaking in sixteenth notes.

Triplets

You can also divide a note evenly into thirds. These notes are called triplets and they look like this:

We can use a variation of our earlier exercise to help get a grasp on triplets. Tap your foot once more in a slow steady pace. Now let's talk about animals! Each time your foot hits the floor, say "frog," then "chicken," then "elephant," then "alligator," making certain to evenly distribute the syllables. "Frogs" are quarter notes, the syllables of the word "chickens" are eighth notes, the syllables of the word "elephants" are triplets, and the four syllables of "alligators" are sixteenth notes.

This may seem a little silly, but it's an important concept to grasp. If you can get to the point where you're tapping your foot evenly and smoothly switching between your animals ("Frog. Elephant. Frog. Chicken. Alligator. Elephant. Alligator. Frog. Chicken. Elephant. Chicken."), then you are well on your way to being able to switch rhythms while playing. Plus you'll be a big hit with little kids!

Signs of the Times

At the start of any piece of music in notation, you will see the bass clef (which we covered in the last chapter) followed by what appears to be a fraction. That's the time signature. Here are some examples:

Reading a time signature is a snap. The upper number tells you how many beats each measure will have. The lower number indicates the length of each beat. Almost all of the music you are likely to encounter will have time signatures of either 4/4 or 3/4 time.

Common Time

4/4 time is the most commonly used time signature. In songs, it's called Common Time. Quite often you will see a "C" used in place of the 4/4 fraction.

In 4/4 time, each measure contains four beats. So any measure can have either one whole note (four beats), two half notes (two beats each), four quarter notes (one beat each), or eight eighth notes (a half-beat apiece). It can also have different combinations of half notes, quarter notes, and eighth notes, as long as it all adds up to four beats. Let's use the first line of "Old MacDonald," which is four measures long, as an example:

● 5.7

def•i•ni•tion

Sometimes a song will not start on the first beat, but rather on the second, third, or fourth, or even on one of the fractional beats. In music notation, this is expressed with **pick up notes**, which will be written before the first full measure starts. When this happens, the song's last measure will usually contain only enough beats to make up for the pick up notes at the beginning. So, for instance, if a song in 4/4 started with a pick up note of a quarter note, then the last measure would normally contain only three beats. When someone counts off a song with pick up notes, he will usually count off a full measure and then the number of beats before the first pick up note. In the example just cited, you would count, "One, two, three, four, one, two, three ..." and then start in on the song.

It's easy to see and hear how you can have a combination of notes to make up the timing of a song. Measures one and three each contain four quarter notes. Measure two has two quarter notes (one beat apiece) and a single half note (two beats), which adds up to four beats. And measure four contains a single whole note.

There are many different time signatures, each of them expressed as a fraction. (2/2 time is called *cut time* and is sometimes written as a "C" with a vertical slash through it.) Besides 4/4 and 3/4 time, here are some that occur in music quite often:

2/2	2 beats per measure	half note = 1 beat
2/4	2 beats per measure	quarter note = 1 beat
6/8	6 beats per measure	eighth note = 1 beat
12/8	12 beats per measure	eighth note = 1 beat
5/4	5 beats per measure	quarter note = 1 beat

Let's try another example using a song you all know:

● 5.8

This one is a little trickier, using half notes, quarter notes, and eighth notes. Try playing it along with the CD to get yourself started, but then also play it on your own as a test of your ability to keep time.

Waltzing Around

3/4 time is probably the second most common time signature. As you've already deduced, in 3/4 time, each measure has three beats, and each quarter note equals one beat. Here is an exercise in 3/4 time:

🔘 *5.9*

This exercise is a combination of half notes, quarter notes, and eighth notes, just like our examples of 4/4 time. But you can hear a definite difference in the time signatures. The accents or emphasis of 4/4 time usually occur every other beat (that is, on the first and third or on the second and fourth beats), while in 3/4 time the accent tends to fall only on the first beat.

3/4 time also presents some interesting questions. You already know of notes that last four beats and two beats, but we haven't learned any that are three beats long. Let's take care of that situation right now.

Ties and Dots

Music is obviously not all whole notes, half notes, quarter notes, and the like. Not only can you have notes that last for three, five, ten, or even more beats, you can also have notes that are one-and-a-half or even three-quarters of a beat long.

Sometimes, too, a note lasts longer than the end of a given measure. If, for example, we wanted the final note of the previous example to last six beats, it would have to extend through three measures.

Fortunately, music notation is equipped to handle all that and more. Let's start out by tying some notes together.

Ties

So suppose you want to have a note that lasts for six beats. The simplest solution, given what we already know, would be to somehow add a half note (two beats) to the four beats of a whole note. And that is precisely what you do, by means of what we call a tie.

Ties have to occur between notes of the same name, otherwise we have what is called a slur, which we will explore in depth at the start of Part 5. Ties can, and often do, occur between notes of the same length. If you wanted to write a note of eight beats in length, for example, you simply tie together two whole notes.

Thinking back about how one might write a note of three beats, the simple answer seems to be just tying together a half note and a quarter note. You'd be right in thinking this, but there's an even easier way to deal with it.

Dotted Half Notes

In music notation, a three-beat note is indicated with the following symbol:

The dot that you see after the half note is shorthand for "add on half of the original length of this note." This allows a dot to occur after any type of note, but you'll rarely see it with a whole note.

A dotted half note, then, lasts three beats—the two beats of the half note, plus an extra one beat (half of two) for the dot. Let's try a piece that incorporates both dotted half notes and ties:

🔊 *5.12*

So far, so good!

Dotted Quarter Notes and More

A dotted quarter note creates a note that lasts a beat and a half, which is one beat for the quarter note and a half beat for the dot. This particular note is used in songs much more often than you might imagine, especially in bass accompaniments.

🔊 *5.13*

Doesn't that sound familiar? How often have you heard a bass player using that particular rhythm? It's a staple of ballads (of all genres from pop to heavy metal), folk and country music, jazz, and more.

To demonstrate the difference the dotted quarter note can make in a piece of music, let's try this melody:

🎵 *5.14*

Let's play this piece again, only with some dotted quarter notes to make the melody more interesting:

🎵 *5.15*

You can probably hear now that this is the melody to "Silent Night." Isn't it amazing what a small change in timing can make? This is why bass players need to know rhythms and timing.

You can also have dotted eighth notes and dotted sixteenth notes, which, as you might imagine, can be tricky, both to read and to play. As beginners, we're not too concerned with those just yet.

Taking a Rest

Silence is an important part of music. Many pros will tell you that knowing when *not* to play is just as, if not more, important than playing. In music notation, *rest symbols* indicate a period of silence. As you might guess, rest symbols only indicate a beat length, since there is no reason for them to give you a note name! Here are our rest symbols:

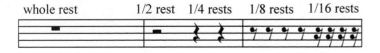

| whole rest | 1/2 rest | 1/4 rests | 1/8 rests | 1/16 rests |

Covering the Basses

So many bass players worry about making noise that they don't put too much time into practicing rests. The idea is to make certain there is a definite rest, a definite moment of silence. Most bass players will lightly touch a string with either the index or middle finger of their right hand to deaden it. Some prefer to use their fretting hand, raising the fretting finger just high enough off the string to stop it from sounding. Both techniques take a little practice, if only to get used to the idea. But before you know it, getting the right lengths of your rests as well as your notes will be second nature to you.

Unlike notes, rests are never tied together and it's rare for them to have dots, but it does happen sometimes. Usually, for example, if someone wants to indicate a rest of three beats, they will use a half rest symbol followed by a quarter rest symbol.

Don't think that being able to execute a rest is a simple matter and won't require some practice! A rest requires that you deaden any ringing strings so there is no sound coming from your instrument. That's not always easy.

Like anything you want to get good at, start with some simple exercises, such as these:

5.17

Let's wrap up this section with one more exercise focusing on rests:

5.18

Playing More Notes Doesn't Make a Song Faster

As a bass player, keeping the beat is important. You have to understand that playing a measure full of sixteenth notes can be the same tempo as a measure of four quarter notes. Listen to and try out this example:

5.19

You can hear the metronome keeping a steady time throughout this example, even though the number of notes and the types of notes being played varies greatly.

People, as a rule, have a tendency to speed up when playing. It's up to you to work on keeping things even. A good bassist helps his band maintain the rhythm. Practicing with a metronome will help.

Taking a Timing (or a Phrase) Apart

Learning how to play particularly tricky timing or short, complicated musical phrases can be the most rewarding experience. It can also be very frustrating if you don't approach it correctly. In Chapter 3 we talked about the importance of proper practice. Timing and tempo are aspects of playing where practice pays off big time.

But it's important to practice intelligently. To many people, practice involves playing a song from start to finish and then playing it again from start to finish. If you're having trouble with a difficult phrase somewhere in the song, this method of practice isn't going to help you very much. Usually what happens is that you play the song the first time, make your mistakes on the difficult part, and then play it again and often make the same mistakes in the same place, even though you know it's coming up in the song.

In the case of working on a song in an unusual timing, it's a good idea to break the measures up into timings that you can work with. Let's work with something in 7/4 timing as a demonstration:

There are number of ways to break up a measure of seven beats. In this example I've done it in two ways. First, we'll split the measure of 7/4 into a measure of 3/4 time and one of 4/4 time, like this:

Next we'll break up the 7/4 measure into one of 4/4 time followed by one of 3/4 time.

Each of these methods gives the original 7/4 measure a different feel in terms of phrasing. Ultimately what will help you decide what to do will be the feel of the piece of music when played. Arranging songs with timing like this can be a lot of fun as well as a challenge.

With riffs and phrases, slow things down as well as break them up. Instead of playing the difficult phrase from start to finish, focus first on the problem area. Break off the whole phrase to start with and then cut up that phrase into smaller, more manageable phrases. For instance, let's say that we were having problems with something like this:

The first thing to do here is to slow everything down and work in a deliberately slow tempo. Taking on the seven sixteenth notes at the end of the first measure is not hard when you count it out slowly. The tricky part here is actually the second measure. You have to hit the two sixteenth notes, one immediately after the other. Fortunately, the second one is tied to a quarter note, which means that the dotted quarter note will be played on the second half of the second beat and the final quarter note on the fourth beat.

Once you manage to straighten something like this out in your head, it's a short step to playing it.

The Least You Need to Know

- ◆ Each measure will contain a specific total beat of notes.
- ◆ Notes will always tell you their length by their shape.
- ◆ Time signatures tell you how many beats are in each measure.
- ◆ There are rest symbols as well, and they all deal with timing.
- ◆ Breaking down a tricky timing or phrase and playing it slowly will help you to play it well at tempo.

Chapter 6

Getting to Your Roots

In This Chapter

- ◆ Reading sheet music and fake sheets
- ◆ Discovering chords
- ◆ Finding the root note of any chord
- ◆ How to find octaves and fifths
- ◆ Learning basic alternating bass lines
- ◆ Some more play-along songs for practice

As you read in Chapter 1, the bass player has to both maintain the rhythm of the song and be a "harmonic center." You learned about reading and keeping rhythm in the last chapter. Here you will learn the basics of harmony, discovering the roots of chords that make up songs. It's even easier than reading music. By the time you finish this chapter, you will be able to play a rudimentary bass part for any song you'd like.

Clean Sheets

And reading music is as good a place as any to start. First, let's think about what a song actually is. Obviously, a song is a piece of music. But how do we tell one song from another? Not necessarily by title, since some songs have the same title. Usually we identify a song by its melody, which, in popular music, is the part that is sung or hummed or whistled. The melody is usually accompanied by a harmony, which is provided by the instruments playing either single notes or chords (more on that in a minute), and by a rhythm, which is played by the drums or some kind of percussion.

As a bass player, your job is to be a bridge between all three of these fundamental parts of a song. This is what makes playing the bass a challenge, but also a lot of fun.

Part of the challenge is that bass players are often given a free hand when it comes to creating their parts. But you obviously can't start in playing any note you'd like! What you need right off the bat are a few important clues, and that's where written music comes in. Chances are likely that you will see bass parts either written out in sheet music or "lead sheets," or that you will be following along with the chord progressions mapped out on "fake sheets," or what I call "chord sheets." Let's take a look at each.

Sheet Music

A typical piece of sheet music is actually piano music, and it often looks like this:

My Bonnie Lies Over The Ocean

Traditional

The top staff is the melody. It is usually written in the treble (or G) clef. The next two staffs are the accompaniment. One is written in the treble clef and one is written in the bass (F) clef, since a pianist plays with both hands—the left hand plays the bass clef part while the right hand plays the treble clef.

In this example, a bass player would play the lower notes of the bass clef part. For the first measure, you would play C (third fret of the A string) and then two Es (second fret of the D string). Measure 2 would be G (third fret of the E string) followed by two Bs (second fret of the A string). You go back to C, then E, and then G in measure three before playing the C note, held for two beats because it's a half note, of measure four.

You can see and hear that you're not playing the melody of the song, but rather providing accompaniment to the melody and the piano part in a rhythmic fashion. You are creating a foundation that the rest of the song can stand upon.

Fake Sheets

Bass players are not always lucky enough to have as much information as sheet music can provide. Sometimes instead of sheet music, the bassist will play from a "fake sheet."

The typical fake sheet will contain the song's melody line (written out in notation on the treble clef) along with the song's lyrics. The accompaniment will consist of chord names written above the staff, like this:

my Bon - nie lies o - ver the o - cean____ My Bon - nie lies o - ver the sea____

You can see the names of the chords change at certain intervals. The first full measure is played with the C chord, the second with F and then C returns for the next three measures. D7 and G are the chords for the final two measures of this example.

It's important to note here that, at first glance, chord names seem very similar to note names. Don't let that throw you off right now; we'll get to that shortly.

Chord Sheets

Fake sheets themselves can be a luxury. If you're playing in a band or just jamming with some friends, you don't usually even get that much. You probably will find yourself playing from "chord sheets" or "cheat sheets." These are simply lines of lyrics written out with chord names placed in strategic spots over the words. A chord sheet for "My Bonnie" looks like this:

My Bonnie Lies Over The Ocean

```
      C          F        C
My Bonnie lies over the ocean
      C          D7       G
My Bonnie lies over the sea
      C          F        C
My Bonnie lies over the ocean
      D7         G7       C
Oh bring back my Bonnie to me
```

Another helpful thing is to always have a pencil or pen handy (you can keep one in your bass case), so that you can make notes for yourself directly on your copy of any music, chord sheet, or lead sheet. This is a great way to remember the little things that make up a song arrangement, such as changes in tempo or dynamics. You can even write in a part you've come up with so that you'll remember it the next time you play the song.

Lead Sheets

Sometimes it's very important to play a single line or a short musical phrase of a particular song. Think of the bass guitar part that opens "Another One Bites the Dust" by Queen (the song was written, naturally, by their bassist, John Deacon). That simple little bass line pretty much defines the song. You couldn't imagine anyone playing the song without incorporating this bass part into the arrangement.

We call these little musical phrases *riffs*. When a riff is so closely associated with a single song, we call it the song's *signature riff*. Signature riffs can be played by

---

Rock Bottom

Fake books have been around quite awhile and are great things for bass players to have. They usually contain hundreds of songs in a single book, simply with the melody, lyrics, and chord progressions. This gives the bass player free rein at coming up with her bass lines. Typical fake books also provide a lot of variety in the song material (where else would you find Stevie Wonder, George M. Cohen, Sting, Richard Wagner, and Lerner and Lowe in the same place?), although it's currently popular to have "genre fake books," written specifically for blues, jazz, folk, and other styles. To get a good idea if a particular fake book is for you, look through the table of contents before buying it. If you know a third to half the songs, you've got a good one.

def·i·ni·tion

You'll be learning more about chords in Chapters 8 and 9, but for now you might want to know a few basic things. If a chord is simply the letter of a note name, like C or F# or Ab, it is a **major** chord. Chords with "m" after the initial letter are **minor** chords. For our purposes in this chapter, you don't have to worry about knowing the difference between the major and minor chords.

Rock Bottom

In the Baroque era of music, the figured bass was a form of musical shorthand similar to today's fake sheets and lead sheets. But it was the bass line that was written out. Numbers from 2 to 8 were written below the bass part and the other musicians, usually keyboard players, had to figure out the chords and fill in the upper parts. That may seem very hard to do, but after a while you get used to the patterns and know the harmony you need instead of figuring it out from scratch each time.

any instrument. You may even have heard high school marching bands play "Another One Bites the Dust" or "Smoke on the Water." But more commonly, a band will try to copy the original instrumentation whenever possible.

Lead sheets, often used by jazz musicians, look like a combination of chord sheets and fake sheets. But instead of notating the melody, they will spell out a signature riff, or any bit of music deemed essential by the arranger. This part could be assigned to a specific instrument, such as the bass, piano, saxophone, or guitar, or given to the band to play as a single unit. Let's say that you were asked to play an arrangement of "Pop Goes the Weasel" in which everyone in the band played the same notes on the "Pop Goes the Weasel" part. The lead sheet would look like this:

(repeat sign - means go back to the beginning and play again or as many times as directed)

In this example, a bass player would be free to play anything in the first 12 measures (notice the repeat sign, which indicates to play the first three measures four times), provided the bass line fit under the C chords played by the rest of the band. Measure 13 calls for the bass to play a single A note (second fret of the G string), followed by a rest of two beats. A half note of D, a quarter note of F, and then a dotted half note each of E and C end the piece.

Instead of a signature riff, lead sheets will sometimes notate specific rhythms to follow, which is indicated by writing out the notes like this:

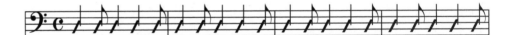

You can see that the "body" of the notes, which are usually small ellipses that indicate which note to play, are now simple slash marks. Which notes you play are not as important as playing this particular rhythm. If no specific rhythm is required, there will be no stems, as in our example on "Pop Goes the Weasel."

If you decide to get into doing studio work as a bass player (or playing any instrument), your ability to read from lead sheets, sheet music, or fake sheets may mean the difference between getting a job (and getting paid!) or sitting at home. That's a pretty good incentive to learn to read music.

Striking a Chord

You've seen in these examples that bass players should be somewhat familiar with chords. Depending on a particular chord, there will be "good notes" to play along with it. There are also plenty of "clunkers," notes that will sound somewhat off, to say the least. How do you know the difference?

First we need to understand what a chord is. A chord is a specific combination of three or more notes. We'll be covering just about every chord there is in Section 3. For now, though, let's try this approach: think of notes as letters. Except for A and I, you cannot make words out of a single letter. Words are made when letters are grouped in specific sets. Similarly, one forms chords by grouping certain notes together.

Play a C note on the third fret of the A string. Now, while holding the C note, also finger the E note on the second fret of the D string and strike both strings at once. You have just played an *interval*, or what some folks call a *dyad*. Finally, still keeping your fingers on the C and E notes, strike the A, D, and G strings with one downward sweep of your thumb. That's a chord, specifically the C major chord. As a bass player, you won't often play chords but it is vital that you know about them. The more you understand about how chords are put together the better a bass player you can become, because chords give you the framework for easily identifying good notes and avoiding the clunkers.

Digging Out the Root

In our earlier examples showing typical fake sheets and chord sheets, you might have mistaken the chord designations for note names. That is a common thing to do, and it's also the first step to smart bass playing. Every chord has what we call a root note, and, conveniently enough, that note shares the same name of the chord.

As you'll see in Chapters 8 and 9, there are many different chords. But each chord only has one root, so if you can name the chord from its symbol, you already know its root, and if you can find that root note on your bass, then you have a note to play.

The cool thing about the root of the chord is that our root note is not affected by whether the chord in question is a major, minor, augmented, diminished, or any other type. The root of C major is C. The root of Cm7sus4 is also C. The root of Eb6 is Eb. Finding the root is that easy.

The following example takes another look at the first line of the chord sheet for "My Bonnie" and add our root notes in a few different rhythmic patterns.

You get a measure of three quarter notes of C to start with, followed by three notes of G. The rhythm of the second measure is a dotted quarter (one and a half beats) followed by an eighth note (half a beat) followed by a quarter note, which is one beat long. Then you get a half note, a quarter note, and another half note of C before taking a rest of one beat.

This may not be the most exciting bass line ever played, but it definitely does the job in terms of both keeping the rhythm and establishing our harmony. Being able to come up with something like this may seem very simple, but it is at the heart of being good at the bass. Once you can handle a basic task such as this, it's easy to branch out and make your part more interesting to both you and the listener.

Basso Profondo

Q: Is it necessary for a bassist to be able to read all the different types of written arrangements?

A: A studio bass player may be asked to play off of sheet music, lead sheets, fake sheets, or chord sheets at a moment's notice. He might even get a lead sheet or fake sheet with Roman numerals written on it instead of chords (as you'll see in Chapter 11).

Likewise if you join a band that's already got a repertoire of songs, you may find yourself faced with any of these types of written music. The more comfortable you are with all these types of sheets, the easier you'll find it to play with others.

🔵 *6.6*

From C to Shining C

def•i•ni•tion

An **octave** is the distance from one note to the next note of the same name. It's called an octave because the higher note is eight notes away from the lower one (you start counting with the original note). You'll be learning more about octaves and other intervals (the distances between notes) in Chapter 7.

The next step, in fact, involves finding more notes that you can use. One obvious choice would be a note of the same name. We've been playing C, the root of the C chord, at the third fret of the A string, but we also know that there's a higher C note at the fifth fret of the G string. That certainly seems like fair game.

The C at the fifth fret of the G string is an *octave* higher than the C played at the third fret of the A string. There is also a C note even higher than that at the 17th fret of the G string. On your typical four string bass, you can usually find any note at three different octave levels.

High Octaves, Low Octaves

Because of the way the bass guitar is tuned, you don't have to hunt around to find the closest octave of any given note. If your starting note is on the E or A string, your octave note will be higher. You will always find it two strings and two frets away, as shown in the following illustration:

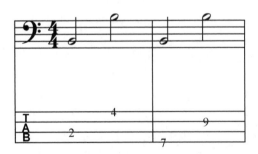

Using the B note as the subject of this example, start by fretting the B note with your index finger at the second fret of the A string. Now place your pinky or ring finger on the G string (two strings away) at the fourth fret (two frets away). That's where the next B note, one octave higher than the original, will be found.

This pattern holds all over the fretboard. If you play the B note at the seventh fret of the E string, then you will find the next B at the ninth fret (two frets away) of the D string (two strings away).

And this works in reverse as well. Use your pinky or ring finger to play the F note at the tenth fret of the G string. Can you find the lower F note? If you're playing the eighth fret (two frets down) of the A string (two strings lower), then you're in the right place!

Taking the Fifth

Another note that you can almost always use when playing from a chord sheet is the *fifth* of the chord. You'll be learning more about fifths and other intervals in Chapter 7, but for the moment, let me show you how to find the fifth of any given root note:

Root   high 5th Root low 5th Root   high 5th Root low 5th

To find a fifth lower than your root, provided that root is on the A, D, or G string, is a snap. It's on the same fret on the next lower (thicker) string. If your root is on the E, A, or D string, you will find the higher fifth on the next higher (thinner) string, two frets away.

Simply being able to add these two notes, the octave, and the fifth, can turn your basic root-only bass line into something much more like music.

Alternate Realities

If you can find your roots, octaves, and fifths, then you can play alternating bass lines. An *alternating bass* pattern does exactly what it says; it alternates from one note (usually the root) to another (usually the fifth) while the band plays a single chord.

For all of the following examples, we'll be thinking that the band is playing a C chord. Let's start with the simplest alternating pattern we can.

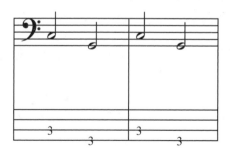

First play the C note at the third fret of the A string. It's a half note in this example, so hold it for two beats. Then play the G note at the third fret of the E string, again holding it for two beats. You can play this over and over again if the song calls for several measures of a C chord.

Rock Bottom

Alternating bass lines are the heartbeat of many folk and country songs, but you can hear them in almost any genre of music. They can add elegance to ballads, be they pop or metal, and they can propel a ska song as it races along at a breakneck speed. Don't discount the alternating bass as simple or beneath your notice. Sometimes it's exactly what a song needs.

Now let's try some other alternating patterns, keeping with our C chord, which means using the C and G notes for the bass lines. Here we are alternating up to G from the root of C:

In our next examples we mix things up a bit, alternating between the root (C) and the fifth (G) in different directions.

And finally, let's try a long combination of our various alternating patterns:

🔘 *6.13*

An Easy Piece to Practice

It's time to put what we've learned in this chapter to practical use. Here is a lead sheet for a simple, four-chord jam-along song:

6.14

This is a classic chord pattern, used in songs from all genres for well over 50 years. The band will play it through four times. The bass will play the first two times through the changes, so that you can hear and play along with the suggested bass line.

When you feel comfortable with this song, feel free to try your hand at playing your own bass lines and rhythms. For now, concentrate on simply playing roots and octaves and fifths, just so you can gain some confidence in playing along with a band.

The Least You Need to Know

- ◆ Chords are three or more different notes played at the same time.
- ◆ The root note of a chord is the note that shares the name of the chord.
- ◆ The octave is always two frets higher and two strings higher than the root.
- ◆ The fifth is always two frets higher and one string higher than the root. It is also on the same fret but a string lower.
- ◆ Alternating bass lines use the root and fifth of the same chord.

Part

The Great Leap Forward

Now that you know your notes, you'll want to learn about chord arpeggios and scales, the basic components of most bass lines. You'll start with the major scale and use your knowledge of it to create almost every chord imaginable. Then you'll put your arpeggios to good use by playing with the band in three jam-along songs.

The Major Scale

In This Chapter

- ◆ Defining scales
- ◆ Creating the major scale
- ◆ The difference between open and closed position playing
- ◆ Finding any major scale on your bass
- ◆ Expanding your major scale pattern across the fingerboard
- ◆ Finding intervals on your fingerboard
- ◆ How practicing intervals improves your ear

The first words of the song "Do, Re, Mi" from the movie *The Sound Of Music* are "Let's start at the very beginning," and, for the musician, the major scale is at the heart of just about everything you could want to know about music. If you know the major scale, you'll be a very short step away from being able to form any chord or chord arpeggio that you want. And, as you'll learn later in Chapter 15, knowing your major scale is equivalent to knowing seven modal scales. I know I keep saying this, but it's amazing how much you can get from music by learning so very little.

In this chapter we'll look at all of our notes and learn how to arrange them into scales, specifically the major scale. We'll also find that learning how to play any single major scale on our bass will give us the ability to play any of the 12 possible major scales.

Yes, I did say 12 major scales! And this would also probably be a good time to tell you that there are many more scales other than the major scale. Don't let this worry you—the major scale is the basis for understanding all of these various possible permutations.

D'oh! Re, Mi—What's in a Scale

Think again about the song from *The Sound Of Music*. We can all sing "Do, Re, Mi, Fa, Sol, La, Ti, Do," but what are we actually singing? We are singing notes in a specific pattern, from the first "Do" to the final "Do," seven notes later. This particular pattern is called the *major scale*.

A *scale* is defined as a sequence of notes starting at one specific note (in this case, "Do") going to the next occurrence of that same note (the final "Do"). This sequence follows any one of several patterns, which are usually a combination of whole steps and half steps. The specific pattern of half steps (each fret of your bass guitar is a half step apart) and whole steps (two frets apart) determines what type of scale it is.

Our "Do, Re, Mi" fits this definition, because we go from one note, "Do," to the next appearance of the same note, "Do." So how do we go about finding the pattern of this scale? First we have to go back a step and remember what we've already learned about notes.

Twelve to a Chromatic Dozen

Cast your mind all the way back to Chapter 4 and you should remember that we have 12 different notes in our musical palette. And to help demonstrate how scales work, I'm going to include the A note at both ends of the sequence:

A	A#/Bb	B	C	C#/Db	D	D#/Eb	E	F	F#/Gb	G	G#/Ab	A

Each of these notes is one half step from its neighbor. That means that, on your bass guitar, they are all one fret apart. If you start with your open A string, which is the A note, then the note at the first fret is A# (also called Bb), at the second fret is B, C is at the third fret, and so on until you get to A at the 12th fret.

Playing each of these notes on your bass, you have, by our definition, created a scale. This is called the *chromatic scale* and this particular scale has 12 notes. Its pattern is to start on any given note and go up 12 half steps, at which point we have come full circle back to our original note.

The important thing to realize is that we could have started on *any* of the 12 notes. Because we began (and ended) with the A note, this would be called the A chromatic scale. If we decided to do the same thing on our D string, we would be playing the D chromatic scale and the pattern of notes, still all half steps, would look like this:

D	D#/Eb	E	F	F#/Gb	G	G#/Ab	A	A#/Bb	B	C	C#/Db	D

The first note of any scale is its root. When we are given the name of any chord or any scale, the name always contains the root. When you know the name of the scale you want, the root note will be your starting point.

Major Accomplishment

For reasons that will, hopefully, make sense a little later, we're going to start with the C major scale. In order to do this, let's first write out the C chromatic scale:

C	C#/Db	D	D#/Eb	E	F	F#/Gb	G	G#/Ab	A	A#/Bb	B	C

Rock Bottom

Don't fall into the trap of thinking that there has to be a certain number of notes in every scale. The *major* scale, as you learn in this chapter, has seven different notes. The *chromatic* scale, which you also see here, has 12. There are scales with five notes and six notes as well. Remember that it is the *pattern* of whole steps and half steps that defines a scale and not the number of notes in the scale.

Now let me give you one more helpful bit of information—the pattern of the major scale. Remember that, by our definition, scales follow any one of several patterns, and those patterns are usually a combination of whole steps and half steps. The chromatic scale was *all* half steps. The major scale consists of the following pattern:

> Root, whole step, whole step, half step, whole step, whole step, whole step, half step

Let's try that out and see what happens. Since we're looking to create the C major scale, C is our root note. One whole step (remember two half steps make a whole step!) up from C is D, one whole step up from D is E, a half step up from E is F, and a whole step from F is G. Finishing the scale, we go a whole step up from G to A, then a whole step up from A to B, and then finally a half step up from B, which is C. Mission accomplished!

Here are the notes of the C major scale:

> C–D–E–F–G–A–B–C

You might notice that the C major scale doesn't contain any accidental notes; that is, there are no flats and no sharps anywhere to be found. That's an important piece of information to file away for later.

Mapping Out the Major Scale

Now that you know the notes of the C major scale, you can play them on your bass. Here is the C major scale written out in both music notation and in bass tablature:

7.1

Because you already know where all of these notes are, you should be able to play this fairly easily. With a little practice , you will even be able to play it with astonishing speed.

Closed Position Playing

Knowing how to play one scale is, for now, simply that: knowing one scale. Wouldn't it be great if knowing one major scale, such as the C major scale, could save us the trouble of learning the other 11?

Covering the Basses

One of the biggest reasons for learning and understanding the major scale is that just about everything in music is described in terms of the major scale. Intervals, which you'll learn about in this chapter, are based on the major scale. Chords and harmonies use the major scale as their starting point. Even other scales are described by their differences to the major scale! The time you put into understanding the major scale at this point in your learning will pay off big time as you grow as both a bassist and a musician.

Covering the Basses

One excellent way to get more familiar with notes up the neck, and you'll be playing a lot of them in closed position, is to say a note's name as you play it. As you practice these closed position scales, initially do it slowly enough to say the note name while playing it. When you play the C major scale, for example, say "C, D, E, F, G, A, B, C" aloud, naming each note when you sound it with your fingers.

This isn't something you have to do constantly, but if you do so when starting in an unfamiliar position on the neck you will soon feel more confident about knowing where the notes are further on up the fingerboard.

On the bass guitar, not only is that possible, it's pretty easy. All we have to do is make a small adjustment to our thinking and then every major scale will be as easy as—you guessed it—"Do, Re, Mi."

Up to this point, you have been playing in what is called *open position* or *first position*. This means that we have kept our one-finger/one-fret style of playing down at the very end of the neck, never venturing beyond the fifth fret. But we know that there are plenty of notes all over the guitar.

We want to find a way to play the C major scale without using open strings. In the language of the bassist, we need to play this scale in *closed position*.

You already possess the knowledge to do this. You know from Chapters 3 and 4 that the note of the open D string can also be played at the fifth fret of the A string. You also know that the note of the open G string can also be played at the fifth fret of the D string. So you can now play your C major scale like this:

Initially, this will take a little rethinking, but not all that much. If you begin with your *middle* finger on the starting C note (third fret of the A string), you will find that you can do this in a one-finger/one-fret style. You'll have to get your pinky into the action, though. Use it for all the notes on the fifth fret (D, G, and the final C), while using your index finger for the notes on the second fret (E and A). Your middle finger is responsible for playing the first C and the F (both on the third fret of their respective strings), and the ring finger takes care of playing the B note located at the fourth fret of the G string.

Needless to say, take some time practicing this. If the stretches are a little hard right now, read on and I think we can come up with a way to help you out.

One Pattern Is Worth Twelve Major Scales

One of the marvelous things about the bass guitar is that any one closed position pattern can be found all over the neck. Once you have a particular pattern in your fingers, you can bring it out pretty much at a moment's notice. Make a mental note that this major scale pattern involves three different strings, so you can't start it with the D or G strings or you'll run out of strings while playing it.

But you can use any note on the A or E strings. Take the C note at the eighth fret of the E string and start right in:

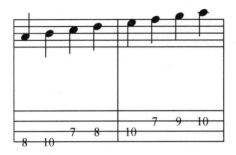

You can see and hear that even though we started in a completely different place on the neck, the fingering pattern is exactly the same. Place your middle finger on the eighth fret of the E string and off you go.

The C major scale you just played (in two different places) can be *any* major scale at all. All you have to do is have the right starting note. So suppose that you want to play an Eb major scale. You don't have to know all the notes that make up this scale, you just have to know where to find an Eb on either the A or E string of your bass.

Knowing this pattern also gives you a chance to work on stretching out your fingers. If you find the stretches too difficult for your pinky at the low end of the neck, start by practicing scales on the higher end. Begin with the Eb scale at the eleventh fret of the E string. When you feel comfortable playing that, then switch to the D scale using the D note at the tenth fret of the E string as your starting point. If you work at it, progressing down the neck as your fingers will allow, you will find yourself playing the F# major scale (starting at the second fret of the E string) in no time at all.

Expanding Your Horizons

Up to this point, you've been playing scales from root to root. Music is fluid, though, and it's important to realize that you have scale notes within your grasp both above and below the root.

This is why, once you've gotten pretty handy with the standard major scale, you then expand it as much as possible within the reach of a given pattern. Let's begin with the closed position C major scale, whose root is on the A string.

Covering the Basses

Music moves in a lot of directions and you should, too! When practicing your scales, be sure to play them both up and down. Use the expanded scale patterns to go beyond the normal pattern of the scale and to familiarize yourself with the notes on "both ends" of the normal pattern. You'll be using these notes a lot when it comes to putting together walking bass patterns, so it's never too early to start thinking about expanding the borders of your scale patterns.

17

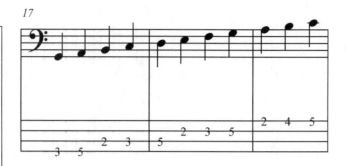

You can see that, without moving your fingers from their original fret positions, you can go below the root all the way down to the G note (third fret of the E string). This is handy for playing alternating bass lines (from Chapter 6). Being able to play the notes in between G and C will make learning walking bass lines (coming up in Chapter 13) a snap.

When the root of the C major scale is on the eighth fret of the E string, you can only go down one note below the root (the B note at the seventh fret of the E string), but you can expand upward, adding on the D, E, and F notes, found at the seventh, ninth, and tenth frets, respectively, of the G string.

In Chapter 18 you'll learn about expanding your scales even farther. For right now, though, take the time to get these patterns into your fingers. You'll definitely feel like you're making progress as a bass player when you can fire off a scale anywhere on the neck of your instrument.

Because this major scale pattern is closed and can be played anywhere on the neck, you will often see it drawn out on a generic grid, meant to represent a fretboard, usually looking like this:

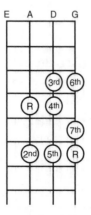

The lines, just as in bass guitar tablature, represent the strings of your bass guitar. The E string is on the left and the G string is on the right. The circles indicate where you should put your fingers in order to get the notes of this pattern. Sometimes the root notes will be highlighted, sometimes, as in this example, the circles will contain the scale degrees (second, third, fourth, etc.). And in case you're wondering just what a scale degree is …

A Brief Discussion on Intervals

Learning the major scale leads logically to thinking about scale degrees and intervals. Knowing about intervals will lay the foundation for painlessly dealing with chords. Perhaps even more importantly, being familiar with intervals is possibly the best thing you can do to work on your ear training—that is, your ability to hear a piece of music and to figure out what is being played.

While scale degrees occur in every scale, the convention is to discuss them in terms of the major scale (yet another reason to make sure you've got it down cold!). Just about all of music theory tends to be taught in terms of degrees of the major scale. It certainly makes it easy to visualize.

Simply put, the scale degree is a number assigned to a note of the scale, and usually done in Roman numerals. The root is I, or one. In the C major scale, the scale degrees are as follows:

I	II	III	IV	V	VI	VII
(Root)	(2nd)	(3rd)	(4th)	(5th)	(6th)	(7th)
C	D	E	F	G	A	B

Thinking of your scale in this way is very helpful if you want to transpose a piece of music, which you'll learn about in Chapter 18. Scale degrees also help us to understand intervals.

An *interval* is the musical distance between notes, measured in steps and/or half steps. Play the C note at the third fret of the A string. Now play the open G string. You are playing the interval of a perfect fifth. When we talk about the distance between C and D, we talk of the interval of a major second. When someone says "a major sixth up from C," he is talking about the A note.

Calling an interval by its proper name can be very important. Major intervals refer to scale degrees. But we also know that there are other notes that aren't in the major scale. Minor intervals are always one step lower than their major scale counterparts. For instance, the distance between C and A is the interval of a major sixth. Going from C to Ab is the interval of a minor sixth. Whenever someone refers to an interval without saying major or minor (with the exception of the fourth and fifth, which we'll discuss shortly), the assumption is that it's a major interval.

Just as important, perhaps even more so, is that intervals, like the major scale pattern, will not change no matter where you are on the fretboard. Knowing this can help accelerate your understanding of chords and arpeggios, which are coming up in the next chapter.

Let's look at each of the 12 different possible intervals.

Rock Bottom

Using Roman numerals is an old convention of musicians. They can be used to describe scale degrees, intervals, and, as you'll see in Chapter 11, chords and chord progressions. In case you never ran into Roman numerals in school, here are the ones you'll need to know:

I = 1
II = 2
III = 3
IV = 4
V = 5
VI = 6
VII = 7

Traditionally, capital letters are used to write Roman numerals, but, as you'll see in Part 4, small letters can be used as well; iii, for instance, is also 3.

Major and Minor Seconds

The interval of the major second is a whole step, or two frets, away from the root (on the same string). Depending on how you're fingering the root (and where it is on the neck), you can also reach the major second on the next higher string but three frets lower. The minor second is simply one fret up, or a half step away, from the root on the same string.

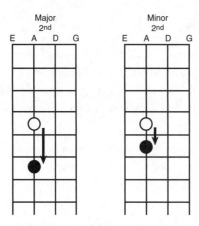

Major and Minor Thirds

The interval of the major third is two whole steps, or four frets, away from the root on the same string. Because of the reach involved, most people play the major third by finding it on the next higher string, one fret lower than the root. The minor third, being three half steps away from the root, can be played either three frets up on the same string or on the next higher string, but two frets lower.

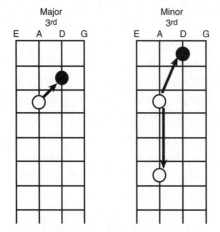

Thirds, as you'll learn next chapter, are incredibly important. Take a moment or two and listen to the intervals of both the major and minor third.

Fourths

The interval of the fourth is two-and-a-half steps (that's five frets) from the root. It's also the easiest one to find on your bass because it's always on the same fret as the root, just on the next higher string.

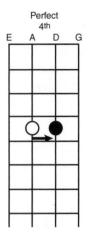

Perfect
4th

In music theory, fourths are usually referred to as "perfect fourths." Simply calling them "fourths" will be fine with most musicians you'll ever meet. Remember, too, that your bass is tuned in intervals of perfect fourths—each string is one fourth higher than the one below it.

Fifths: Perfect, Augmented, and Diminished

Fifths, on the other hand, can be a perfect mess. Not really, but here the names of the intervals are tip-offs to the four basic chords that we'll be learning about next chapter. The *perfect* fifth is three-and-a-half steps (seven total frets) up from the root. As you learned last chapter, you can find it on the next higher string, two frets up from the root. The diminished fifth is three whole steps from the root, and you can find it on the next higher string, one fret up from the root.

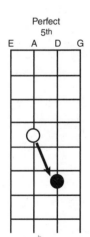

Perfect
5th

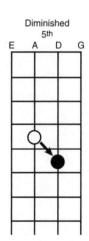

Diminished
5th

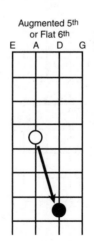

Augmented 5th
or Flat 6th

def•i•ni•tion

The diminished fifth is also known as the **tritone**. It is special in that it is exactly the halfway note between a root and its octave. Tritone comes from "tri," meaning three, and "tone," which refers to a full step in music. In the opening of "Purple Haze," by Jimi Hendrix, the bass plays an E while the guitar plays Bb, which is the tritone of E, creating a very distinct sound. Tritones are used extensively in jazz music but can be found in many other genres as well.

The augmented fifth, which is also the minor sixth, is four whole steps higher than the root. Most people find it on the next higher string, three frets up from the root. You can also reach it easily two strings higher and two frets lower than the root.

Sixths and Minor Sixths

The interval of the major sixth is four-and-a-half steps (or nine total frets) from the root. The easiest place to find it is right above the major third, but one string higher. As mentioned, the minor sixth is the same interval as the augmented fifth, which you found just a moment ago.

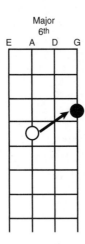

Major
6th

Major Sevenths and Flat Sevenths

The interval of the major seventh is five-and-a-half steps (11 total frets) up from the root. The easiest place to find it is two strings higher than the root and one fret high as well. The flat seventh, which is sometimes called the minor seventh, is another easy one—two strings higher than the root and on the same fret.

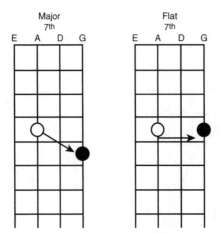

Major
7th

Flat
7th

Notice that I use the term "flat seventh" instead of "minor seventh." This is to avoid confusion when we start talking about minor chords. I think that, aside from the third, it's best to not use the term "minor" if you can avoid it. Usually I would also say "flat second," but it seldom comes up in conversation the way minor sevenths do.

The final interval, the perfect octave, you already know from Chapter 6. It is located two strings and two frets higher up from the root.

Intervals and Ear Training

Don't think of intervals as something you have to learn. In all seriousness, you can play bass without knowing them. But taking the time to listen to intervals will improve both your playing and your listening.

Most people don't have perfect pitch; that is, if you play a certain note, very few people will be able to come up to you and say "That's C#!" You don't need to have perfect pitch to be a musician—most professionals, in fact, don't. But having *relative* pitch is a skill that most people can, with practice, develop.

The interval of a fifth, for instance, is pretty distinct. It doesn't matter if it's from C to G, E to B, or Ab to Eb, the interval of the fifth has a unique sound. As do all the intervals.

Listening is an important part of the musician's world. If you're trying to figure out a bass part from a recording (remember that there's not all that much bass guitar music out there), being able to hear that the bass player raised the note a fourth or a sixth can help you to puzzle out a tricky phrase without music.

The key word is, of course, practice. Quiz yourself on intervals by playing them to yourself. Better yet, have a friend do it with you and you can quiz each other. Making ear training part of your practice time will yield a lot of benefits.

The Least You Need to Know

- ◆ A scale is a specific pattern of notes.
- ◆ The major scale is the basis for much of the music theory that you will learn.
- ◆ Any pattern learned in a closed position can be played anywhere on the bass.
- ◆ Patterns of intervals are constant across the fingerboard of the bass.
- ◆ Learning to recognize intervals can help you improve your listening skills.

Basso Profondo

Q: Is it necessary for a bassist, or any musician, to have perfect pitch?

A: Few professional musicians have perfect pitch. But that doesn't mean they don't have good ears! It's far more important for musicians to have "relative" pitch than perfect pitch. Relative pitch is the ability to hear (and play) different intervals, given a starting note. Jazz bassists, and others, often listen to their band mates for improvisational inspiration, and being able to hear and identify intervals is where it all starts.

Chapter 8

Chords and Arpeggios

In This Chapter

 ◆ Where chords come from
 ◆ The four basic chord types
 ◆ The importance of the third
 ◆ Playing power chords
 ◆ Using triads to create chords
 ◆ Discovering inversions
 ◆ Creating chord arpeggios

With the knowledge of the major scale secure in your brain and with your skills at recognizing intervals, you are now ready to create chords. Even though bass players do not often play full chords, they quite often play patterns called *arpeggios*, which contain notes that make up chords. If you're going to improve as a bassist, knowing how chords are constructed is essential.

Musicians tend to learn how to construct chords in one of two ways, both of which we'll cover in this chapter. Both are easy to learn and remember, and you'll probably find yourself wondering what all the fuss over chord theory is about. Having all of this knowledge at your beck and call is just one of the cool things about being a bass player.

Once you know how to make the four basic types of chords, you can construct chord arpeggios, which involves playing the notes of any given chord in sequence, much like a scale. And, again like the scale, you'll find some simple patterns you can use anywhere on the fretboard.

Four Chords and the Truth

Just as there are many types of scales, there are also many different kinds of chords. At the heart of it all, though, are four basic types—major, minor, augmented, and diminished. All the other chords you might have heard or seen are embellishments of this quartet of chords.

◆ **Major chords** are probably what most people hear in their minds when they think of chords. They are bold and full-bodied and simply invite the listener to sing along.

◆ **Minor chords** sound sad and wistful, as if something important is somehow slightly askew. They can be quiet and introspective or loud and angry.

◆ **Augmented chords** feel unsettled. Listening to one, you get antsy, waiting for the music to move someplace more secure, less edgy.

◆ **Diminished chords** also seem unsettled, but in a more mystical and melancholy way. They are not as jarring as augmented chords; the unease they convey is slighter, easier to deal with.

Unless you play a lot of jazz or older songs (and we're talking about songs from before 1950 here), 90 percent of the chords you run into will be either major or minor. But as a bass player, you should be familiar with all four because you never know when an augmented or diminished chord might pop up.

A-One and A-Three and A-Five

The notes that make up chords form specific patterns, much in the same style that scales are created. Our four basic chords all use the root, third, and fifth of any major scale.

That may seem like a contradiction, but it's not. Remember our discussion on intervals from the previous chapter? There are different types of thirds (major and minor) as well as fifths (perfect, diminished, and augmented). The four basic types of chords are made up this way:

Major	root	major third	perfect fifth
Minor	root	minor third	perfect fifth
Augmented	root	major third	augmented fifth
Diminished	root	minor third	diminished fifth

Applying this information to the C major scale, we can come up with the four basic types of C chords:

C major	C	E	G
C minor	C	Eb	G
C augmented	C	E	G#
C diminished	C	Eb	Gb

Remember the C chord we played last chapter? Let's try that exercise again and this time, we'll check out how the other three basic chords sound:

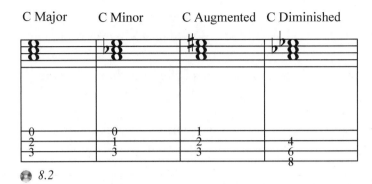

C Major   C Minor   C Augmented   C Diminished

🔴 *8.2*

The Power of Three

If you want to start a wild debate among musicians, ask how many notes it takes to make a chord. This isn't like asking, "How many drummers does it take to change a light bulb?" For some people, it's a very big question. One group will argue that two notes are enough while the other faction will insist on having three.

Bass players, thankfully, don't have to take sides, but they do have to understand where the argument comes from. Remember the C chord we played last chapter? Let's try that exercise again, and this time we'll throw a little twist into it.

7

First play the C major chord and then the C minor. Now play only the root (the C note at the third fret of the A) and the fifth (the open G string). Does that sound major or minor to you?

Actually, it's neither. For most musicians, it's the interval of the third that defines any chord. As you can hear in this example, without a third it's impossible to tell if a chord is a major chord or a minor one. But sometimes, that ambiguity is precisely what a musician wants.

Power Chords to the People

When you play just the root and the fifth, you create what today's musicians (especially those in the rock, metal, and punk genres) call a *power chord*. Because it is easy to finger and because of the overtones this interval generates, particularly at loud volumes and with a little distortion, the power chord is a staple of many genres of today's music.

Rock Bottom

The term "power chord" is relatively new, but the musical idea of playing intervals of perfect fifths to accompany a melody or lead line certainly isn't. Some musical instruments, such as the bagpipes, were created specifically with the fifth in mind. The "bag" part of the bagpipes emits a constant power chord while the "pipe" part plays the melody.

Many stringed instruments also use this idea. The Appalachian dulcimer, also called the mountain dulcimer, has two strings tuned to the interval of the fifth. These are continuously strummed while a third string, strummed at the same time as the others, provides the melody.

If you are working off of a fake sheet, lead sheet, or chord sheet, power chords are identified as "5" chords. "C5," for instance, would be a C power chord. "Ab5" would be a power chord with Ab as its root.

Power chords are easy for the bassist to play. Simply form the interval of the fifth, as you learned in Chapter 7, and play both strings at the same time. In many bands, particularly if the band only has three members (usually guitar, bass, and drums), the bass player will play power chords to help fill out the sound. Here is an exercise that will help you practice your power chords:

21

8.4

As with any exercise, start slowly so you can work out exactly which fingers you want where. Usually with a power chord formation, you will use your index finger to fret the note of the lower string and either your pinky or ring finger to play the note on the higher string. With a little persistence, practice, and repetition, you'll quickly pick up speed.

Try a Triad

Some people find it easier to think of chords only in terms of the interval of thirds, both major and minor. If you're a visual person, this makes sense because, in musical notation, basic chords look like thirds stacked on top of one another. Here is a C major chord written in music notation:

You already know that C to E is the interval of a major third. You can also easily figure out that going from E to G is three half steps, which we learned is a minor third. So you can think of the notes of the C major chord (C, E, and G) as a major third with a minor third stacked on top of it.

When we stack two thirds on top of each other, we get what is called a *triad*. Conveniently enough, each of the four basic chords is one of the four possible combinations of triads that can be created:

Major	root	major third	minor third
Minor	root	minor third	major third
Augmented	root	major third	major third
Diminished	root	minor third	minor third

Thinking of chords being constructed in this manner is very helpful when you get to some of the more complicated types of chords like the ninth, eleventh, and thirteenth, which you'll be learning in the next chapter.

Inversions

Chords don't have to start on a root note. When the root of a chord is in the bass (being played by the bass player!), the chord sounds full and steady. But you could play a different note of the chord, such as the fifth or the third, instead of the root. Doing so creates an *inversion* of that chord. You can play a basic triad three ways: the original "root note in the bass" way; the *first inversion*, which means that the third is in the bass; and the *second inversion*, which means that the bass note is the fifth.

Here are the inversions of the C major chord for you to study and listen to:

C Major   1st Inversion   2nd Inversion

Play this example on your bass and you will hear that while these are all still a C major chord, the bass note creates very different moods for all three. The first inversion sounds transitory. You might say that it sounds like the bassist is trying to get someplace else, someplace away from the C chord. Chances are you'd be right, too. We'll learn much more about that in Chapter 13.

The second inversion also sounds a bit transitory but not as much. It's like the bass player got stuck in the second part of an alternating bass line and couldn't find his way back to the root.

Knowing your inversions is like knowing how to expand your scale beyond the basic notes of the pattern. Being able to start on any given note and to create a chord arpeggio is an invaluable tool for the bass player. And, having said that, it's time to learn about arpeggios.

Major Arpeggios

I mentioned at the start of this chapter that bass players don't often play full chords. That's a bit misleading. While the bassist may not play all three (or

def•i•ni•tion

Occasionally, a piece of music will deliberately call for a particular inversion of a chord. This is done by means of a **slash chord**. Slash chords look like two chords written together with a "/" sign between them. The chord being asked for is always on the left side of the slash mark and the requested bass note is to the right of the slash mark.

For example, let's say that the writer or arranger of a song specifically wants the second inversion of the C major chord. She would write out the chord as "C/G," in other words, the C major chord (the "C" to the left of the slash) with the G note (the "G" to the right of the slash) in the bass. We will discuss slash chords at length throughout Part 4.

more) notes of a given chord at once, she very often runs the individual notes of a chord together, one after another, in a sequence called an *arpeggio*.

After learning how to find the root and then playing alternating patterns with the root and fifth of any given chord, playing arpeggios gives the bass player more interesting material to work with. In many genres of music (reggae springs immediately to mind), the bass lines consist of little more than elegant arpeggios, cleverly laying down the rhythm while establishing the chords for the vocalist and other musicians.

Playing a major arpeggio is like playing a major scale while leaving out certain notes. Here is a C major arpeggio, played with the root at the third fret of the A string:

Because this is a closed pattern, we can play the arpeggio of any major chord you'd care to name. Here is a B major arpeggio:

Also, just as with scales, you can expand your arpeggio pattern to include notes of the chord above and below the normal pattern; in other words, you can create inversions. Here are several inversions of the G major chord:

After all the time and effort you put into practicing the major scale, you should find playing major arpeggios a breeze. But with the arpeggios of the other three basic chords—the minor, augmented, and diminished—you might find it easier to think of these chords in terms of their intervals.

Minor Arpeggios

Minor arpeggios can be tricky at first, but with a little practice, it's easy to get the hang of them. Let's look at a few:

G Minor Arpeggio   1st Inversion   2nd Inversion

The trick here is to start with your index finger on the root. This will allow you to jump to the minor third, three frets away, with either your pinky or your ring finger. Then you can cover the fifth and high root with the same finger. If you're only going up three notes, you might want to try the second example in the illustration. Finding the fifth after the minor third (in this case) is easy if you think of the fifth as being a major third from the second note.

Also remember that inversions are fair game. The third minor arpeggio in the above example is a second inversion, even though we're playing the root note first. It's simply an easy way of getting through what might otherwise be a difficult fingering.

Augmented Arpeggios

The augmented arpeggio is going to remind you of one of our exercises from Chapter 4.

Since each step is a major third from the other, you can play any augmented arpeggio as a diagonal line across the fingerboard. And also because all the

Covering the Basses

Be sure to practice playing your arpeggios in both directions, going down as well as up. Also try to expand a note or two in either direction if the fingering will allow.

And if you keep up the "say the note as you play it" strategy, you'll discover an interesting bonus: in no time at all you'll have the notes of specific chords memorized, which will help you know where the notes are on the fingerboard.

It's just like when you learned to read music notation—if you give yourself a little goal to accomplish each day, such as knowing the notes of a C major chord, in less than a month you will have more than enough musical knowledge to last a lifetime.

intervals are the same, each inversion will have the same shape. This one, while it may initially be slightly difficult to finger, will be very easy to remember.

Augmented chords are made up of the root, the third (an interval of a major third), and the augmented fifth (which is a major third away from the third). The interval of the major third is two whole steps, or four half steps. This is special, because there are a total of 12 chromatic tones, as we learned in Chapter 7. This means that the three notes of the augmented chord perfectly divide the 12 chromatic steps.

What all this means to you as a bass player is that any one augmented chord is simply an inversion of two other augmented chords. Here's a little chart to show you:

Chord	Root	Third	Augmented fifth
C Augmented	C	E	G#
E Augmented	E	G#	C (actually B#)
G# Augmented	G#	C	E (actually D##)

If you get into jazz, you'll find yourself using augmented chords quite a bit. They add a lot of spice to pop songs and ballads as well.

Diminished Arpeggios

More often than not, you're going to find music calling for a diminished seventh chord or half-diminished seventh chord instead of the regular diminished. Those are coming up in the next chapter. But you should still take a moment to familiarize yourself with the basic diminished chord arpeggio:

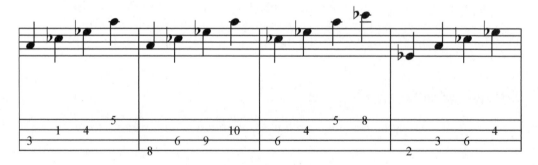

This is another one where your fingers will be hopping! As with the minor arpeggio, starting with your index finger on the root will help. And again like the minor chord, thinking in terms of the second inversion will also make playing a diminished chord arpeggio a little smoother.

The Least You Need to Know

♦ There are four basic chords—major, minor, augmented, and diminished.

♦ Power chords contain just the root and fifth of the chord name.

♦ Inversions are chords with either the third or fifth as the lowest note, in place of the root note.

♦ Arpeggios are chord notes played in a sequence.

Chapter 9

Other Chords You'll Need to Know

In This Chapter

- Learning the different types of seventh chords
- Creating suspended chords
- Building additional chords
- Taking chords in context
- Taking chords in stride

Creating any chord becomes a matter of "following the instructions." Everything starts with our four basic chords—the major, minor, augmented, and diminished—and from there we simply add additional notes to the original triad. Which notes? That is just a matter of reading the chord name, which contains all the instructions you need. There will be no reason to get confused by something like A7sus4 when you know a few small tips concerning the "shorthand" used to describe a chord.

In addition to explaining our remaining chords, this chapter will include arpeggio patterns for each type so that you can practice them on your bass. As in our last chapter, you will get specific examples in closed position patterns so that you can use them to create arpeggios for any given chord. It's never too early to be thinking about taking a solo, and having numerous chord arpeggios at your fingertips will ensure that you never run out of ideas when it's your turn to take center stage.

Seventh Heaven

It's almost impossible, especially for those who play the various subgenres of rock, country, blues, and jazz, to *not* run into seventh chords. They are everywhere!

At first, seventh chords may seem like a world of confusion because there are so many different types of them. But once you learn the conventions of naming seventh chords, and once you get the arpeggios into your hands and head, you will find the various seventh chords to be terrific tools for creating things like jazzy walking bass lines, rocking bass fills, and bluesy riffs.

Dominant Sevenths

The most common type of seventh chord is the *dominant seventh*. The dominant seventh is the same interval as the flat seventh or minor seventh, which we learned about in Chapter 7. This chord is so common, in fact, that the convention is to use a dominant seventh whenever you see a "7" after a chord name, unless specifically told otherwise. A7, for example, is shorthand for A dominant seventh.

To create a dominant seventh arpeggio, start with the major chord triad and add the interval of the flat seventh between the fifth and the high root, as in this example using the C7 arpeggio:

Like our other arpeggios, this one is a closed pattern you can play anywhere on the neck. You know this drill by now, so go ahead and work out other dominant seventh arpeggios starting on their various component notes.

In the meantime, let's look at something of interest. Unlike our triads, which all involved three notes, or our "power chords" (from Chapter 8), which only use two, the dominant seventh chord and arpeggio has four different notes. This makes it possible for you to move all over the fingerboard, especially when you expand your arpeggio like this:

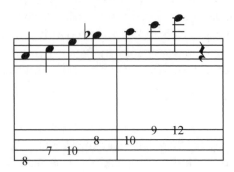

Start with your middle finger on the eighth fret and play as you would a normal C major arpeggio, using your index finger to get the E at the seventh fret of the A string and your pinky to play the G note at the tenth fret of the same string. Now use your middle finger again to play the Bb note located at the eighth fret of the D string, and then slide that same finger up to the tenth fret to play the C note found there. Sliding your middle finger up to the tenth fret allows you to finger the rest of the arpeggio, the E and G notes at the ninth and twelfth frets, respectively, of the G string with your index finger (on the E) and pinky (on the G).

Even though the arpeggios you'll learn in this chapter give you more notes to play, it's important to realize that you don't have to play them all. Here, as an example, is a standard blues bass line, created from a descending C7 arpeggio that omits the third (the E note):

This is one demonstration of how riffs and fills are created from arpeggios. As you learn and practice the examples in this chapter, feel free to experiment and come up with musical phrases of your own. Remember to write down the ones that you like, so you don't have to go through the process of creating them a second time!

Major Sevenths

If C7 is shorthand for C dominant seventh, meaning we add a Bb (the interval of the flat seventh) to the C major triad, what do we do if we want to add the regular B note? Happily, the shorthand for this is very straightforward. Adding the interval of the major seventh to any major triad is indicated by "maj7." So, Cmaj7 means taking the C major triad (C, E, and G) and tacking on the B note (major seventh), as shown in the following illustration:

Major sevenths are often used in jazz and ballads, but can show up in all sorts of songs. They have a mellow sound and flow very naturally on the bass, especially in descending arpeggios.

Minor Sevenths

If you see a chord marked "Cm," you know that the "m" stands for minor. So it makes sense that Cm7 is shorthand for C minor seventh. But is the seventh

Covering the Basses

There are a few general rules to chord shorthand. Unless indicated otherwise, assume a chord is a major chord. E, for instance, will mean E major. A small "m" after a chord indicates minor. Em, therefore, is E minor. "Aug" or "+" are usually used to name augmented chords, and "dim" is short for diminished. There are some exceptions and they are noted in this chapter.

dominant or major? A good way to think of chords is to understand that the "m" always deals with the third. Because the "7" stands on its own, we can say that it's a dominant seventh. Cm7 then, or any minor seventh chord, is formed by starting with the *minor* chord arpeggio and adding the dominant seventh to it, like this:

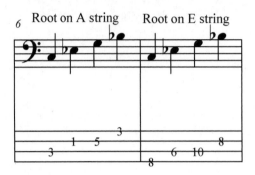

You may find some of the stretches of the minor chord a little hard at first. They will come with practice, but don't forget that you have the option of using inversions. Here are the first and second inversions of the Cm7 chord:

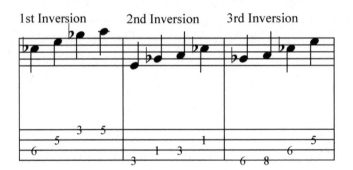

You will also note that we now have a "third" inversion. This is because the Cm7 chord has four notes. The third inversion begins with Bb.

It is also possible to have a minor major seventh chord, although you probably won't run into a lot of these. The designation for this oddly cool sounding chord is usually written "m(maj7)," as in Cm(maj7). Here is the arpeggio for it:

Augmented Sevenths

Augmented chords often have dominant sevenths attached to them, especially in jazz pieces. Instead of being written out as "Caug7," you often see these chords designated as dominant sevenths with "#5" added on. "#5" is shorthand for augmented, since our augmented chord is the root, third, and augmented fifth. So, in keeping with our examples in C, here is the C7#5 arpeggio:

It is truly rare to see an augmented chord with a major seventh tacked onto it. But it is possible. Usually when this occurs, the chord is given a different name that makes it easier to read and play, as you'll learn shortly.

Half-Diminished Sevenths

When you add a dominant seventh to a diminished chord, it is called a half-diminished seventh and usually goes by the designation "m7b5" or "m7(b5)." The "m" indicates a minor third and the "b5" is the interval of the diminished fifth, which gives us a diminished triad to start with. Just add on the dominant seventh and you're all set.

Diminished Sevenths

The designation "dim7" gives us one more type of seventh to learn. As you might suspect, the "dim" stands for diminished, and it means we should start with a diminished triad. But the "dim" also means to diminish, or lower, the *dominant seventh* an additional step as well. The easiest way to remember this is to think of the "dim7" as four minor thirds stacked upon one another, such as in the following.

Like our augmented arpeggio from Chapter 8, this one seems more like a finger exercise. Diminished seventh arpeggios are excellent ways of moving up and down the neck in a hurry, as you can tell from the expanded arpeggio in the example above.

Like the augmented chords, diminished sevenths are special because their four notes are all three half-steps apart, which divides evenly into the 12 chromatic half steps of music. So each diminished seventh chord shares its notes with three others. Using Cdim7 to give us a starting point:

Chord	Root	Minor 3rd	Diminished 5th	Diminished 7th
Cdim7	C	Eb	Gb	A
Ebdim7	Eb	Gb	A	C
Gbdim7	Gb	A	C	Eb
Adim7	A	C	Eb	Gb

Suspending the Third

In our last chapter, we examined power chords, which contained no interval of the third. Besides simply dropping the third, it is possible to replace it with another note, usually the fourth or the second. These are called *suspended chords* and are often used in pop, rock, and country music. More often than not, they will be designated by "sus" with either a "4" or a "2" to indicate which interval to use as a replacement for the third.

Using the C major chord as an example, Csus4 would be a chord made up of C and G (the root and fifth of the C chord) and F, which is the fourth and replaces the E (third). Csus2 is C, G, and D.

Suspended chords, like power chords, are neither major nor minor since there is no third in them. You shouldn't ever run into a designation like Cmsus4, but you never know! If you do, just treat it the same as you would Csus4.

Suspended Fourths

Far and away, the suspended fourth is the more common of the two suspended chords. You will frequently see "sus" markings without a number after it at all and the convention is to treat a chord written this way as a "sus4" chord. Here is the Csus4 arpeggio:

You will also find suspended chords of both types with dominant sevenths added to them. Usually the dominant seventh will come first in the designation, as in C7sus4. Again, if there is no "4" or "2" after the "sus," assume that the fourth is to be used. Like the "plain" sus4 chord, these arpeggios are easy (and fun) to play.

Suspended Seconds

As mentioned, the "sus2" indicates replacing the third of the major triad with the interval of the second. So our Csus2 and C7sus2 arpeggios will be played like this:

Occasionally you might run into a suspended chord that uses both the second and fourth in place of the third. Should you ever encounter a chord like Csus2sus4, you will know to use this arpeggio.

Suspended chord arpeggios are great for breaking up long stretches of a single chord. For instance, if you are faced with six measures of D major, throw in a measure or two of a Dsus4 o r Dsus2 arpeggio, or even a measure of each. It will keep things fresh for both you and your listeners.

Building an Addition

Our four basic chord types are fine, but often people like to add a little more flavor to a chord. The addition of an additional note or two, usually taken from the major scale of the original root, can add all sorts of textures to your basic chords. Most often than not, these embellishments occur to your standard major chords, so we'll focus on those in this section.

Sixth Sense

The sixth chord, particularly the major sixth chord, is a staple of jazz and old-time pop music. To build the major sixth arpeggio, start with your major triad and add the interval of the sixth after the fifth, as in this example illustrating the C6 arpeggio:

Nine Lives

Many chords in jazz and blues are simply triads stacked to the sky. When you see chords like ninths, elevenths, and thirteenths, think of them as seventh chords with more notes added. C9, for instance, means to take your C dominant seventh chord and add the ninth note of the scale (which is the same as the second) to it after the seventh.

This chord uses five notes, so it's best to think about using all four strings for the arpeggio. As you can see, you have to move around a bit for something like this.

The major ninth works on the same idea, but uses the major seventh instead of the dominant seventh, as in this example:

<table>
<tr><td>def•i•ni•tion</td></tr>
</table>

The use of the seventh, whether a dominant seventh or a major seventh, is what distinguishes a ninth chord from an **add9 chord**. To create an "add9," just take the major chord and stick on the ninth. Cadd9, for example, is C, E, G and D. In some music you might also see "add9" chords written as "2" chords, such as "C2." Treat any chord like this as you would the sixth chord.

Elevenths and Thirteenths and Accidentals

Likewise, elevenths and thirteenths start with the dominant seventh arpeggio and then add the ninth, and then the eleventh and then the thirteenth. As you might imagine, this really involves jumping around the fingerboard.

At this point, it's smart to think about dumping some of the notes in order to have a little breathing room. Usually the fifth is the first to go, but it's often your call as to what notes to keep and which to drop. As a rule, the root, third, and seventh tend to stay and you can add on from there.

Finally, you might also run into the odd accidental, something like C7#9 or C7b13. There's no need to panic if you use your head. The best strategy is to start with the basic chord, in this case the C7, and just add the note in question, like this:

As before, dropping the fifth will help make these a little more manageable.

What's in a Name

One of the things that can frustrate beginners is that there seem to be seven million different chords and you are expected to know them all. This isn't really the case at all. You will often run into a chord that has the same notes as another, but a different name.

For instance, the C6 chord is made up of C, E, G (the C major triad), and A (the sixth of C). These same notes also make up the Am7 chord.

The bass player, by filling in the all-important bass note, is often responsible for maintaining the "context" of a chord progression, and his or her choice of notes can make a lot of difference in how a song sounds. This is why knowing the notes of various chords, at least the basic ones, can be so important.

As you will learn in Part 4, chords often fulfill specific tasks in a song. The more you read chord progressions in music, the more you will notice repeated patterns and the more the sense of "musical context" will take hold. Don't worry too much about it at this point—simply use the skills you have to build your arpeggios and don't get overly concerned with names.

In a Pinch

Finally, one last bit of advice concerning chords: there's never a reason to panic as long as you know the root. And knowing the root is the easiest thing in the world.

When faced with a complicated chord, you can always opt to simplify things. Playing a C major arpeggio, for example, under a C9 chord will sound absolutely fine. Just playing the C note or even a C and G alternating bass pattern will also fit the bill nicely.

As you continue to practice, you will gain more and more confidence in your ability to perform arpeggios, and when that happens you'll become more daring with your bass lines. It's all part of the natural evolution of the bassist.

Rhythmic Assistance

You may have noticed that all the arpeggio examples in this chapter were either written in straight quarter notes or as a string of eighth notes. This is a perfectly fine way to start, but remember that, in a real song, you're probably going to play your arpeggios in all sorts of rhythmic patterns.

When you feel you have a particular arpeggio down cold, take the time to play around with it. If it's a four-note arpeggio, start out with a half note and then use a triplet for the other three. Sandwich two sixteenth notes between two eighth notes or string together some dotted quarter and eighth notes.

You can also take rhythms that you like and experiment with different ways of playing your arpeggios with the same timing. You have all sorts of options.

Never forget that you can put together wonderfully fancy arpeggios, but it's all for naught if you've lost the rhythm of a song! In Part 4 you'll be putting both your rhythmic and arpeggiating skills to good use, so it's not to early to start practicing.

The Least You Need to Know

- You can create more complicated chords by adding the scale degrees dictated by the chord name.
- There are many types of seventh chords. The dominant seventh is the most common.
- Suspended chords replace the third with either the fourth or second.
- Ninths, elevenths, and thirteenth chords automatically include the dominant seventh.
- When in doubt, play the root!
- Practice using arpeggios with various rhythms.

Basso Profondo

Q: There seem to be a lot of different kinds of chords! Do I need to know them all?

A: One of the cool things about playing bass is that you can often be as simple (or as complicated) as you like. As long as you know the root note of any chord (which you learned in Chapter 6), you cannot go wrong. As you get more comfortable with knowing chords and arpeggios, you will find yourself creating more complicated and interesting bass patterns. You'll also find yourself knowing the makeup of each chord the more you use it.

Chapter 10

Using What We've Learned So Far

In This Chapter

- ◆ A jam-along song with two chords
- ◆ A jam-along song with three chords
- ◆ A jam-along song with four chords
- ◆ Assessing your performance
- ◆ Dealing with mistakes

Now the fun really begins! In this chapter you're going to jam along with the band on three different songs. The idea is for you to create your own bass part to play along with the band. I will give you some suggestions, three or four per song, that you can either play or use as guidelines.

These aren't really "songs," they're just short chord patterns that repeat over and over (and over!) again. We're not worried about the melody line or anything but the rhythm and the chord pattern.

If you're worried that you're going to make a mistake, I've got news for you—you will. As far as I can tell, there's only one way not to make a mistake, and that's not to play. I don't think that should be an option. Enjoy your mistakes and learn from them! We'll talk more about that at the end of the chapter.

Get Ready

It's always a good idea to warm up before playing or practicing. Stretch and shake out your arms, hands, and fingers; roll your shoulders; get loose and relaxed. It's also a good idea to warm up the mind. This is just practice, after all—not a big concert performance. If your mindset is to learn and have fun, you'll have a good time playing. If you're preoccupied with other things, wait awhile and try playing again later.

Have paper and a pen or pencil and be prepared to take some notes. Too many people learn this the hard way! They might come up with a killer bass line while playing a song and think, "That's really cool!" Then when they try to play it later, it's gone! If you come up with something, stop, retrace your steps, and do it again. And again. Then write down what you did. You can do so in notation or bass guitar tablature or even in plain English ("I hit the A string, waited a beat and then hit the C note really quickly …"). The point is to give yourself the best chance to remember and re-create what you did. Some people record their practices for this very purpose.

All of these songs, by the way, are slow to moderate in tempo. This is to give you a chance to work on them without worrying about keeping up with the band. Enjoy yourself!

Song #1

Our first piece only has two chords and is at a medium-slow (as opposed to deathly slow) pace. Give Song #1 a listen while you look over the chord/rhythm chart:

Cmaj7   Bm7   Cmaj7   Bm7

This is a repeat sign. It means go back to the beginning.

🔊 *10.1*

> **Covering the Basses**
>
> Ending a song together is a good sign that a band is tight. Listen for the audio clues in each song for your ending point and do your best to end with the band.

Because this song uses only two chords, it's easy to think of it as simple. But I've tried to give you a challenge by using two moderately complicated chords. The heavy bar at the far right with the two dots is called a *repeat sign*. When you get to it, simply go back to the beginning and keep playing.

The rhythm of this song is also fairly simple. Each measure has two sets of a dotted quarter note followed by an eighth note. This is a classic slow-to-moderate song groove. The song ends with one final hit of the Cmaj7 chord. Play the root note, C, and let it ring.

Speaking of which, this might be a good time to make sure you know your two-chord arpeggios for this piece. The notes of the Cmaj7 chord are C, E, G, and B. The notes of the Bm7 chord are B, D, F#, and A. Each chord lasts for one measure of four beats.

Suggestion #1

Here are some suggested bass lines that you can use to play along with Song #1:

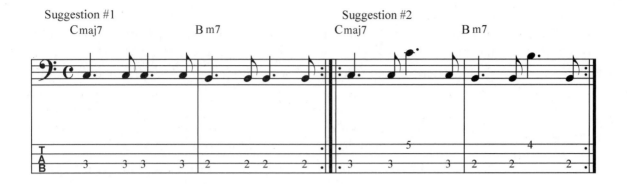

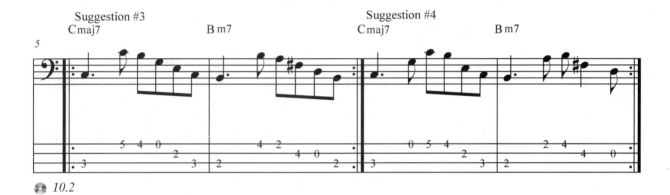

🔵 *10.2*

The first suggestion is as simple as they come. All you do is hit the root note with the timing of the general rhythm pattern. Starting out as simply as possible gives you the chance to get settled into the rhythm and the basic harmonic feel of the song.

When all else fails, you know you have this easy, steady bass line to come back to. As you play along with the song, a good idea might be to come back to Suggestion #1 from time to time in order to give yourself a break.

Suggestion #2

Suggestion #2 also involves only the root notes, but the third root is an octave higher than the other three. This is a good way to get your fingers a little bit more acclimated. Playing octaves, as you know, requires you to be ready for the high octave while playing the low one. You're already thinking ahead!

With all of these suggestions, feel free to change them around a bit. A cool thing to do with Suggestion #2, for instance, would be to use two high B notes in the middle of the measure of Bm7.

Suggestion #3

Experiment with all sorts of different ideas. In addition to trying different notes, you can also work at changing around the rhythm a little. When you do that, though, it's very important to keep the overall rhythm in mind. Suggestion #3 is a good example of how to do this. You begin with the dotted quarter note and

Covering the Basses

Starting out with a simple bass line is always a good plan. As you become more familiar with a song, you can add more complicated parts to it. You will do the same as you learn more scales, arpeggios, and riffs. Don't worry about whether you sound good, worry about whether the song sounds good!

eighth note, but then finish the measure with four eighth notes. If you're worried about not getting the right notes, then start by using just the root note with the new rhythm. Always feel free to fall back on what you know.

Each measure of Suggestion #3 involves a descending chord arpeggio. With this first song, I also suggest using the open strings (whenever indicated by the bass guitar tablature) until you feel comfortable. Once you can handle the timing, try playing these arpeggios in a closed position, fingering the G note at the fifth fret of the D string and the D note at the fifth fret of the A string.

Notice that I try to keep the last note of each measure pretty close to the first note of the next one. This is an example of what is called voice leading, and we'll be touching upon this fairly soon in our next chapter.

Suggestion #4

Suggestion #4 is similar to Suggestion #3, but the differences are important. In the measure of Cmaj7, the chord arpeggio is broken up. You hit the G note second and then the high C and skip the G on the way down the arpeggio. This is to remind you to feel free to rearrange your arpeggios. They don't always have to be in order, going up or down. Taking bits and pieces of them is how cool-sounding bass lines are created.

The arpeggio is broken up in the measure of Bm7 as well. Not only that, but the timing has been changed again. Notice how hanging on to the F# note for a whole beat changes the feel of the bass part without dramatically altering the overall rhythm.

As I mentioned, the whole point of this chapter is for you to play and have fun. Nobody's going to come up and tell you you're playing it all wrong. You have to figure out what works and *why*. Listen to yourself with the band. Are you in sync with the rhythm and the feel? It's easy to be your own worst critic, so stay loose, remember you're still a beginner, and you'll get better each time you play and practice.

Song #2

We'll pick up the tempo in Song #2, but only a little. This time you've got three chords to deal with:

10.3

The rhythm of this song is also fairly simple—each measure has the same pattern of a quarter note, followed by a dotted quarter note, followed by three eighth notes.

Covering the Basses

Sometimes *not* playing can add a lot to a bass line. Taking a rest every now and then, or adding notes of longer lengths, gives an interesting addition to a normal bass line.

Suggestion #1

Now that you've heard the song, you can listen to the suggested bass lines:

Suggestion #1

Suggestion #2

Suggestion #3

🔊 *10.4*

The first suggestion is, once again, sticking with the root note of each given chord and mirroring the basic rhythm pattern. Note that the rhythm isn't copied exactly—instead of a quarter note for the first beat, I suggest using an eighth note followed by an eighth rest. This brings a little more punch to the second beat. This is a very simple little trick that can add a nice touch to a pattern, particularly if you get the whole band going along with it.

Suggestion #2

Stick with the basic rhythm pattern in Suggestion #2 and add some chord arpeggios. On the measure of Am (the second measure), I leave out the C note of the arpeggio and just use the A and E notes, because the C is prominently used in the third measure. Keeping it "on ice" makes things sound a little more interesting. It's a little thing, but that's what playing around is all about—seeing which little things you like and want to keep in your mental musical filing cabinet.

Suggestion #3

In Suggestion #3 we totally abandon the basic rhythm pattern and use four quarter notes for each measure. You might think this would derail things, but actually, the bass is now serving as the band's metronome, steadily keeping the beat. This is an excellent way to test yourself on holding true to the tempo of a song.

Another technique used in this suggestion is the reverse-direction play of the arpeggio. In the first measure, go up with a G major arpeggio, then go up to the A at the start of the second measure and descend with the A minor arpeggio. Go up again with the C major arpeggio (starting on your C note) during the third measure, then come down again with the G major arpeggio for the last measure.

Notice that the last G major arpeggio is actually the first inversion. Since B is right next to C, it made musical sense to start the arpeggio on B and then descend. An added bonus to this is not hitting the G note twice, once at the end of measure four and then at the start of the song again when we repeat it. Starting and ending this arpeggio on G is certainly something you *can* do and it will sound fine, but after trying it out a couple of times, this way sounded better to me. Try it for yourself and listen to your preference. You might want to start it on D!

Song #3

Our third song's a little more of a rocker. The tempo is slightly faster and the rhythm pattern doesn't stay the same throughout, so pay attention! To top things off, it's got four different chords to worry about:

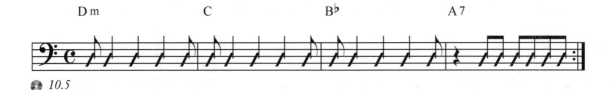

10.5

The rhythm of this song, while simple, can be tricky. The first three measures start out with an eighth note followed by three quarter notes. This means that you'll be playing off the beat the entire measure—after the first note, that is.

The last measure begins with a quarter rest. The whole band (with the occasional exception of the piano and lead guitar) will stop for a whole beat and then play six eighth notes in unison. Being able to do something like this in a group setting makes a band tight.

Suggestion #1

Guess what? You already know what Suggestion #1 is going to be by now. But that doesn't mean you should skip practicing it! So go ahead and play the root notes with the basic rhythm and get settled in. Have a listen to the other two suggestions while you're at it:

Suggestion #1

Suggestion #2

Suggestion #3

🌐 *10.6*

Just a quick note: It would have been easier to make the last measure start out with an eighth rest followed by seven eighth notes. But I wanted to give you something that required a little concentration!

Suggestion #2

There's nothing very tricky here, just your friendly chord arpeggios. The rhythm stays the same while you move from the root to the fifth and down to the third and to the root again. The overall chord pattern is descending, going from Dm to C to Bb and then to A7. Suggestion #2 emphasizes this descending pattern by playing the root on the last eighth note of each measure. Giving it an extra accent on your right hand will help make this particular pattern stronger.

Suggestion #3

Suggestion #3 replaces the first quarter note with two eighth notes, so you start out moving. Here the bass part is ignoring the thirds of the arpeggio, giving the song more of a "power chord" feel. Try to use the frets indicated by the bass guitar tablature on this suggestion. It will help you with practicing the "root fifth root" position of your fretting hand.

Taking Stock

So, how did you do? Sit down and take stock. Be objective and honest, but also be certain to bring up one good point for every one that might need some attention. If you keep a practice journal or a playing log, write down some notes and observations.

For example, let's say you could have played the A7 arpeggio in Song #3 a little cleaner. Make a note of that and practice accordingly. Don't play the song over and over; just work on the measure of A7. Start out slower and play the arpeggio in a style and manner that feels comfortable and right. If you can't play it clean at a slow pace, it's a safe bet that it won't be clean at speed, either.

Make (the Most of) Mistakes

You can't play without making a mistake, but you can play without other people knowing you made one! If you play a wrong note and then stop, throw up your hands, and shake your head, pretty much everyone will know you goofed. But if you play through your mistake without even blinking, most people won't hear it. It's true. Music goes by fast and mistakes are simply things of the moment. If you don't broadcast the mistake to your audience, it will probably slip by.

So when you practice, even with these jam-along tracks, practice not only playing but also how you deal with making mistakes. When you play a wrong note, keep on making music with the band. And be certain to give problem sections extra attention in your next personal practice time.

Come Back

Perhaps the most important thing to keep in mind is that every musician is a work in progress. Don't play along with these songs once and then toss them aside. As you move on in this book and learn more techniques and more theory, come back and try these songs again. Coming back to work on an old song is not a step backward. It gives you a chance to see that you're progressing very nicely.

The Least You Need to Know

- If you can, try to listen to a song before playing it.
- Start out with simple bass parts and then work on more complicated ones.
- Try to keep notes (at least mental ones) of what worked and what needs work.
- Play through your mistakes. Most of your listeners won't notice you made one unless you tell them.
- As you learn more, go back to an old song and see what you can add to it.

Part 4

Movin' and Groovin'

Your next evolutionary step in becoming a solid bass player is to create *movement*. In this section you will take your knowledge of chords and arpeggios and use it to create *moving* bass lines that smoothly flow from one chord to another. You'll learn what keys are, how to tell what key a song is in, and which scales and arpeggios a particular key may call for.

You'll also learn some simple riffs you can use in various standard chord progressions, and briefly explore the use of modes. And, of course, you'll get to show off all your new knowledge with some jam-along song tracks.

Home Sweet Home: The Concept of Keys

In This Chapter

◆ Learning about tension and resolution

◆ Discovering the key of a song

◆ Reading key signatures

◆ Finding the triads of any major key

◆ Understanding the Circle of Fifths

With your knowledge of the major scale and of how various chords are put together, you now have all the tools you need to become a steady, solid bass player. You've already used your newfound skills to play the jam-along songs in Chapters 6 and 10.

Listening to other bass players, you also know that there can be more to a bass line than simply playing the root note of a chord or a chord arpeggio. Cool bass lines move from place to place, following along with the chord progressions of a song.

The next step in a bassist's natural evolution is learning how to move. Once you know a little more about how songs are put together, you will be able to come up with bass lines that flow with the music. Bass lines that groove.

Rather than just showing you some tricks that you can copy and use in some circumstances, I'd like to teach you how songs and chord progressions work so you'll be able to create as well as copy. This section of the book will give you the knowledge you need to grow from a "static" bass player to a "moving" one.

What Key Is It In?

Whether you know it or not, almost all songs have patterns. There are rhythmic patterns—places where a particular beat or rhythm will pop up over and over again. As a bass player, it's very important to pay attention to the rhythmic

def•i•ni•tion

In the simplest terms, a **chord progression** is the movement from one chord to the next in a piece of music. A song may be thought of as a single chord progression, as in most blues songs, or it may also be seen as a combination of progressions—usually a different progression for the different parts of the song.

pattern. But songs also contain harmonic patterns, chords that are used and repeated in specific sequences throughout the song. These patterns are called *chord progressions*.

Chord progressions are the harmonic accompaniment for a song. The singer will sing the melody (or a lead instrument will play it), while the rest of the band provides the backing chordal harmony. Usually, the chord progression is a specific pattern of chords and, as a rule, the progression dictates the key of a song.

If you didn't know better, you'd think that musicians were all part-time locksmiths—they're constantly going on about keys. Knowing the key of a given song can tell you a lot, like which major scale to play in or which chord triads to use.

The trouble is that this simple question doesn't always have a simple answer. For now, let's explore the general rules of keys. When we later discuss modes in Chapter 15, you'll see some of the exceptions to the rule.

Resolving Your Tension

For the moment, don't worry about the question, "What's a key?" Instead, think about this: how do you know when a song is finished? And we're not talking about when the music stops.

Pick up your bass and try this experiment: I want you to play the following melody line, which you'll recognize as "Mary Had a Little Lamb," on your bass:

6

🔘 *11.1*

It feels really wrong to end the song there, doesn't it? How about if we tried this instead:

6

🔘 *11.2*

No, that doesn't work either. In both these cases, we have not come to a satisfying
ending point. Something just feels wrong. Not surprisingly, in music, this feeling
of unease, that we haven't gotten where we want to go yet, is called *tension*. When
the tension gives way to a feeling that we've gotten to the right place, this is
called *resolution*. Just to put our minds at ease, let's resolve "Mary" right now:

6

🔘 *11.3*

Can you hear and feel the resolution, the relief of the tension? Whether you
know it or not, whenever you listen to a piece of music, you're picking up on the
subtleties of the interplay between tension and resolution. Most music, whether

it's a pop song or a symphony, is like a roller-coaster ride. You start out at ease, then you experience all manner of little tensions and releases, not to mention a few big ones, and then you get back to the safe feeling of your starting point.

In other words, you've come "home."

Keys to the Highway

The feeling of being home is a good analogy for the key of a song. If your song is in the key of C major, then playing a final C major chord at the end will make you feel as though you've made it home safely. If you're in the key of D minor, then you want to end on a D minor chord. There will always be exceptions, but for most cases, this will hold.

The important thing to note here is that it's a chord we're concerned with, not a note. You're going to do the "Mary Had a Little Lamb" melody once more, but this time with a backing track:

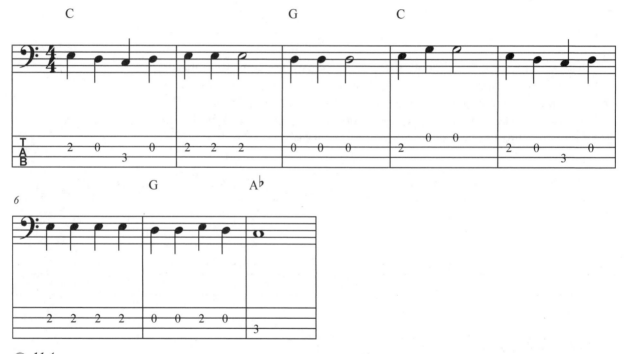

11.4

Did you hear that even though you played the right note at the end (the C) that the song still lacked resolution? That's because the organ ended on an Ab major chord, not C major. The C note is part of the Ab major chord, but playing the Ab major chord didn't help to make the song end well.

The whole purpose of a key is to give you a sense of balance, to provide a place where tensions can be resolved. Keys provide your ears with a sense of home.

Accidentals on Purpose

Let's do another experiment. Play the C major scale, but start on G and play all the notes—G, A, B, C, D, E, F, and then the G again, like this:

When you played this on your bass, you undoubtedly noticed that it doesn't sound right at all. Actually, it sounds fine up until you get to the F—then things just fall apart. Believe it or not, this is because you are so tuned into the major scale that it affects your hearing!

Now try doing the same thing but this time play F# instead of F:

Now that sounds correct, doesn't it? In fact, it sounds like a major scale. Specifically it's the G major scale and whether you know it or not, you've just picked up a particularly vital piece of information. The G major scale has one sharp in it—F#.

This interval of a half step between the seventh and the root is very important to your ears. The seventh, in music theory, is called a *leading tone* because the half step is naturally leading your ears up to the root. This is why our earlier example of the G scale using F in place of F# sounded strange and unsatisfying. But in this last example, you get a feeling of finality when you reach the last G. That's the leading tone doing it's job!

Up until now, you've been playing scales by patterns and probably haven't worried too much about the notes involved. But if you go back to your major scale pattern and start playing around the neck and notice the notes you're playing, you'll find out something very interesting. The C major scale is the only one that has no flats or sharps in it.

Basso Profondo

Q: How can knowing chords and keys help me as a bass player?

A: Knowing the makeup of any chord will give you more options when creating bass lines. "Leading tones" are a perfect example of this. Suppose you have a chord progression of A to D. You know that the A chord is made up of A, C#, and E. You also know (or will shortly know) that C# is the leading tone in the key of D. Using that C# in your bass line, perhaps as part of an arpeggio, right before landing on D will provide an excellent sound. Try it yourself: First play a few As followed by a D. Then play A followed by C# and then D, and see which one you prefer.

Key Signatures

The easiest way to tell the key of a song is to look at a piece of sheet music. At the start of the music, right before the time signature (covered in Chapter 5), is the *key signature.* The key signature is a single sharp or flat, or a group of sharps or flats (never both), appearing on the staff right before the time signature. They look like this:

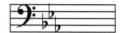

The first key signature, since it has one sharp (and that is F#), indicates the key of G major. The second one, with the three flats, is Eb major. The third has neither sharps nor flats, so it's C major. The fourth is the key signature for E major. It has four sharps.

Putting the key signature at the start of a piece of music (and at the start of each line) indicates that those sharps and flats apply to the note in question whenever you come upon it in the song. This beats having to write a sharp sign for every note of F in the key of G. If the songwriter or arranger wants you to play an F instead of an F#, he will indicate this by using the natural sign, as in this example:

Here you would play F#s in the first measure, Fs in the second and both F# and F in the third. Remember that a natural sign (or any accidental) only lasts for a measure unless otherwise indicated. Having key signatures makes reading and writing music a lot easier.

Keys, and consequently key signatures, follow distinct rules. If your key signature has one sharp, it's an F# and nothing else. You can't have a piece of music with a key signature of only C#. Why? Because there isn't a major scale that can be constructed with just a C#. This is important because it means that once you've learned the key signatures, you will always know the number of flats or sharps in any given key. And you will also know which notes are the flats or sharps.

Here are key signatures for all 12 major keys. We'll start with C and work through six of the "sharp" keys:

Key of C Major - No flats, no sharps

4 Key of G Major - 1 sharp (F#)

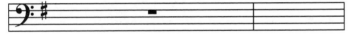

7 Key of D Major - 2 sharps (F# and C#)

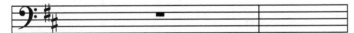

10 Key of A Major - 3 sharps (F#, C# and G#)

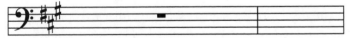

13 Key of E Major - 4 sharps (F#, C#, G# and D#)

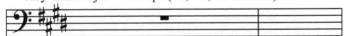

16 Key of B Major - 5 sharps (F#, C#, G#, D# and A#)

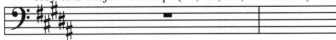

19 Key of F# Major - 6 sharps (F#, C#, G#, D#, A# and E#)

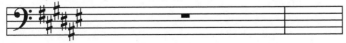

Now let's start again with C and work through six of the "flat" keys:

Key of F Major - 1 flat (Bb)

37 Key of Bb Major - 2 flats (Bb and Eb)

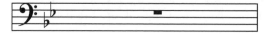

40 Key of Eb Major - 3 flats (Bb, Eb and Ab)

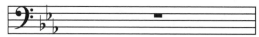

43 **Key of Ab Major - 4 flats (Bb, Eb, Ab and Db)**

46 Key of Db Major - 5 flats (Bb, Eb, Ab, Db and Gb)

We could, off course, write out more key signatures with either flats or sharps. If there were seven sharps in the key signature, that would be the key of C# major. Seven flats would mean the key of Cb major. But it's rare for the bass guitarist to venture far from the keys we've written out.

Triads of Any Major Key

When you know the key a song is in, you can also make a very educated guess about the chords that will be used in that particular song. The chords used in many songs are *diatonic* to the key of the song. Diatonic means that they stay with the notes of the major scale of that song.

You could start with your major scale and figure out the triads for each scale degree, but there is a much easier way. Let's use the C major scale as an example and look first at the scale degree:

I	II	III	IV	V	VI	VII
C	D	E	F	G	A	B

First we're going to discard the seventh. Building a triad from the B note using only the notes of the C major scale will give you a B diminished chord. In most songs (and we're talking about most pop, rock, country, and such—jazz doesn't count here), you won't run into many diminished chords. But you will run into lots of major and minor chords.

For the moment, let's not think of them as chords, but rather as colors ....

Primary Colors—The Major Chords

If you're working in a major key, then your chords at the first (root), fourth, and fifth scale degrees will almost always be major chords. I have to say "almost" because there are instances where a songwriter might use a minor instead.

But "almost always" is pretty good odds when it comes to music. Using the key of C major again as an example, we can fill in the following chords:

I	II	III	IV	V	VI
C			F	G	

If you've played guitar or piano, this probably is making a lightbulb go off in your head. It's almost impossible to find a song in C major that doesn't have an F or G major chord in it.

Let's try another key. If we wanted to pick out our "primary color chords"—that is, the chords at the first, fourth, and fifth position—in the key of A major, we'd write out (or mentally recite) the A major scale and know that they are as follows:

I	II	III	IV	V	VI
A			D	E	

This may not seem like much to you now, but what if I told you that just about any blues song is just a pattern using the I, IV, and V chord in a given key? You could then sit in at your local bar's next open-mic night and play along anytime someone says, "This song is a 12-bar blues in E." You'd know that the only chords are going to be E, A, and B (the I, IV, and V in the key of E) and could play the roots of the chords or even some chord arpeggios accordingly.

By the way, we'll be looking at the specific chord progressions of most blues songs later on in Chapter 23.

Secondary Colors—The Minor Chords

The triads built starting on the second, third, and sixth degrees of the major scale are all minor. Going back to C major as an example, that would mean we'd be looking at these chords:

I	ii	iii	IV	V	vi
	Dm	Em			Am

The two patterns of major and minor chords will be the same in every major key. The first, fourth, and fifth degrees will have triads forming major chords while the triads formed starting at the second, third, and sixth degrees will be minor.

> **Covering the Basses**
>
> When you know the I, IV, and V chord of any key, you will be able to play literally *thousands* of songs! Most blues and classic rock and roll music—plus a huge amount of country, folk, reggae, swing, and numerous other genres—are simply slight variations of the I–IV–V chord progression. Do yourself a favor and take a moment to memorize the I, IV, and V pattern in numerous keys, particularly those you find yourself playing in fairly often.

I	ii	iii	IV	V	vi
Major	minor	minor	Major	Major	minor

Did you notice that I used "small" letters for the Roman numerals for the second, third, and sixth degrees? This is another musical convention. When writing a song out in terms of its chord progression, the standard is to use Roman numerals—capital numerals for major chords and small numerals for minor ones. Regular numbers, like 7 or 9, can be added to the Roman numeral to indicate a modified chord, such as a seventh chord or a ninth chord. So if the chord progression in a piece of music reads …

I–I7–IV–iv–I–V7–I

… and you were told to play this in the key of C, you would use the following chords:

C–C7–F–Fm–C–G7–C

Let's go back and look at all of our diatonic major scale triads in the key of C major:

I	ii	iii	IV	V	vi
C	Dm	Em	F	G	Am

How about in the key of F? Using the F major scale and this same template of triads, we can see that these are the chords we'll get:

I	ii	iii	IV	V	vi
F	Gm	Am	Bb	C	Dm

Thinking about chords in this fashion can be very useful. It allows you to work chord changes in any key without thinking about it very much. Since you're already pretty up on your major scale pattern, think of how easy it would be to play a I–vi–IV–V bass line. All you would have to know is what key the song was in, which would give you your starting note. Test it out in a few different keys.

Whenever you can, try to see a specific chord progression in terms of its generic components. For instance, if you're in the key of D and the progression is D to G to Em to A, think of it as I–IV–ii–V. Getting a general mindset will help you to see the patterns of progressions everywhere. And because the bass is very conducive to pattern playing, you will find it easy to take a bass line you like with one specific progression and play it in a different key, as you'll see in Chapter 13.

Not all songs are strictly diatonic when it comes to the chords they use. This means that in some music you will find things like an A7 chord in the key of C. But for the most part, you will find that a huge number of songs are strictly diatonic, making this system of triads more than worth your while to know.

Rock Bottom

Another method of writing out chord progressions is called *Nashville numbers*. Regular numbers are used in place of Roman numerals. An "m" after a number would indicate a minor chord and modified chords typically have little numbers after them that look like exponents.

Will the Circle Be Unbroken

Another very useful tool when it comes to remembering keys and dealing with chord progressions is the *Circle of Fifths*, which looks like this:

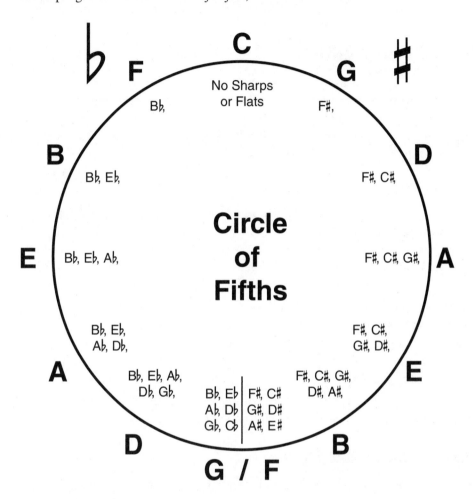

The key of C major (and all of these are major keys, by the way) is at the 12 o'clock position. Each key shift to the right (clockwise) adds a sharp to the key signature. The key of G major, as we noted earlier, contains one sharp (F#). The key of D major has two, A major has three, and so on.

If we start with C major and go to the left (counterclockwise), you add one flat to each new key signature. F major, then, contains a single flat; the key of Bb major has two; the key of Eb has three; and so on.

This is called the Circle of Fifths because of the special relationship between the root note of a key and the fifth degree of its scale. In the key of C major, G is the fifth degree. In the key of G major, D is the fifth degree. A is the fifth note in the key of D major, and you get the idea. Going clockwise around the circle, you always go to the fifth of the previous note or key. This relationship carries you completely around the circle.

Rock Bottom

Some people think of the Circle of Fifths as the "Circle of Fourths" because if you go in the opposite direction, counterclockwise, you land on the IV chord of the key preceding it. In the key of C, for instance, F is the IV chord. Bb is the IV chord of F and Eb is the IV of Bb. Just as with the V chord in the clockwise direction, the relationship of the IV chord will be constant in the counterclockwise direction around the circle.

The Circle of Fifths, upon closer examination, will also clue you in on other relationships between chords and keys. Pick a key, any key. You will see that the IV chord of that key is in the next space going counterclockwise while the V chord is the next space in the clockwise direction. So if you knew that a particular song involved only I, IV, and V chords, you could easily play it in any key.

Back Home Again

There's an even better use for the Circle of Fifths. Let's think once more about the idea of being home in a key. No single chord progression makes us feel so totally resolved as we do when listening to the V chord followed by the I chord. Well, actually one—playing the V7 chord followed by the I. But even playing just the root notes of those chords gives a satisfying resolution. If any song happens to end on a V to I change, then the chances are truly good that the song is in the key of the I chord.

An added bonus to becoming familiar and comfortable to playing in keys is that your ear will get better at telling you when something is wrong. When you set the tonality of a song, and when you know the general sound of the chord progression, it becomes easier to hear "clunker" notes, just as you did in our earlier examples with "Mary Had a Little Lamb."

Being able to trust your ear and to hear when something is wrong is a great first step toward being able to avoid a mistake. When you are practicing and play a wrong note, you might first chalk it up to a slip of the fingers. But that slip, with repetition, can become habit. You need your ears to tell you when something is wrong with your hands.

Having confidence in your ears is something that, like almost everything else about playing bass, comes with practice and patience.

The Least You Need to Know

- Chord progressions are the specific pattern of chord changes used either in a song or a part of a song.
- Most songs are written in a single key, which gives you the tonal center of that song.
- The key signature will tell you what key a song is written in.
- The triads formed from the major scale will give you the chords you are mostly likely to find in any given song.
- Chord progressions can be thought of in general or generic terms as well in specific chords.
- The Circle Of Fifths shows various relationships between keys and chords.

Minor Madness

In This Chapter

- ◆ Discovering songs in minor keys
- ◆ Creating the natural minor scale
- ◆ How to find the relative minor of any major key
- ◆ The differences between the three minor scales
- ◆ Building chord triads from the three minor scales

In Chapter 7 you learned the major scale and the system of musical intervals used to create scales and chords. The importance of the major scale cannot be understated, because just about everything in music and music theory is described or defined in terms of the major scale.

Even minor chords, as you discovered in Chapter 11 (and have used in some of our examples and jam-along tracks), come from natural intervals of the major scale. Songs in major keys will frequently contain minor chords, as you learned by making triads from the major scale in our last chapter.

This chapter will delve into minor keys—examining how they are created and why it's important for the bass player to be familiar with each of the three minor scales. We'll also take the time to build triads from each minor scale. You might find that you prefer to play bass on minor key songs, as they often lend themselves to very interesting bass lines.

Minor Problems

Not every song is in a major key. In many pieces, the tonal center, that feeling of "home" we discussed in our last chapter, revolves around a minor chord. These songs tend to sound sadder, a little more emotional than songs in major keys.

It may help to think of some songs in minor keys. "Greensleeves" (also known as the Christmas carol "What Child Is This?") and, speaking of Christmas carols, "We Three Kings of Orient Are" might be familiar to most people. Or perhaps the little snippet on the next page, which some of you might know as "The Volga Boatman."

🔘 *12.1*

Even playing only this melody on your bass, you can hear that you wouldn't want a major chord to accompany these notes. There's such an ominous and dour feeling to this song—a major chord would sound totally out of place.

The minor chord, as you learned in Chapter 8, contains its root, a *minor* third (as opposed to the major third), and the perfect fifth. This simple change to the third makes a very dramatic difference in the tone and character of the chord. But simply substituting a minor chord for a major one rarely makes for a pleasing overall chord progression in a song.

Songs in minor keys can be tricky to play because the scales, and consequently many of the chords, don't follow the same patterns as the major scale. To make matters even more interesting, there are *three* different minor scales that one can use, and each one has a sound all its own.

You may not know it in your head yet, but your ear will tell you that there's usually a lot more going on in a minor key song than can be explained by one simple scale pattern. Quite often, these songs seem to use chords that come out of left field but still sound right.

Much of the minor key feel does come from repeated use of the root chord. Like most songs, a song in a minor key will end on its root chord and create a solid sense of tonality. Are there other ways of creating that feeling of home for a song in a minor key?

The Natural Minor Scale

There certainly are. First, though, we should take a look at the minor scale, or at least at one of the three different minor scales. You already know the major scale, so the next step would be to learn the *natural minor* scale, since it uses the same notes as the major scale but uses a different note as its root.

For instance, here's the C major scale:

The A natural minor scale uses the same notes as the C major scale, but starts and ends on A (hence the "A" of "A natural minor"). It looks and sounds like this:

def•i•ni•tion

The **natural minor scale** is also called the **Aeolian mode**. As you'll learn in Chapter 15, it is one of the seven different modes you can create from the major scale.

You can hear what a difference starting on a different note makes when playing a scale! We'll be exploring more about this in Chapter 15.

For now, though, the important thing to realize is that you cannot simply start on any note of the major scale to get the minor scale. Remember that the major scale is built on a specific pattern of intervals. If you pick a different note as your root and then use the same notes of the major scale for the rest of the scale, you will get entirely different patterns of intervals. Compare the intervals of the A major scale to those of the A natural minor:

🎵 *12.4*

Notice that the half steps are now at different scale degrees. In the major scale, the half steps occur between the third and fourth degrees and between the seventh and the root. In the natural minor scale, they happen between the second and third degrees and between the fifth and sixth degrees. Even though we are using the same basic pattern, that of the major scale, for both scales, starting on a different root note gives the natural minor scale its own unique sound.

Just as we built the major scale with a specific pattern of whole steps and half steps, we can do the same with the natural minor scale. Pick a note as your root and then proceed in the following manner:

> Root, whole step, half step, whole step, whole step, half step, whole step, whole step

Natural Minors Are All Relative

To create a natural minor scale from any major scale, you use the *sixth* note of the major scale as your new root. Using the sixth note always creates this specific pattern of whole and half steps, which you just learned, that defines the natural minor scale.

Some people find it easier to think of the relative minor as being a step and a half lower than the root of the major scale. On the bass, this certainly makes sense. If you are on the root note of any major chord, the root note of the relative minor will be on the same string, but three frets lower. Eb, for example, can be found on the sixth fret of the A string. To find the relative minor of Eb major, go to the note that is on the third fret of the A string. It will be C, and C minor is indeed the relative minor of Eb major.

Thinking of the natural minor scale in terms of the notes of the major scale also allows the bass player to think in terms of patterns instead of notes. The A natural minor scale, in closed position, starting with the root (A) on the fifth fret of the E string, looks like this:

Like the major scale and the chord arpeggios in closed position that you've already learned, this is a moveable pattern. If, for example, you wanted to play a C natural minor scale, all you need to do is find the C note on either the E or A string and repeat this pattern, as shown in the illustration below:

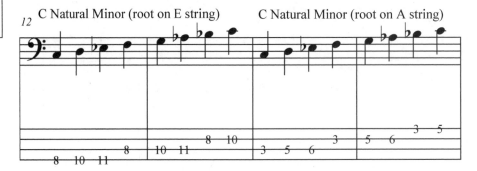

When you learned the major scale pattern in a closed position (back in Chapter 7), you learned how to play all 12 possible major scales. You didn't know it at the time, but you also learned how to play all 12 possible natural minor scales! That seems like a pretty good deal, doesn't it?

One of the appeals of the natural minor scale is its fingering. The root note, when found on the E or A strings, is fretted with the index finger, and many people find this more (pardon the pun) natural to play than the major scale pattern. And because all the notes of the major scale are used in the natural minor scale, some musicians find themselves inclined to think of the "minor position" of the major scale first.

That might seem to be a lot of work, but it's really not. Remember that the natural minor is formed from the sixth note of the major scale. The natural minor scale is, in fact, called the *relative* minor of the major key. And if you know the sixth note of any major scale, then you can create the relative minor scale without a second thought.

A Relative Minor for Every Major

Every major scale contains a natural minor scale. Starting on the sixth note of any major scale will give you the natural minor scale of your starting note. So, for instance, if you take your F major scale (F, G, A, Bb, C, D, and E) and start on the sixth note, D, you get the D natural minor scale, which is D, E, F, G, A, Bb, and C. D minor is the relative minor of F major.

The natural minor scales even follow a similar pattern when it comes to key signatures, much like the Circle of Fifths you read about in our last chapter. Now that you have learned that each major key has a relative minor, it's important to realize that the key signatures are now doing double duty. For instance, because A minor is the relative minor of C major, both of these keys will share the same key signature—that is, one with no sharps and no flats. If you see a key signature with three flats, then you know that the song is either in Eb major or C minor.

Here is a handy chart, done in the same order as the Circle of Fifths, to help you make conversions from any major key to its relative minor:

Major key	Number of #s or bs	Relative minor
C	0	A minor
G	1 #	E minor
D	2 #s	B minor
A	3 #s	F# minor
E	4 #s	C# minor
B	5 #s	G# minor
F# (Gb)	6 #s (6 bs)	D# (Eb) minor
Db	5 bs	Bb minor
Ab	4 bs	F minor
Eb	3 bs	C minor
Bb	2 bs	G minor
F	1 bs	D minor

So now that you know each key signature gives you two possible home keys, how do you know which one to use? Part of the answer involves reading. You will usually be playing with chord charts, and if a song ends on the relative minor, chances are it's meant to be played in the minor key.

But part of the answer also involves listening, and that's where our two other minor scales come into play.

The Harmonic Minor Scale

Do you remember our example of the G major scale without the F# from our last chapter? The natural minor scale also has no leading tone, that half step between the seventh note and the root, which seems so satisfying to our ears.

To some people, this leading tone seems essential to defining a scale. And the *harmonic minor scale* allows you to have both the minor third and minor sixth of the natural minor scale *and* the leading tone of the major seventh. Let's look and listen to the A harmonic minor scale:

🔊 *12.7*

The harmonic minor scale sounds fairly exotic, especially going from the sixth note to the seventh. By using the major seventh instead of the flatted seventh of the natural minor, the distance between the sixth and seventh note is now a step and a half. This is very unusual in Western music and it gives the harmonic minor scale a sound usually associated with music of the Far East or the Middle East.

Using the harmonic minor scale, particularly when playing it beneath a multi-measure passage of a single minor chord, creates all sorts of interesting bass lines.

The Melodic Minor Scale

Much of what we consider "musical" comes from our history, from all the songs and other pieces of music that have been written and played in our culture throughout the ages. And most of those songs, in terms of musical history, involve singing. The voice is the oldest instrument. The *melodic minor scale* is probably the most pleasant to the ears, perhaps because it is also the easiest one to sing or hum along with. It is also the only scale that uses different notes when it ascends than it does when it descends.

Going Up

Starting at the root and moving upward, the melodic minor keeps the minor third, but uses the major sixth and the major seventh:

The use of the minor third, the only note that has changed from the major scale, is enough to give this scale its minor feel. To many people, the melodic minor is the best sounding of the three minor scales because it seems closest to the major scale—at least it does when it's ascending.

Coming Down

Descending from the root, however, the melodic minor uses the same notes as those of the natural minor scale. Although this may seem strange on paper, it does sound very satisfying to the ears. In the following example we'll go both up and then down, and you can judge for yourself:

🌐 *12.9*

There are people who play the melodic minor scale using the same notes in both directions, but it's not as common as you might think. A lot of that has to do with the chord progressions found in songs with minor keys. And to get at the heart of the chords used, we need to go back to our triads.

Triads from the Minor Scales

Since each of the three minor scales uses different notes, we get three different sets of chords when using triads taken from each minor scale. One reason songs in minor keys can be so surprising is that songwriters often use chords taken from two or even all three minor scales in a single song. While there are songs in minor keys that stay diatonic, there are many more songs whose chord progressions flit from the chords of one minor scale to the chords of another.

When making triads from any of the three minor scales, it's easy to see why we get such a variety. The only triad that doesn't contain a sixth or seventh (the two notes which differ in each minor scale) is the root triad, consisting of the root, minor third, and perfect fifth. Consequently, while the root chord remains the same, we get some very interesting variations at the other positions of the scale.

Natural

Let's take a look at the triads we get when using the notes of the natural minor scale. For the sake of comparing the three minor scales, we'll use the key of A minor for each of the examples in this section.

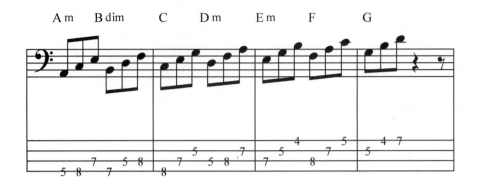

Because the natural minor scale uses the same notes as the major scale, there are no real surprises here. We have three major chords—the III, VI, and VII—and three minor ones—the i, iv, and v. The ii chord is a diminished triad. When you encounter the ii chord in a song in a minor key, you can pretty much bet that the chord immediately after it will be the v chord.

It's interesting to note that, in the natural minor scale, the root, iv, and v triads are all minor, just like their root, IV, and V counterparts in the major scale are all majors. There are many songs that will use the minor root and the minor fourth, but a minor triad on the fifth is not all that common.

The other interesting thing is that VI and VII chords are major triads. There are a great many songs that use a "minor root—major seven—major six" progression, particularly in the various genres of rock music.

Harmonic

The harmonic minor scale, with its major seventh being the only different note between it and the natural minor scale, gives us both some surprises and some comfort:

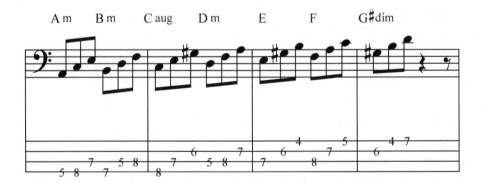

Here we have two minor chords (the root and the iv), two major chords (the V and VI), and two diminished chords (the ii and vii). We also get an augmented triad for the third position, which is rarely used in most music, outside of some classical pieces. Having a minor fourth and a major fifth, as we'll see in the next section, makes this set of triads very comforting.

Melodic

As you've learned, the only difference between the major scale and the ascending melodic minor scale is one note—the minor, or flatted, third. But while that leads to having many triads in common with the major scale, the overall tonal quality is strikingly different:

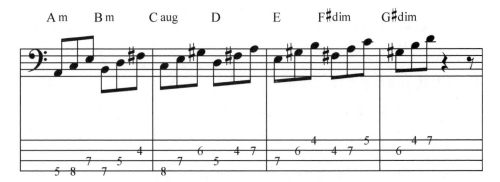

The root triad, obviously, is minor. The second, fourth, and fifth triads are identical to their major scale counterparts. That is, the second is a minor triad while the fourth and fifths are major. Going from a minor root to a major fourth is a popular progression in many Latin songs.

In the melodic minor, we still have an augmented triad at the third position, just as in the harmonic minor. The chords built on the sixth and seventh degrees of the scale are diminished triads. Remember that the descending melodic minor scale would use the same triads formed by the natural minor scale.

Minor Resolutions

The feeling of home, which helps you to determine the key of a song in a major key, also helps you establish the tonality of a minor key. But depending upon the scale or scales being used, that sense of tonality could involve a very different cadence than the V to I, which is so commonly used in songs in major keys.

The V to I progression, an excellent way to attain the feel of home in the major keys, can be used to the same effect in songs written in minor keys. But if the V chord is a minor chord, the resolution will not seem nearly as strong or satisfying as it would if the V chord were a major chord. Gm or Gm7 resolving to Cm sounds weak compared to using a G or G7 to Cm.

Another strong-sounding resolution, and one that is used very frequently in rock, pop, and folk music, is going from the major VII to the minor root. Because of the choices of triads offered by the three minor scales, there are all sorts of choices to be made in terms of chord progressions.

And this is where the songwriter tends to most often leap from the triads of one minor scale to another. It is very common, for instance, to play a song in Am whose chord progression is Am (root), G (VII in the natural minor scale), F (VI in the natural minor scale), and then E or E7 (V in the harmonic or melodic minor scale). The E7 makes the strongest resolution back to the root of A minor.

A bass player usually has to be on his toes when playing songs in a minor key. Knowing a little more about which scales and which chords are likely to show up can keep you from getting lost or confused. More importantly, this knowledge can help you create bass lines that are appropriate to a song's specific chord progression. Take a little time to familiarize yourself with the mysteries of minor scales and you will find that playing songs in minor keys can brighten your day.

In Chapter 16, at the end of this section of the book, you will find two jam-along songs written in minor keys. They might very well become your favorite practice pieces!

The Least You Need to Know

- ◆ Songs can be written in minor as well as major keys.
- ◆ Every major key has a relative minor.
- ◆ There are three different minor scales.
- ◆ Because there are three different minor scales, you will have three different sets of triads to work with when building chords.

Chapter 13

Wandering from Home: Chord Progressions

In This Chapter

- ◆ Thinking about chord progressions and movement
- ◆ Examples of I–IV, V–I, and ii–V–I progressions
- ◆ Using chromatic notes to spice up bass lines
- ◆ The descending bass line
- ◆ Knowing when not to move

Music is motion. Songs progress from an introduction to a verse to a chorus and so on until they reach an ending. Even if a song has only one chord or riff played over and over, there is usually some kind of movement going on.

And the bass player is a key part of moving the song along. So far you've learned about rhythm and scales and chord arpeggios and keys, all of which are important parts of a solid musical foundation. But now it's time to put your knowledge to the task of making music *move*.

In this chapter you'll learn about the most basic chord progressions used in songs and about how it's up to you to make the trip from Point A to Point B— or from A major to D major—as interesting as possible. You also see how the knowledge you have about chord construction and about scales will aid you in coming up with interesting bass lines of your own.

Progressive Thinking

Most songs involve a number of chord changes. They start out on one chord and progress to a second. They might return to the original chord, or they might move on to a third. Whatever the pattern is, it usually repeats throughout a piece of music. If the first verse of a song is two measures of D minor followed by a measure of G minor and then one of A7, you can usually bet the second verse will follow the exact same pattern.

Covering the Basses

You can learn a lot about chord progression simply by listening to music. It's not important to have perfect pitch, which means having the ability to identify, say, a C chord going to Dm7 just by ear. As mentioned in Chapter 7, most musicians don't have perfect pitch—some actually think it's more of a hindrance than a help. But having *relative pitch* is something you can develop with critical listening. Most chord progressions have distinct sounds. It's almost impossible not to recognize a V–I progression, for example, once you know how to listen for it. A great way to practice (and it's easy and fun, too!) is just to sit down with some music that you have chord sheets for. Follow along with the chord sheets and just listen to the progressions. Then try to pick out what the bassist is doing. Developing your ear in this manner will put more and more ideas into your head that you can use when you're playing.

When you just start out playing music, chord progressions may seem to be random choices. But as you play more songs, you find different chords seem to go together. The I chord will often be paired with the IV or V chord, for instance. The iii chord seems to be followed quite often by the IV or ii chord. You'll get to the point where the concept of triads that we covered in Chapter 11 makes a lot of sense because the primary and secondary chords tend to stick together.

As you gain more experience playing, you'll even start to see that a lot of progressions are relatively predictable. Any V chord or V7 chord is, more likely than not, going to be followed by the root chord. In the key of C, for instance, C will almost always be the next chord after G or G7. ii chords are usually followed by V chords. IV chords quite often come after I chords.

While it's important to remember that anything is possible in terms of a chord progression, it's just as important to keep your eyes and ears open for progressions that seem to pop up over and over again. Songs tend to be repeating patterns and having an idea as to what the pattern may be can make your job as a bassist a little easier.

Just as there are only so many notes and chords, there are also only so many ways of connecting one chord to another. But moving from chord to chord involves rhythm as well as notes, and this added dimension opens up as many possible bass lines as you can dream up.

Walking the Bass Lines

As a bass player, you have the ability to lead a listener from one chord to the next. And you can do so in a manner as complex or simple as you choose. You could, if you chose to do so, be a bass player who only plays the root notes of chords. Heaven knows there are many of them out there! It does get boring after a while though—for the bassist as well as for the listener.

Likewise, you can use alternating bass lines or chord arpeggios in every song you play. This would be more interesting than only playing root notes, but it can still become predictable after awhile.

Using notes from scales to move from the root note of one chord to the root note of another makes for much more interesting playing. And, when used in combination with chord arpeggios, scales can create some very fluid bass lines. And because you are already familiar with your scale fingering, bass lines involving scales tend to be easy to play.

For example, say you've been working on a song in the key of G where the progression is G to Bm to Em. You could move the bass line from G to Bm by using the A note of the G major scale to "connect the dots," so to speak. We simply want to get to the B of the Bm chord at the right point in the song. Likewise, you can use the C and D notes of the scale to move you from Bm to Em.

The objective of a bassist is not only to come up with a riff that sounds good with a particular chord, but also one that moves smoothly from one chord to the next. You can play the most fancy and flashy riffs in the world, but it doesn't do you much good if they don't fit in with the chord progression of the song at hand.

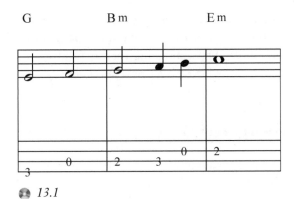

🔊 *13.1*

Remember that patterns are the bass player's bread and butter. When you come up with a bass line that you like for a particular chord progression, take an extra minute to learn it in closed position. Then you'll be able to use the pattern on any occasion the chord progression comes up, regardless of what key it's in.

Let's go back to that G to Bm to Em progression in the last example. Putting the chord progression into generic terms, it would be a I–iii–vi progression. And if we use a closed position on this progression, it would be played like this:

Now suppose that you were playing a different song, one in the key of Bb, which had a Bb to Dm to Gm progression. That is also a I–iii–vi progression. You can play the pattern you just came up with but use Bb as your starting point:

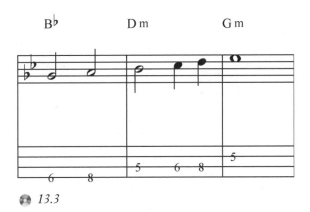

🔊 *13.3*

What you've just done here, taking a progression in one key and then playing it in another, is called "transposing," and you'll be finding out more about it in Chapter 18.

As you learned in Chapter 11, being able to think of chord progressions in both specific and generic terms is a big step to becoming proficient at the bass. But it's a simple step that involves nothing more than you taking the time to be observant of what you're doing and to know a little about notes and chords—which you already do!

Leaving Home (I–IV Progressions)

Far and away, the I–IV and V–I chord progressions are used more than any other. Musically speaking, the IV chord is like a home away from home. It's a comfortable place to stop, and you feel like staying there a bit before moving on back to your "real home." Think about a song like "You Are My Sunshine." When you get to the chord at the end of the second line in the chorus ("You make me happy …"), it sounds like a very natural place, musically, for a bit of a pause.

Going from the root chord to the IV chord can be done very simply—just climb up the notes of the scale. You can also go in reverse when moving from the IV chord back to the root, like this example in the key of C:

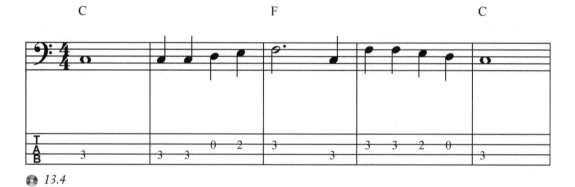

🔘 *13.4*

It doesn't get much simpler than this! But you can get as fancy or complicated as you'd like. Try this example:

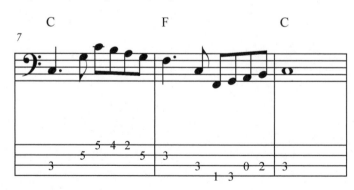

🔘 *13.5*

Here you combine a bit of the alternating bass line (from Chapter 6) with a descending scale line to get from C (the I chord) to F. Once at the F note, you use a descending alternating bass line and then an ascending scale line to get back to C from F.

Combining scale notes with chord arpeggios gives you even more possibilities when it comes to moving around on your bass. These next two examples show a couple of interesting approaches to the I–IV progression:

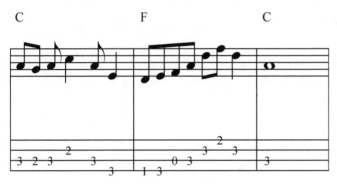

🌐 *13.6*

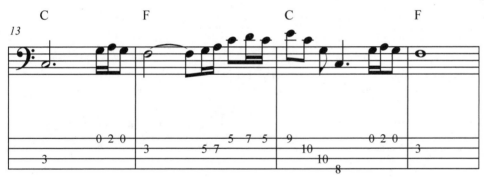

🌐 *13.7*

In the first example, the first measure ends with a descending C major arpeggio, which leads to the F at the start of the second measure. Measure two begins with a short scale run (F to G to A) before using an F major scale arpeggio, starting on the A and going up past F to A and back to F.

The second example is a wonderful demonstration of the bass guitar as a melodic lead instrument. It may sound pretty fancy, but it's simple using the notes of the C major scale, combined with a descending C major chord arpeggio at the beginning of the third measure. An important thing to listen to in this last example is that the second measure begins on the high E note, which is the third of the C major chord, instead of the root note of C. Starting on the third and then landing and pausing on the root note later on in the measure helps to create the tonality of the major chord in a way that catches your attention.

Covering the Basses

Timing is a critical component of any bass line. You want to be certain that you land on the chord change at the right time. Most chord changes occur on the first or third beats of any given measure. Obviously, this isn't true of every song you'll ever play. Listening to a song's chord changes will help you plan ahead for your own bass lines.

def•i•ni•tion

Much of the seeming "magic" of creating bass lines comes from **targeting** the root note of a given chord or another of the chord's component notes. Part of the beauty of working with arpeggios and scale notes is that you are usually a short distance away from the next note that you need for a bass line. In a seemingly strange chord progression like going from G major to Eb minor, think of Eb as your target. The closest note to Eb is either E or D and D happens to be part of the G major chord. Ending your G bass line on D puts you right next to your target note and makes for a seamlessly smooth bass line. We'll discuss targeting much more in Chapters 15 and 20, which deal, respectively, with modal scales and improvising.

Return Trip (V-I Progressions)

The V–I progression is even more common than the I–IV. As we discussed in Chapter 7, the V–I progression, also known as the "perfect cadence," practically defines the tonality of a piece of music. It's no accident that the fifth is used almost always as the "alternate" in the alternating bass line.

You will run into the V–I progression in practically every song you play, so it's good to get some ideas about how to play it. Remember that just because something's been done a million times, that doesn't mean you can't come up with a fresh twist on it.

Here are some examples of the V–I progression. Let's work in the key of D this time out, meaning that D will be the I chord and A will be the V.

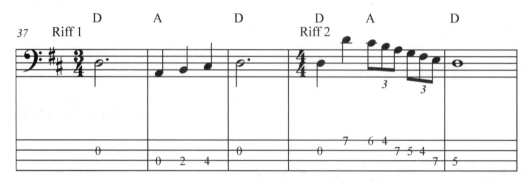

🔘 *13.8*

Riff 1 is very straightforward, using notes of the D major scale to climb from A to D in the second measure. While Riff 2 does the same thing, it's interesting in that the C# note is the start of the descending scale run. Remember that C# is the third of the A major chord, so this is a perfectly sound thing to do.

Not playing, or inserting rests (from Chapter 4), is yet another way of making bass lines stand out. Riff 3 starts out each measure with a rest of a half beat. This creates an emphasis on the off-beat, which gives a spicy feel to the rhythm.

Speaking of rhythms, Riff 4 uses a repeated rhythm of two sixteenth notes followed by an eighth note to liven things up a little. A final note of interest: both of the last two riffs use the G note to give the A chord more of an A7 feel. V7 chords are even better than V chords for creating that perfect cadence. And even if the rest of the band is sticking with the V chord, the bassist can nudge things along a bit by adding the "7" of V7.

A Little Jazz on the Way (ii–V–I Progressions)

Not too far behind the V–I progression in terms of common usage is the ii–V–I progression. This particular progression is a staple of jazz songs of all types, not to mention country, pop, rock, and other musical genres. The ii, and especially the ii7 chord, leads the ear very nicely to the V, which, as you've already discovered, in turn leads the ear right back to the root.

Here are a few examples of ii–V–I done in the key of F major. Remember that in the key of F major, Gm is the ii chord, C is the V chord, and F, naturally, is the I:

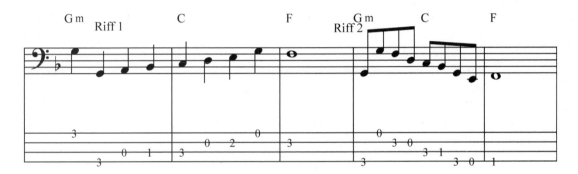

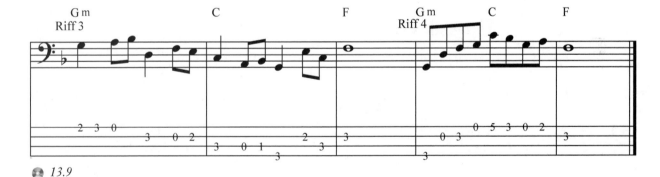

13.9

Getting Outside Help with a Bass Line

Don't feel obligated to stick with the notes of your major or minor scale while creating a bass line. After all, you've got 12 to work with, why restrict yourself to just seven? You can also take notes from outside the scale, using these notes as leading tones to the root of the chord (or whatever your target note might be) coming up next in your progression. *Chromatic progressions* bring more spice to your playing.

Chromatic I–IV Riffs

Here, in the key of A, are some examples of I–IV progressions that use chromatic notes from outside the A major scale:

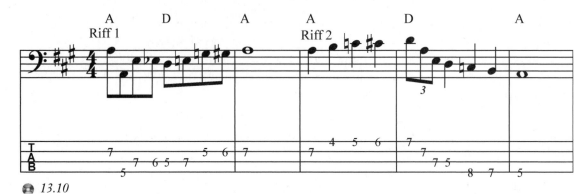

🔊 *13.10*

The first riff starts out sounding like a typical major-scale walking bass line. But instead of going from A to B to C#, it goes from A to B to C natural (the minor third of the A major scale) before hitting the C# on its way to the D that begins the second measure. Then, after playing a descending D major chord arpeggio, the C natural is used once again to descend to A. This use of the minor third gives the progression a very bluesy or jazzy feel.

Chromatic notes also give the second riff a little more punch, using first Eb as a leading tone to D and then using a G natural to lead up to the G# that brings us home to A.

Chromatic V–I Riffs

Let's try the key of Eb major to demonstrate some chromatic V–I riffs:

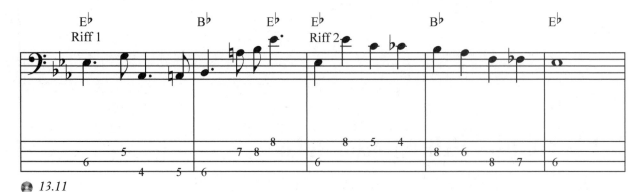

🔊 *13.11*

Chromatic ii–V–I Riffs

And to wrap up this section, we'll return to the key of C major for some chromatic examples of the ii–V–I progression.

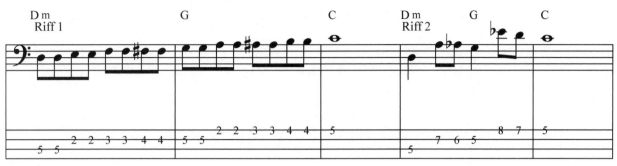

🔵 *13.12*

A Classic Walk Down the Stairs

No look at standard progressions would be complete without a discussion of the descending bass line. Quite often you will hear a bassist play something that sounds like a descending major scale, but all the chords over it seem to change with every note.

Your ears aren't playing tricks on you! This is a classic technique that all bass players use. Here's an example in the key of C:

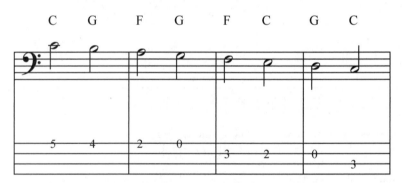

In this example, the bass is playing a descending C major scale. The first note, C, is the root of the C chord. Even though the next chord is G, the bassist uses B as his note, because he knows that B is the third of the G chord. Likewise, using A as the bass note for the F chord works perfectly fine. G, because it is the fifth of the C chord, will serve as the next bass note and there's no problem with F because it's the root of the F chord. E (the third of the C chord) and D (the fifth of the D chord) lead you right back to C.

This is a good example of how knowing what notes make up any given chord can help you create a bass line that might otherwise involve playing nothing but root notes. Say that you were given a chord sheet that used the following chords:

    C–E7–Am–A7–D7–G–C

You might be tempted to play all roots or to wander all over creation with a moving bass line, but it would also be possible to do something with a simple elegance.

> ### Basso Profondo
>
> *Q: If there are only so many types of chord progressions, how can I create interesting bass lines?*
>
> A: There are many ways to make a bass line fresh, even if the chord progression is older than Bill Wyman! Think of a chord progression as a short trip, like from your house to school or work. You could drive the major highway, you could take a lesser-traveled back road, you could even ride your bike.
>
> Making imaginative use of rhythm and remembering that you can move chromatically as well as diatonically can help you keep coming up with new ideas. Listening to other bass players is also a great way to find new approaches to tried-and-true chord progressions.

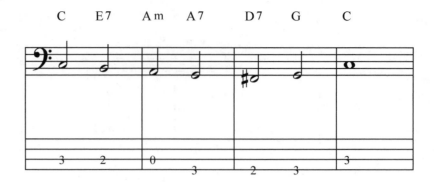

Here the B note is part of the E chord, while the G is part of the A7. Using the F# (the third of the D7 chord) lends a bit of a jazzy, chromatic touch and leads you very nicely back to G for the penultimate chord.

And speaking of chromatics, the following is a chord progression you're likely to see a lot if you play pop music:

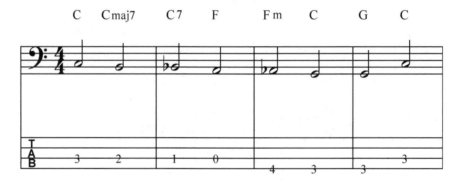

You can find this use of major seventh, dominant seventh, and minor chords in all sorts of music, and it lends itself very handily to the descending bass line. The IV–iv change (from F to Fm in this example) is especially pleasing with the bass, emphasizing the move from the third of the IV chord (the A in this case) to the minor third (the Ab).

Staying Put

As much fun as moving bass lines are to come up with and play, you can also make a dramatic bass line by staying on a single note while the rest of the band changes chords. Here is a good example of that:

You will find this driving, droning type of bass line quite often in various genres of rock music. It creates a pulsing, almost hypnotic effect to the beat of the music.

Just as knowing your scales and chord arpeggios can help you to create moving bass parts, knowing which notes make up any given chord will assist you in getting better as a bass player. Being able to stay on a single note while chords change can be exactly what a song needs to give it (and you!) a bit of a breather.

Which, in kind of a strange way, brings us back to the I–IV progression. Sitting on the root note of the I also gives you the fifth of the IV chord, and you will find many songs that start out in this fashion.

The Wander of It All

If you think about it, there are a finite number of chord progressions. A good number, yes, but it's still definitely a finite one. And that number is even smaller when you limit it to how many chord progressions actually sound good. The chances of you finding a piece of music with a G major to Db minor to F diminished to A major are truly slim, though certainly not impossible.

But given that there are (relatively) few chord progressions, there seem to be a vast number of bass lines. How can that be?

Remember that bass lines involve rhythm and rests as much as they involve notes. You can play a simple bass walk from C to F, for example, in as many different ways as you can dream up. A little pause here, a couple of quicker notes there, and presto! You have a new bass line to call your own.

Playing around and coming up with a number of bass lines for any one progression is a great way to start. But don't stop there! Say you have a cool riff for a progression in 4/4 timing. Come up with one for the same chord progression but in 3/4 timing instead. Take the riff you came up with for a rock song and see if you can't make a country one out of it (there'll be more on various musical genres in Part 6).

Besides learning riffs from books, listening to other bass players is a great way to get ideas. But the best thing of all is simply to try things out and see what you come up with. Even if you come up with a killer riff only to find out that someone else has already recorded it—remember that you came up with it on your own. That means there's more where that one came from!

The Least You Need to Know

- Bass players move songs along—bass lines are meant to move from chord to chord.
- I–IV and V–I are the two most-used chord progressions.
- You can use chromatic notes as well as diatonic ones to create a bass line.
- Both descending bass lines and droning bass lines can be used to great effect in music.

Rock Bottom

The use of a single note in the bass while a melody or chord is constantly changing above it has quite a bit of history in music. And we're talking about music from all over the world. Instruments as different as bagpipes, sitars, and mountain dulcimers all use a droning bass to provide harmonic support for the melody lines being played on these instruments' higher registers.

Further from Home: More Chord Progressions

In This Chapter

◆ Working with longer chord progressions

◆ Examples of bass lines for standard chord progressions

◆ What modulations are

◆ Using the V chord from another key

◆ The use of the turnaround

Now that you're getting good at two-chord progressions, such as the I–IV and V–I, and three-chord progressions such as the ii–V–I from our last chapter, it's time to work on longer strings of chords.

The same ideas we discussed earlier still apply—you want to take a look at an overall progression and figure out where you want to be and when. You'll need to think of timing as well as scales and the notes that make up the various chords in the progression. Do you want to work diatonically, using only the notes from the major scale in question, or will you bring in chromatic tones to spruce things up a bit? It's all up to you.

Do Wop Do Wah (I–vi–IV–V)

Let's start with a classic progression—the I–vi–IV–V. You will hear this in a lot of styles, but '50s doo-wop or old ballads will bring it most readily to mind. Think of a song like "Stand by Me" or "Last Kiss"—they are simply the I–vi–IV–V progression played over and over again. Recent songs like Simple Plan's "Welcome to My Life" also use this progression.

Let's start out by working in the key of D major. That means the I–vi–IV–V progression will be D to Bm to G to A. In all of the first four examples, we'll work in 4/4 time and have each chord last for two beats one time through the progression before ending with four beats of D. And let's begin with something that swings a little:

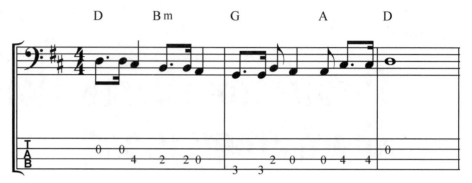

14.1

You can see and hear that the I–vi–IV–V progression is a perfect fit for the classic descending bass line. Moving downward from D to B involves a skip of two notes of the D major scale, as does the jump from B to G.

Our second example begins with a rest of one beat and then uses the alternating bass line approach to get going:

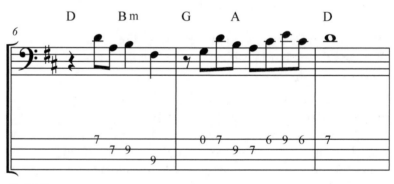

14.2

The second measure also begins with a rest—this time it's a half-beat rest—and finishes off with arpeggios of the G and A chords before ending on D.

Now let's add a few chromatic touches to the mix:

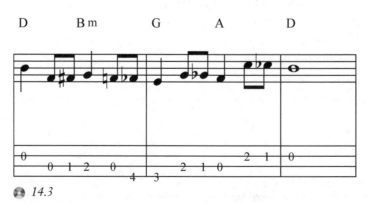

14.3

And in this next example, we'll use a dotted quarter- and eighth-note rhythm to punctuate the use of chromatic leading tones:

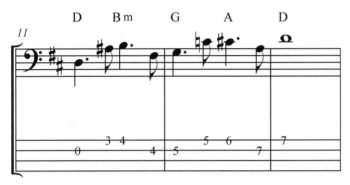

🔊 *14.4*

Hopefully these four examples will also illustrate that even though a chord progression has been done more times than you can count, there are still many ways of coming up with fresh bass lines for it. Using various rhythms and rests, playing it strictly diatonic or bringing in chromatic touches, the bass player should never worry about being stale.

Stringing on Thirds (I–iii–IV–V and variations)

Using the iii chord as a step between I and IV can be found in songs like "Puff the Magic Dragon" and other folk songs, but the I–iii cadence, particularly in songs written in minor keys, is also a favorite of many alternative rockers like Nirvana. In ballads and other songs in major keys, following the I chord with a iii is like playing the Imaj7. In the key of C, for example, Em (E, G, and B) is the iii chord, and Cmaj7, as you know, contains C, E, G, and B. This makes for a very mellow change.

Our first example, written in Bb major, uses an ascending major scale over the first part of the progression:

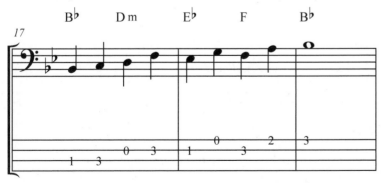

🔊 *14.5*

After the first three notes of the Bb major scale, this riff then jumps up from D to F, which is part of a Dm chord arpeggio. It then repeats the mini-arpeggio in Eb and F to finish the riff.

Just to make things a little more interesting, let's try doing the next example in 3/4 time:

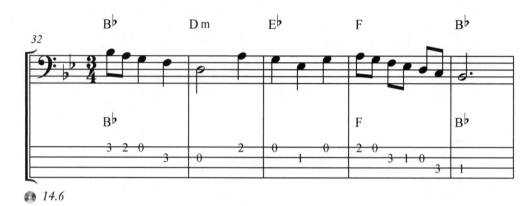

🔘 *14.6*

And now let's play two examples with chromatic touches, one in 4/4 and one in 3/4 timing:

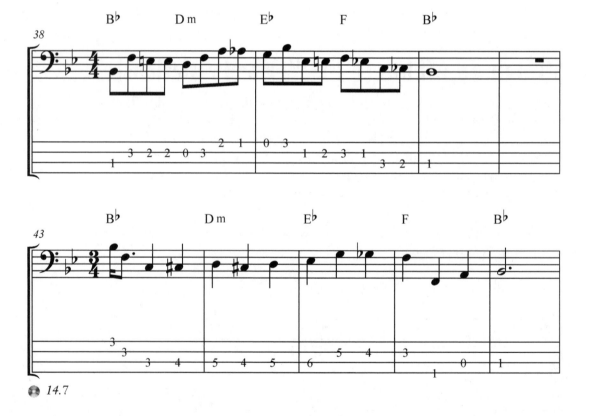

🔘 *14.7*

In most of the harder styles of rock, the subtleties of the iii chord are passed over for the edginess of the flatted third. You're much more likely to run into progressions and bass lines like the next two.

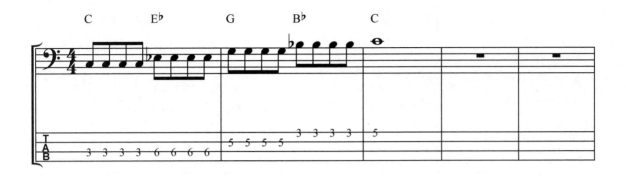

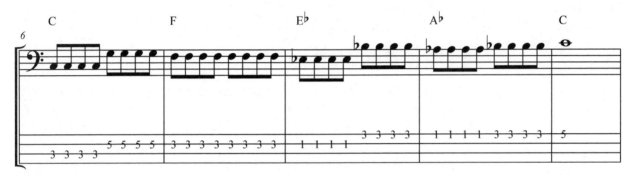

🔘 *14.8*

Major and Minor Rock (I–bVII–IV Progressions)

Speaking of rock, a classic progression of rock music is the I–bVII–IV. You will hear this in songs like "Taking Care of Business" and "Addicted to Love," among many, many others. It's also used quite often in bluegrass music. The signature sound of this particular progression is going from the original root chord down a full step to the major chord of the bVII. In our examples, we'll use the key of G major, so the chords will be G, F, and C.

Like all of the progressions we've covered so far, there are still many ways for the bass player to approach this one. Obviously, you can go for a "root-only" rock style, but you can decide to be rather melodic, as in the following example:

🔘 *14.9*

Or you can also be very busy, almost in a boogie-woogie style of playing:

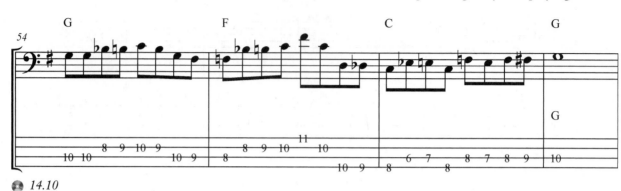

14.10

A Little Modulation

Tonal centers of songs can be moving targets. A song that starts in the key of G major, for instance, can end up in the key of Bb major, D minor, or just about anywhere. But the vast majority of songs tend to start in a key and end in the same key.

That doesn't mean, though, that things can't happen between the beginning and the ending of a song! Occasionally there will be slight changes of key, called *modulations*. A bass player needs to be aware of modulations because any change of key can bring new scales or nondiatonic chords into play.

Songs in minor keys, for example, might suddenly seem to be in a major key. Again the traditional folksong "Greensleeves" is a good example. It obviously starts in a minor key but about two thirds of the way through, at what could be called the song's chorus, it sounds positively major for a few lines before ending on a minor note.

Another common place for a modulation would be at the end of a phrase halfway through the verse of a song. Typically, the midpoint of a song's verse would use a V chord, which would resolve to the root chord at the start of the next phrase. In order to make the V chord seem like more of a resting place, it's often preceded by the V chord of its own key, a "V of V" chord, if you will.

The easiest way to spot a modulation is by the V chord of the key into which you're modulating. If you see a chord that is not diatonic to the key you're in, chances are likely that it's a "V of" chord and will herald in a short modulation. The most common types of this chord are discussed next.

V of V

If you're playing a song in the key of C and a D7 chord pops up, the chances are very good that the next chord following will be G. Because D is the V chord in the key of G and G is the V chord in the key of C, D7 in the key of C is called V of V.

In folk, country, and bluegrass, the V of V chord occurs quite frequently. Usually the second line of songs in these genres will end with a V chord, and the V of V is perfect for ushering it in.

V of ii

V of ii is often used to replace the vii chord, particularly in jazz songs. A song in the key of G, for instance, might go from G to E or E7 and then to Am.

V of vi

Likewise, the V of vi will be used in place of the iii chord when resolving to the vi. This chord will most often be found in songs that modulate between a major key and its relative minor. Using the key of F as an example, you might find a progression like F to A7 (V7 of vi) to Dm (the vi chord).

V of IV

Musicians rarely think about the V of IV chord, even though it's probably used more often than any other! It's simply the dominant seven of the I chord–I7. Many songs will use the I7 chord to fill out I–IV progressions, mostly because the additional seventh note provides such a great-sounding resolution. This is why a bass player can often use the flatted seventh note of the major scale in a I–IV progression.

Deceptive Cadences

Occasionally, you will run into *deceptive cadences*. These are usually "V of" chords that resolve to something other than what you were thinking. A classic example is the I–V of V–IV–I progression, where the V of V chord resolves to IV instead of V. Many rock songs, particularly from the '60s and '70s, use this progression.

Another deceptive cadence that turns up quite often involves the V of vi chord. Instead of resolving to vi, it is followed by the IV chord.

Deceptive cadences can liven up a song and they certainly keep a bassist playing a song for the first time on her toes!

Turning Things Around

Another little musical quirk for the bassist to watch out for is the *turnaround*. Turnarounds occur frequently in blues songs, and many jazz standards as well.

The turnaround is aptly named. After a song has completed a verse or a chorus, it's usually on the I chord. In order to give the next verse (which more often than not starts on the I as well) a kick-start, the music will do a quick change to the V chord, making the start of the new verse more immediate. For the bass player, the turnaround will often include a chromatic step up or down to the root of the V chord.

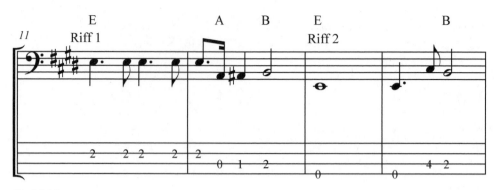

🔊 *14.11*

In jazz, turnarounds tend to be a little more complicated, as in the following example:

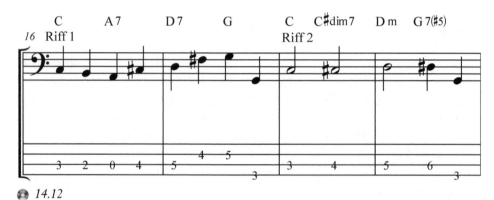

🔊 *14.12*

Rather than a quick change from the I to the V, or the I–IV–V, these turnarounds involve progressions of four different chords. If you get lost on a turnaround, remember that you're going to end on the V—be there on time and you'll be fine!

Because the bass is a vital part of creating the tonal center of any song, it's important to be aware of the different things that can happen. If you're playing a song for the very first time, there's going to be a chance that a modulation or turnaround will fool you. But having the basic knowledge of modulations and turnarounds will keep you from being fooled the second time around!

The Least You Need to Know

- ◆ Many chord progressions are indicative of a song's style.
- ◆ Modulations are temporary changes of keys within songs.
- ◆ A nondiatonic chord is likely to be a "V of" chord.
- ◆ "V of" chords can be deceptive!
- ◆ A turnaround is a quick change from the I to the V chord before starting a song again.

Chapter 15

Going Modal with Scales

In This Chapter

◆ Learning the pentatonic scale

◆ Discovering modal scales

◆ Making use of "the box"

◆ Using a song's chord progression as a guide to scales

Some bass players obsess about scales and, to a point, that's certainly understandable. As you've learned in the last two chapters, scales can help you move from one chord to the next. If you're comfortable playing the major and various minor scales at different positions on your fingerboard, you're going to be a very solid bass player.

Knowing scales also provides you with easy fingering choices for most chord arpeggios, such as those we covered in Chapters 8 and 9. Most bass lines revolve around a particular scale or arpeggio.

Occasionally, though, the major or minor scale you're playing might not fit your needs on a given song. You could be playing, for example, a song that seems to be in A minor, but has some chord changes that are outside of the A minor natural scale. Or perhaps there's a song in the key of C that includes a lot of Bb major chords. Some "tweaking" or other adjustment of a scale may be in order.

In this chapter you'll learn about the pentatonic scale and about modal scales. Don't panic and think this is a lot of material to cover! You've already learned these scales simply by knowing the major and natural minor scales. Instead of thinking about it as learning more scales, look at this chapter as a guide to rethinking the scales you already know in order to create cool bass lines.

Who Says a Scale Has to Have Seven Notes?

For most bass players, there is rarely any need to play every note of a given scale. Usually a riff or a walking bass line will simply involve part of a scale, as you discovered in our last two chapters. If you think about it, chord arpeggios are simply notes taken from part of a scale—namely the notes specific to forming a particular chord.

Pentatonic scales operate in a similar fashion. As you might guess, the pentatonic scale has five notes (that's the "penta" part, as in pentagon or pentagram) in it. And not just any five notes, naturally! There is a specific pattern to follow.

The Major Pentatonic Scale

To play a major pentatonic scale, start with the root in major scale position—that is, using your index finger to fret it. Then play the second, third, fifth, and sixth degrees of the major scale and end with the octave. In the following example, you'll use C as your root note:

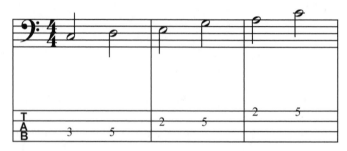

If the major pentatonic sounds familiar to you, it's probably because it's used so often in rock and pop music. The opening bass line to the classic Motown hit "My Girl" is simply a repeated ascending major pentatonic scale.

This is a very happy-sounding scale that sounds great under a major chord. It also goes well with major seventh, dominant seventh, and sixth chords.

Because the major pentatonic has no fourth, you have to be careful about using it in any progression that involves the IV chord. But it will certainly serve you well in a I–vi–ii–V progression or anytime you are playing a song that switches a lot between I and vi. If, for example, a song had a chord progression going back and forth from C to Am, then you could play riffs taken from the C major pentatonic scale under those changes all day long.

The Minor Pentatonic Scale

Just as every major scale has a relative minor, you can also make a minor pentatonic scale for each major pentatonic scale. Since A minor is the relative minor to C major, you'd be correct in assuming that the A minor pentatonic scale uses the same notes as those in the C major pentatonic scale. All you need to do is start on A instead of C, as in the following example:

Finger the minor pentatonic the same way you would the natural minor, using your index finger to fret the root. You'll find that this pattern fits your fingers very nicely up and down the neck of your bass guitar.

It's important to think of the minor pentatonic, or any scale for that matter, in terms of its component intervals. Looking at scales in this fashion can help you determine where and when to use a particular scale in a song or chord progression.

The minor pentatonic starts with the root note and continues on in this pattern:

> Root, minor third, fourth, fifth, flat seventh

This is essentially a minor seventh arpeggio with the fourth degree of the scale thrown in for good measure. Obviously, this scale will sound good being played under a minor or a minor seventh chord.

Because there is no sixth, you can also use the minor pentatonic to come up with bass lines for any progression involving a change from a minor root to its fourth, for example, going from Cm to F or Fm in the key of C minor.

In this case it doesn't matter if the fourth is a minor (as in the iv triad taken from the natural minor scale) or major (as the IV triad taken from harmonic or melodic minor scales), because the minor pentatonic scale only contains two of the three notes of the iv or IV chord. In this example, the C minor pentatonic scale has the notes C, Eb, F, G, and Bb. Therefore the only notes available in this scale for an F chord, major or minor, are F and C. This is a case where the harmony of the F chord is implied rather than stated directly.

You will also learn in Chapter 23 that the minor pentatonic can be used to great effect for blues songs in major keys.

What's in the Box?

One of the reasons that the minor pentatonic scale is so popular with bass players and other fretted instrument players is that its pattern naturally creates a box on your fingerboard. By "box," I mean a section where you can reach every note of the minor pentatonic scale within the span of two frets. Let's expand our last example and take a look:

Here we've taken the A minor pentatonic and extended it across all four strings. Now let's examine the notes on the G, D, and A strings:

def•i•ni•tion

Depending on which book you read, who you have as a teacher (if you have a teacher), or with whom you talk shop, you may find all sorts of differing "boundaries" for **the box.** Most people will think of it in the terms described here, but some players, especially those who have no trouble spanning three or four frets, consider the box to be three frets wide instead of two. Some teachers prefer to teach the box as being four frets wide, in order to accommodate all the notes of the major scale.

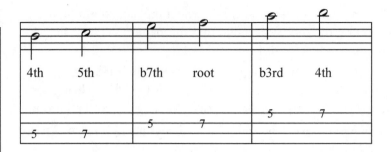

You can see that every note of the A minor pentatonic is either on the fifth or seventh fret of the top three strings. The root (A) sits at the seventh fret of the D string, with the fourth (D) above it at the seventh fret of the G string and the fifth (E) below it at the seventh fret of the A string. The fifth fret has the minor third (C) on the G string, the flatted seventh (G) on the D string, and another fourth (D) on the A string. That's quite convenient!

Bass lines and riffs taken from *the box* occur in almost every type of music. You will especially hear them in various blues and rock songs. The box is also a handy starting point for the fledgling bass soloist, as you'll see in Chapters 19 and 20.

Turning One Scale into Seven Scales—Modal Thinking

For every bass player who obsesses about scales, another will obsess about modes. A *mode*, simply speaking, is a major scale, but with a small twist. In Chapter 12, you created the natural minor scale by using the same notes of the major scale and starting with the sixth note as its new root. The natural minor scale is also called the *Aeolian mode*. Since the major scale has seven different notes, you can create a different modal scale by starting the major scale on a different note.

Just talking about modes will scare off many beginning bass students, which is unfortunate because they are very easy to understand when you take a moment to sort them out. The hardest part about learning modes is dealing with their names, which come from Ancient Greece. Once you get past that, modes are a lot of fun and can add a lot of spice to your playing.

Ionian Mode

For all of the following examples, we're going to use our old friend, the C major scale. When playing the C major scale, starting on C and moving on up to the next C, we are also playing what's called the *C Ionian mode*, or C Ionian scale.

For the record, unless you're taking part in a music theory class, it is unlikely that anyone will ever talk to you about the Ionian mode. Just keeping thinking "major scale" and you'll be fine. You'll also keep your mind free of too much clutter!

Dorian Mode

Take the C major scale and start on the second note, the D, instead of the C and play all the notes until you hit D once again.

This is the *D Dorian scale*. It's a D scale because you began and ended on D. Because you began on a different note of the major scale, you changed the pattern of the whole steps and half steps in your scale. Any Dorian scale will use the following pattern:

> Root, whole step, half step, whole step, whole step, whole step, half step, whole step

Songs in Dorian modes will sound much like songs in minor keys. The major difference is that they will always have major IV chords, like the triad taken from the harmonic and melodic minor scales.

Phrygian Mode

Now let's start the C major scale with E, the third note. This will be the *E Phrygian scale*, and it will sound more exotic than any of the modal scales you've heard so far:

In the Phrygian mode you go right from the root to an interval of a minor second, which is very unusual in music. The Phrygian modal pattern is as follows:

> Root, half step, whole step, whole step, whole step, half step, whole step, whole step

Playing a Phrygian scale under a minor or minor seventh chord of the same root (using the E Phrygian while the band is playing Em7, for example) will add a little spice to the mix.

Lydian Mode

Using the F of the C major scale as our starting and ending point will give us the *F Lydian scale*, which sounds the closest to the normal major scale:

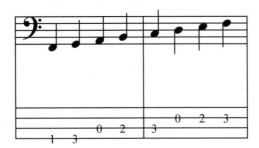

The Lydian mode sounds so much like a major scale because the third note is major and there is a half step between the seventh and the root. Here is the pattern of the Lydian mode:

> Root, whole step, whole step, whole step, half step, whole step, whole step, half step

This leading tone, as we discussed earlier in Chapter 12, gives our ears a "major scale" feel. The Lydian and Ionian (major scale) modes are the only two of the seven modal scales that use half steps between the seventh note and the root.

Mixolydian Mode

The *Mixolydian mode*, which you will hear a lot in rock music, is created when you start out on the fifth note of the major scale. So in our example, you want to begin and end your C major scale on the G note:

The pattern for any Mixolydian scale is:

> Root, whole step, whole step, half step, whole step, whole step, half step, whole step

While this sounds a lot like the major scale, the flatted seventh is a dead give-away that you're in a mode of some sort. If you are soloing or improvising under a dominant seventh chord, the Mixolydian scale will work very nicely.

Aeolian Mode

We covered the *Aeolian mode* in Chapter 12 when we learned how to make the natural minor scale. But in case you've forgotten, here is the A Aeolian scale, which is what you get when you start the C major scale on the A note:

Like the Ionian mode, you are more likely to find yourself discussing the "natural minor" scale than using the formal Greek name. But it doesn't hurt to be up on things!

Locrian Mode

Starting with B, the seventh note of the C major scale, will give you the *B Locrian scale*, which looks and sounds like this:

The Locrian mode sounds very jarring, owing to the many minor intervals of its makeup. Here is the pattern for any Locrian scale:

> Root, half step, whole step, whole step, half step, whole step, whole step, whole step

Here the only notes that are the same as those in the major scale are those at the root and fourth positions. It's small wonder that this scale sounds quite unusual.

> **Covering the Basses**
>
> Some people find it a lot easier to *not* think about modes and to instead think about targeting. If you are in a situation which calls for the D Dorian, as an example, you might simply think about playing the C major scale but be targeting notes of the D minor chord, namely D, F, and A. If you're a person who finds chord components easier to deal with than scales, this might prove to be a good approach for you.

In the examples used so far, we've stayed in the same key of C major and used our new root note to create the modal scale. Here are the seven modes once again, but this time each one starts with the same root note, A for this example. This juxtaposition will allow you to better hear and appreciate the different tones and textures each mode has to offer:

 15.12

A good way to get a feel for these various modes is to play arpeggios of their various seventh chords—that is, make an arpeggio of the root, third, fifth, and seventh degree of each mode. These arpeggios give you a good overall feel of the mode itself, and you will also hear how each mode has its own unique sound.

Chord Progressions as Guideposts

Modes are a great tool for a bass player, but the real trick comes in knowing when to use any given modal scale. If you're jamming over a single chord, then just about anything will work. But if you're playing a song with a specific chord progression, then you need to put the knowledge about chords you've gained to use.

Many rock songs, for instance, have progressions of I–IV–I. In the key of C, this would mean C, Bb, F, and C. Playing the C major scale wouldn't really work because you don't have the Bb note at your disposal. But playing a C Mixolydian scale would have all the notes you need.

As mentioned earlier, Dorian scales work exceptionally well with progressions of minor roots changing to major fourths. If you see the song you're playing goes from Em to A7 to Em again, then you can use the E Dorian scale to your heart's content.

Taking a little time to analyze the chord makeup of a song will help you to get a better grasp of which modal scale can be used. As you play more, you will see patterns and you will start to automatically know which mode will best serve you in a song.

But be sure not to fall into the trap of thinking that one scale will fit all your needs in a single song. While this may be true of a lot of music, it's certainly not the case with all songs. Suppose, for example, you were going to be playing bass on a song with the following chord progression:

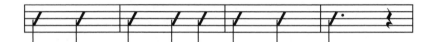

Fmaj7   E7   Am   Gm7 C9 Fmaj7   E7   Am

Here you would run into any number of problems if you chose to use a single scale. Your best bet would be to break up the chord progression into pieces that go well together. E and Am, for instance, are the V chord and root of the A harmonic minor scale and the notes of the Fmaj7 chord (F, A, C, and E) would also fit that scale. The Gm7 (G, Bb, D, and F) and C9 (C, E, G, and Bb) are parts of the F major scale, or C Myxolidian scale. So breaking up this progression into the following parts might work well:

Fmaj7   E7   Am   Gm7 C9 Fmaj7   E7   Am
43
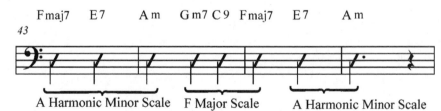

A Harmonic Minor Scale   F Major Scale   A Harmonic Minor Scale

Approaching each song you play with an awareness of its chord progressions, coupled with a knowledge of what notes make up those chords, will always give you the freedom to create interesting and compelling bass lines.

Basso Profondo

Q: Am I the only one who finds modes confusing?

A: Hardly! A lot of people find it easier to play modal scales by thinking of them as *major scales with different tonal centers*. Instead of worrying about how to play a D Dorian scale, for instance, you can think of it as a C major scale, except that your tonal center is D instead of C. You'd want to target notes of the Dm arpeggio (D, F, and A) instead of those of the C major (C, E, and G). Like much of the material we've covered, the more you use it in a practical way, the easier it is for it to become second nature.

The Least You Need to Know

- The pentatonic scale uses five notes instead of seven.

- "The box" provides an easy way to finger all the notes of a pentatonic scale.

- There are seven different modal scales that you can create by using each of the notes of the major scale as a starting point.

- A song's chord progression will help you decide which scale or mode (or perhaps more than one!) to use.

Progressive Jamming

In This Chapter

- ◆ A jam-along song in D major
- ◆ A jam-along song in A minor
- ◆ A jam-along song in C Dorian
- ◆ The "second take" approach
- ◆ Listening for an opening

It's time once again to put what you've learned in this part of the book to practical use. This chapter contains three new jam-along songs which you can play with the band. Each song will be presented as a rhythm lead sheet, and there will also be some bass line suggestions to help you get started. But the idea is still to have you create your own bass parts to play.

These new jam-along songs are structured a little more like songs. Each will have different sections, usually four to eight measures apiece. Some of the chord progressions will be relatively easy, and some will involve a little thinking.

Be Prepared!

A good strategy would be to approach these new jam-along songs in much the same way you did those in Chapter 10. First listen to the music—get a sense of the timing and the chord changes. Also try to get a feel for the mood of the song. Is it happy? Sad? Agitated? Mysterious? Part of being the bass player is keying in on a song's emotion as well as its tempo and harmony.

Start simply. The first time through you might play just root notes of the chords, getting acquainted with the chord progressions and rhythms of each section of each song. Then try some simple patterns involving chord arpeggios. When you feel up to it, take a stab at using some of the scales and modes you've learned from this section of the book.

And, just as you did in Chapter 10, take notes on your playing. When you come up with a few bass lines that you especially like, write them down. There's little as frustrating as trying to remember a bass part that you knew was absolutely perfect yesterday but is somehow out of your grasp today.

And be certain to take time to tinker. Think about your fingering—about whether playing in a different position on the fingerboard might help you get some notes quicker or cleaner. Does your bass line breathe? Do you need more notes, less notes, longer notes, more rests? The more you learn to refine, the more refined your playing will become—in live settings as well as in practice.

Song #1

Our first piece is in D major. The chord progression is typical of many pop, rock, and country songs, but it does offer an interesting twist in the song's last section:

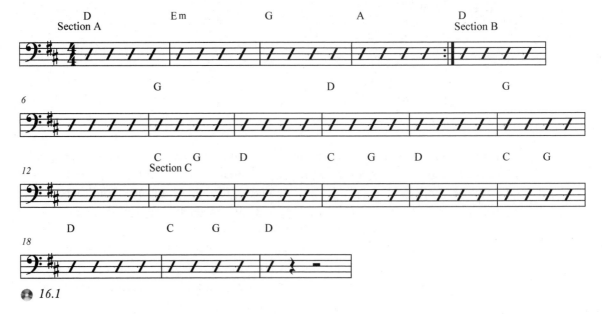

16.1

Section A is four measures long and has four changes, each chord lasting four beats (one measure). The progression, I–iii–IV–V (D, Em, G, and A, in this example), stays nicely in the key of D major. The D major scale and D major pentatonic scale will certainly work if you decide to try to come up with some moving bass lines. You play this section twice, as indicated by the repeat sign at the end of measure four.

In the I–IV (D to G) progression that makes up Section B, the chord changes occur every two measures. This gives you more time to play around with your bass lines. But don't get so carried away that you are taken by surprise by what happens next.

The last section of this song, Section C, involves the bVII–IV–I progression, C to G to D in the key of D. You studied a variation of this in Chapter 14. Here, the change from C to G is quicker; each of these chords lasts for only two beats, while the D gets four.

If you might be already thinking in terms of scales for this section of the song, the appearance of the C chord in this progression would suggest using either the D Mixolydian (which is exactly like the D scale except it has a C instead of C#) or the D minor pentatonic.

On the CD, the band plays through the song once. The drummer will count off four beats and the rest of the band will start right in.

Suggestion #1

The first three measures of Song #1 can be a great demonstration of the ease of playing "the box." Playing in D major, using the D at the fifth fret of the A string as an anchor, you can find almost all the notes you need on either the fifth or seventh fret of the E, A, and D strings:

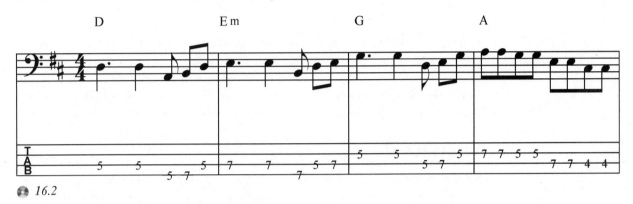

16.2

Using the same rhythm throughout the first three measures helps make this suggestion relatively easy to play. All you do is hit the root note with the timing of the general rhythm pattern. Starting out as simply as possible gives you the chance to get settled into the rhythm and the basic harmonic feel of the song.

You can use the fourth measure, where the A chord is played, to cut loose a little bit. The above suggestion uses a descending A7 arpeggio, all in eighth notes. Another possibility would be to play a descending scale run from A to D, like this:

Getting in a little flurry of notes every now and then gives some variation to your bass line. It is certainly possible to maintain the same rhythm of the first three measures.

A

This sounds perfectly fine. You could easily use an alternating bass pattern as well, or simply play only the A note. Playing a single note gives you all sorts of options, too. You could play the A as a whole note to fill the measure, or play a single eighth note to start the measure and let the rest of the band fill in the rest. The choice is totally up to you. It's all part of the fun of arranging the bass part.

Suggestion #2

Section B, because of the two measures between each chord change, lends itself nicely to all sorts of bass lines. You could be very busy, filling in every available space with eighth notes and sixteenth notes. You could also be very sparse, playing a whole note of D on the first measure, a whole note of F# on the second, a whole note of G on the third, and so on.

Here's another idea:

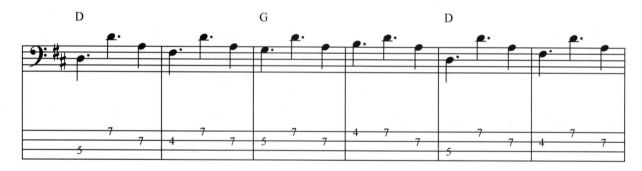

16.5

This suggestion begins with a quarter note of D, just as in Section A, but then uses an alternating bass pattern to slow up the tempo and emphasize the D major tonality, particularly by using the F# to start the second measure. Even when the chord changes to G in measure three, it's played against the D and A of the D major chord, which makes a nice unifying motif.

The second time through the chords of this section, be thinking about the C natural chord that's coming up at the start of Section C. This suggestion uses B as a natural lead-in to the C note.

Suggestion #3

The C to G to D pattern of Section C is played a total of four times. So here are four different ideas about approaching it:

🔊 *16.6*

Every measure that involves the C to G change is done the same way. The bass mirrors the rhythm guitar and drums by using two quarter notes of C, followed by two eighth notes of G and then a rest of one beat. Playing the exact same timing as the rest of the rhythm section makes the band sound very tight.

On the first pass at the measure of D, this arrangement uses an ascending alternating bass pattern of D, A, and D. It's very simple, but still involves some nice rhythmic movement. And it also emphasizes the D tonal center of Section C after the song has detoured slightly with the C chord.

By contrast, though, the second time through the measure of D is total motion. Starting on the D note, the bass line moves down one note to C and then plays what is essentially a D Mixolydian scale from that C to the C of the next measure. This is a good example once again of how the bass is creating and stressing the tonal center of this part of the song.

The box is brought back for the third pass of the D measure, shown in the following illustration. This particular riff can be heard in all sorts of different musical styles. And even though there's a C natural in the descending bass line, the D tonality is still front and center because of the two Ds which start the measure, not to mention the one at the end.

The band ends the song on the final playing of the C to G to D progression, so hitting and holding the D note will be fine.

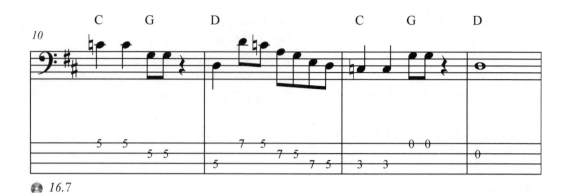

16.7

Song #2

Song #2 is a little bit of a workout in the key of Am. It also consists of three different sections, with the first section being repeated at the beginning of the song. Here's your chart:

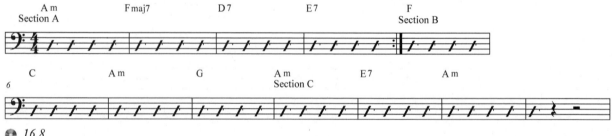

16.8

The chord progression of Section A involves a switch between at least two of the three minor scales. Am to Fmaj7 works fine with either the A natural minor or the A harmonic minor scale, but the D7 is definitely a part of the A melodic minor. The E7 in measure four can be part of either the A harmonic or A melodic minor.

Section B provides you with a good example of modulation. Here the song sounds more as if it's in a major key, specifically C major (the relative major of A minor). In the key of C major, this would be a IV–I–vi–V progression, which is a slight variation of the I–vi–IV–V progression you studied in Chapter 14.

The final section is very straightforward, using a i–V–I to reestablish Am as the tonal center of the song.

The band plays this song through twice. On the first pass, the Am chord of the final measure is hit on the first beat, the drummer plays a turnaround, and then the song begins again at Section A, which, just as the first time, gets repeated.

Suggestion #1

After listening to the song, you might want to take some time and think about what you want to do. Playing root notes, alternating bass lines, and chord arpeggios will all work very well, and there are also numerous other ways to approach playing this piece.

One possibility would be to use the A note as a drone throughout the first three measures since it is a common note in all three chords (Am, Fmaj7, and D7). Pursuing that line of thought a bit further, you might also decide to play something like this:

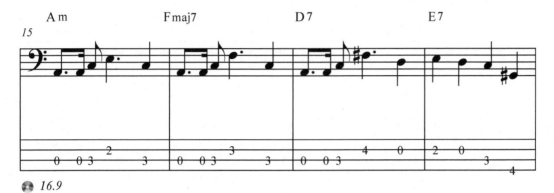

 16.9

This suggestion is simply using chord arpeggios for the first three measures, but it takes advantage of the fact that both the A and C notes are part of each of the three chords. In the third measure, the arpeggio ends on D in order to lead it to the E, which is the root note of the E7.

In the fourth measure, notes of the A harmonic minor scale are employed in order to use the G# as a lead to A for the second go-around of Section A. But the second time through, the progression goes from E7 to F (the first chord of Section B). That's a perfect example of a deceptive cadence, which I'm certain you remember discussing in the last chapter. It's a simple enough thing to lead from the E to the F like this:

This is one good reason why it's important, whenever possible, to try to scan through a song before playing it. Going from G# to F, as you might have had to do here, is not the easiest move for either the fingers or the ears!

Suggestion #2

By this time in your bass studies, you should have few problems coming up with ideas for Section B of this song. So why don't we skip ahead to Section C?

I'd like to use this section of Song #2 to demonstrate a use of the melodic minor scale in both ascending and descending forms.

🎵 *16.11*

🔑 Covering the Basses

The more you are able to use the things you learn about music in a practical way, such as in playing a song, the easier it becomes to grasp concepts that seemed obtuse at first glance.

Whenever you learn something new, whether it's a bit of music theory or a tricky finger technique, do your best to include it in every practice until you know it hands-down. It may seem like overkill at first, but it's a good way to make certain you have the knowledge in your hands when you need it next.

In this suggestion, Section C begins by repeating the initial rhythm and mimicking the Am chord arpeggio of the first measure of Section A. Measure two starts with an ascending E alternating bass pattern, but then switches over to a scale run using the final notes of the A melodic minor scale. The descending A melodic minor scale (and you remember that it contains the same notes as the A natural minor scale) follows in the penultimate measure, leading back to the final A note at the start of measure four.

Listen to how the Am tonality is carried both in the ascending and descending melodic scales, despite their different notes.

Song #3

Our third song's a puzzle and an exercise as well as a moving little number. It's only got four chords (remember when dealing with two chords was hard?), but the challenge will be dealing with it harmonically.

A quick look at the song reveals that it is in essentially two parts—a progression of Cm to F7 that repeats at the beginning and then a progression of Cm to Eb to F to Bb that repeats in the middle before returning to the Cm to F7 to Cm at the very end.

You can see from the key signature that the song should be in Bb major or its relative minor, which is G minor. But that's obviously not the case because, as you can hear, the music definitely centers around the tonality of the C minor chord.

Think about C's relation to Bb in the key of Bb—it's the second note and, in the key of Bb major, it has a minor triad.

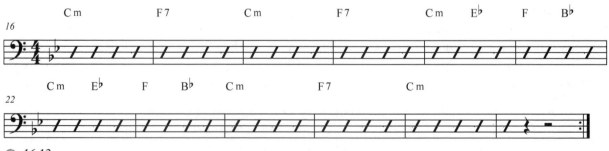

🎵 *16.12*

This would be an excellent place to use the C Dorian scale, since it uses the same notes as the Bb major scale but starts on C instead of Bb. And, indeed, you will see that the suggestion for this jam-along song is a walking bass line taken straight from the C Dorian scale.

On the CD, the entire song is played twice, much in the same way as the previous song, with the drums providing a short break between the first and second go-around.

Suggestion #1

In order to remind you that keeping good timing is vital to your role as a bass player, this suggestion uses straight quarter notes all the way up to the next-to-last measure. You get to be the band's metronome once again!

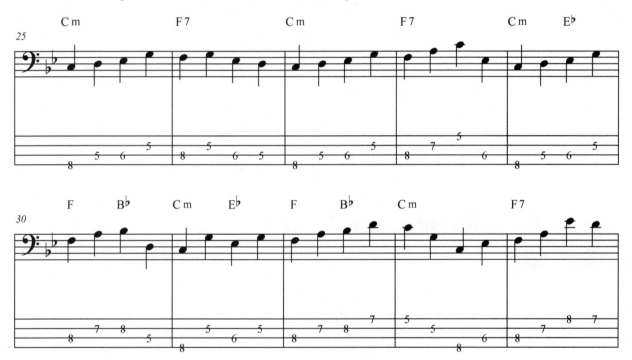

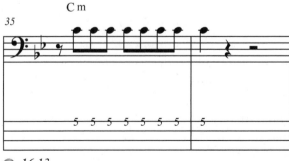

🔘 *16.13*

The last two measures of Cm find the band playing eighth notes in unison. The suggestion above stays with the C note but you could certainly use a scale or chord arpeggio or alternating bass pattern in its place.

Suggestion #2

The second suggestion is more of a practice tip. Before playing this song, try running your fingers through the following extended C Dorian scale (both up and down) a few times:

All the notes you need to play Suggestion #1 for this song are right here between the fifth and eighth frets of your bass. You can do a lot of movement without going very far!

This last song might seem, on paper, to be the easiest of the three, but it will take some time and practice to get it up to speed. Go very slowly at first—painfully slowly if need be. And don't forget to practice the C Dorian scale before you play the song. You'll be surprised at how quickly you'll be able to catch up to the rest of the band.

Taking a Second Take

You should know part of the drill by now—after you're done playing around with your new songs, take the time to assess what you accomplished and to plan how to get better. Are you getting a grasp of the bass player's mentality?

Just as important—are you finding yourself coming up with ideas after the fact? One of the frustrating things about playing a live performance is thinking afterward of all the things you could have done. But unless you're playing a gig tomorrow with a band you've never played with before playing songs you've never heard, this shouldn't be the case with you.

A good bassist develops his bass lines. Hearing a song through once can give you ideas. Playing a song will determine which ideas work and which don't. And, quite often, playing it again will lead to more ideas for your bass lines. Each repeated listen or performance will sharpen your ears and usually lead you to coming up with better and better lines.

Whenever you're playing with others in a friendly jamming situation, don't be afraid to ask to play a song again. And again. But then sit down and take stock. Be objective and honest. And also be certain to bring up one good point for every one that needs attention. If you keep a practice journal or a log of your playing, this would be a great time to write down some notes and observations.

Listening for an Opening

Listening to a song beforehand can also provide you with some vital information—are there natural "breathing" spaces that can be used for a short bass fill or two? While playing the bass often requires you to be steady and repetitive, it's rare for any song not to provide ample opportunities for a little flash.

The key word here is "little." Often, you may find that you need to hold the beat and tonality for three beats in any given measure of four-four timing. But that gives you the fourth beat to use as you will. Sometimes, as in the songs in this chapter, you might find yourself with even two beats or a whole measure to call your own!

But the important thing to remember is that the song always has to come first. The best bass players bring spark to a song without bringing attention to themselves. Making a flashy little bass riff seem like a natural part of a song is an art, just like playing the bass itself. And it is something that takes practice, just like anything else about your instrument.

This is still another example of something you can practice without even having your bass at hand. Whenever you listen to a song, no matter where you might happen to be, it's easy to make a mental note of where you, as the bass player, could find a space or two for an unobtrusive scale run or a colorful chord arpeggio.

And don't just listen to other bass players for clues. Every song, no matter what style of music, has natural breathing spaces. The more music you listen to, the more your ears will get attuned to these little gaps just waiting for you to fill them. We'll be exploring this more in Chapters 19 and 20, but right now is a fine time to start listening and thinking about it.

The Least You Need to Know

- Taking a moment or two to analyze a song's structure can help you decide how to play it.
- Try to use the new ideas you learn about music in a practical way, such as in a song, whenever you can.
- Warming up your fingers with a scale or two in an unfamiliar key or mode often makes the song a little easier to play.
- Songs often have natural pausing places—perfect spots for a short bass riff.
- As you learn more, go back to an old song and see what you can add to it.

Basso Profondo

Q: Are there any rules or tricks for knowing when to come in for a fill or when not to?

A: It's not so much a trick or rule as it is getting a good feeling for a song. If you're playing something for the first time, play as simply as possible. Listen for natural pauses in the phrasing of the lyrics or in another player's part. Listen to the rhythm of the drummer. You will hear places where the bass can fill in.

Taking the time to listen is important. If you just charge through a song without listening, you may miss an opportunity to create a harmony line with another player or help the drummer punch through a catchy rhythm. Remember you're part of a group and take part in creating the arrangement as a group.

Part 5

Moving On Up

Being well-versed in the basics, you're now ready to start creating your own bass solos and improvisations. First you'll look at some slurring techniques, such as hammer-ons, pull-offs, and slides, which will add some spice to your playing. You'll also discover how to play further up the neck of your bass guitar, giving you the freedom of movement to create spectacular bass lines.

Finally, you'll combine these new techniques with your old skills and knowledge and start working on improvising and soloing.

17

Spicing Up Your Playing

In This Chapter

- ◆ Defining slurs and grace notes
- ◆ The three basic tricks—hammer-ons, pull-offs, and slides
- ◆ Discovering palm muting and dead notes
- ◆ Playing double-stops
- ◆ Using anticipations in rhythmic patterns

Every musical instrument has personality quirks, things particular to that instrument or to the family of instruments to which it belongs. You can take your hand and smash it down on the low keys of the piano, for example, creating a musical thunderclap, or use a drumstick on the rim of a snare drum to give it a crisp, clicking beat.

The bass guitar is no exception—being from the same musical family, you can use many of the same left- and right-hand techniques guitarists use on their instruments. Given the nature of the bass guitar, these techniques not only bring variety to your playing, they can also bring speed and grace to tricky passages of music.

More importantly, most of these playing techniques are very easy to learn and master. With a little dedicated practice, you can quickly improve your basic playing, adding spice and style to your bass lines.

Slurring Your Words

Way, way back in Chapter 3, you first started playing notes on your bass guitar and you've been using the same basic method since then—the left hand frets a note on the fingerboard (or not, if you wanted to play the note of an open string) while the right hand strikes the string to produce the note. This method of playing, once you've practiced it a little, produces a clean, clear articulation of each note.

def•i•ni•tion

A **slur**, in its simplest form, is going from one note to another without articulating the second note by plucking the string again with your right hand. Your left hand (the one on the neck of the bass guitar), by means of one or more techniques, creates the second note.

Sometimes, though, you might want something slightly less clear and less articulated. And sometimes a piece of music may call for notes played slightly faster than you're capable of doing with your right hand. Using slurred notes becomes an option.

A *slur* is a combination of two or more different notes. Usually, they are played in such a way that the right hand is involved in striking only the first note. The other note or notes of the slur are sounded by the use of various left-hand techniques, such as hammer-ons, pull-offs, and slides.

In musical notation, slurs are indicated by an arced line, which connects two or more notes. At first glance, slurs look like tied notes (from Chapter 5), but the arcing line connects different notes instead of the same one. The following illustration shows you the difference between slurs and tied notes:

Music specifically written for the bass guitar will also usually include special notations to indicate what type of slur to use. There are several slurring options open to the bass guitarist, depending on the notes involved in the slur, where the notes are located both on the fingerboard and in relation to one another as well as the type of musical effect the bassist wants to achieve.

Saving Grace

Slurs are also used to create "grace notes," which are very short notes that ornament or "grace" the note that follows it. In music notation, a grace note is a tiny note immediately before a regular sized one, like this:

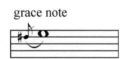

Some teachers like to call grace notes "oops notes" because they are very much like quick mistakes. In the above example, you begin with your finger fretting the F# at the fourth fret of the D string. As soon as you strike the string with your right hand, you want to get to the G note at the fifth fret. It's like you suddenly realized that you were on the wrong note and had to get to the right one as quickly as possible.

And getting off the grace note quickly is, more often than not, a job for the left hand. Let's take a look at the three basic types of slurring used by the bass guitarist: the hammer-on, the pull-off, and the slide.

If I Had a Hammer-On ...

One thing you can say about each of the three slurring techniques is that they are well named! Each name, in fact, tells you exactly how to perform the technique.

Let's start with the hammer-on, and a very simple exercise:

🔘 *17.3*

Begin by striking the open G string with your right hand. Now "hammer" the tip of your index finger of your left hand onto the second fret of the G string. Don't strike the string again with your right hand, let the left hand make the note ring out as it hammers the string. You should get a clear, clean, ringing tone.

Don't worry if it takes a little time to get the hang of this technique. Depending on how much you practice, developing the finger strength and the touch will vary from person to person. But it won't be long before you're merrily hammering away.

Be sure to work on hammer-ons with each finger, from your index finger down to the pinky. Here's another easy exercise to get you going:

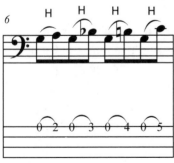

🔘 *17.4*

def•i•ni•tion

Slurs, when notated in bass guitar tablature, will usually be identified by type. An "H" between two notes, for instance, indicates the use of a hammer-on. A "P" (sometimes "PO") means to perform a pull-off, and an "S," or "SL," denotes a slide. In musical notation, slurs may also be noted in the same fashion, but not always.

Double and Multiple Hammers

The technique of hammering-on can provide some added speed to your playing, particularly when you get adept at playing more than one hammer at a time. When you feel that you're making progress with single hammer-ons, then you can start in on practicing hammer-ons involving more than one finger.

Performing a double or multiple hammer-on begins with the same steps as a single hammer:

● 17.5

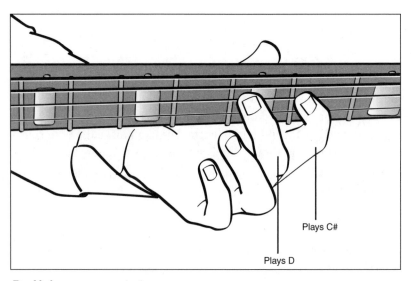

Double hammer-on postioning.

Start with striking the open A string with your right hand. Then use your index finger, hammering it onto the fourth fret of the A string, to sound the C# note. Then hammer your middle finger onto the fifth fret to sound the D note. Again, be persistent and patient with your practicing.

When you're comfortable performing doubles, move on to three- and four-fingered hammer-ons. Here is an extended version of our previous exercise:

● 17.7

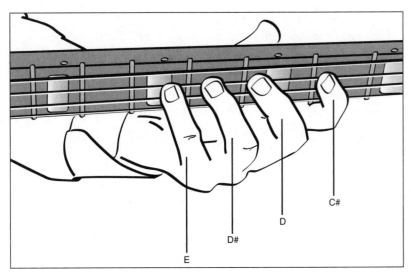

Multiple hammer-on positioning.

Begin with the same steps you used in the previous exercise and then use your ring finger to hammer the sixth fret of the A, which is the D note, and your pinky to sound the E at the seventh fret of the A string.

You will notice that the sound you get from each note will diminish with each finger. That is normal and will change as you develop more strength in each digit. Your amplifier will help you out a lot when playing hammer-ons and other slurs because it picks up just about every little thing you do on your bass guitar. But it's important to have the technique in your hands so that you have control of your dynamics. How articulate each note is and how much volume and sustain it has should be up to you and not merely a by-product of your equipment.

Pulling-Off a Fast One

The pull-off is sort of a reverse hammer-on. Some teachers call the pull-off a "hammer-off." Let's start once again with the simplest possible example:

17.9

Place the index finger of your left hand on the second fret of the G string and then strike the string with your right hand. This will sound the A note. Now pull your index finger off the fret, which will in turn sound the open G string.

The trick here is to "pull" your finger off, not merely lift it off. Raising the finger straight off the string will not give you much of a sound for the second note. But if you pull the finger down slightly, you tug on the string and that tugging is what makes the second note (the open G in this example) ring out.

Just as with the hammer-on, you want to develop each of the fingers of your left hand to the point where each one can perform a decent-sounding pull-off. Use the following example to get yourself started:

🔘 *17.10*

Multiple Pull-Offs

Double and multiple pull-offs are a little trickier, but get easier with practice. The key lies in proper finger placement. Take a look at the following example:

🔘 *17.11*

You want to start this off by having *both* your index and ring fingers on the A string before you play your first note. Place the index finger on the fourth fret and the ring finger on the fifth fret. Now strike the A string with your right hand, sounding the D note, and then pull off your ring finger, leaving your index finger in place. The pulling ring finger sounds the C# note because your index finger is still on the fourth fret. Pulling off your index finger will sound the open A string.

The Trill of It All

After learning how to play hammer-ons and pull-offs, the next step is to combine the two techniques. Test your newfound slurring skills on the following exercise.

🔘 *17.12*

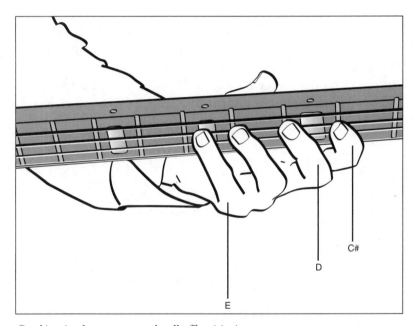

Combination hammer-on and pull-off positioning.

Start by striking the open A string with your right hand. Then hammer-on the index finger of your left hand on the fourth fret, followed by the middle finger on the fifth fret and the pinky on the seventh fret. Keep each finger firmly on its fret after hammering it on. After sounding the E note with your pinky, immediately pull it off to get the D note again, courtesy of the middle finger still holding on at the fifth fret. Pull the middle finger and the C# note will sound because you still have your index finger at the fourth fret. Pulling the index finger will give you the open A string's note. Congratulations! You've played seven notes with one strike of your right hand!

As I mentioned, developing sufficient finger strength to play hammer-ons and pull-offs with confidence and ease takes practice, patience, and persistence. A little concentrated effort on your behalf should result in great-sounding slurs.

When you use a repeated hammer-on and pull-off between two notes, it's called a *trill*. The following illustration shows you a trill in both music notation and bass guitar tablature.

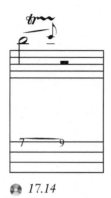

🔘 *17.14*

Here you first strike the D note (having the index finger of your left hand on the seventh fret of the G string) with your right hand and then immediately use the ring finger of your left hand to hammer-on and pull-off on the ninth fret of the G string. Depending on your finger strength, you could keep this up all day! But the object is usually to allow the trill to last for the specified duration of the note in question.

Slip-Sliding Away

Another commonly used slurring technique on the bass guitar is called the *slide*. It involves playing a note and then sliding your finger along the string from the initial note to the new one. The following illustration will give you an idea of how the bassist accomplishes this:

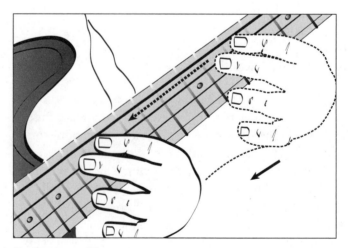

Performing a slide.

Sliding is very much a matter of feel. After you strike the first note, you want to ease up the pressure on the finger of your left hand very slightly. There should be enough pressure to be able to hear a continuous sound of moving from one note to the next, but not so much pressure that you cannot effective glide your finger along the frets. Look and listen to the following examples.

 *17.16*

The first example in this illustration starts with playing the D note at the fifth fret of the A string. Use any finger of your left hand you'd like to fret the note. After striking the string with your right hand, slide the finger up along the neck until you reach the A note at the 12th fret. Once you've gotten there, increase the pressure on your finger once again to give the A note a little more sustain.

You can, of course, slide down the neck as well as up, as shown in the second example. And the third example demonstrates sliding in both directions between two notes.

Slides can be used to all sorts of effect by the bass guitarist. They can be long and flowing; elegant and haunting; or short, crisp, and harsh. And, as you'll discover in Chapter 18, slides can help you connect together scales and chord arpeggios both up and down the fingerboard, enabling you to use the entire neck of your bass guitar freely and easily.

Slides to Nowhere

Occasionally you may come across some bass guitar tablature or music notation that looks like this:

 *17.17*

If you're not given a specific starting point for a slide, then where you start is up to you. More often than not, starting one or two frets away from your target is a good idea. In the above example, beginning the slide on the Bb or B note (the third and fourth frets, respectively, on the G string), would be perfectly acceptable. And it would sound good.

> ### Rock Bottom
>
> In both music notation and bass guitar tablature, slides are often indicated by slash marks. A "/" preceding a note means that you should slide up to the note in question and "\" would mean to slide down to it. You can obviously make a good guess of the direction of a slide by observing where the second note of a slide is in relationship to the first.

Sometimes, you're asked to slide down from a note to an unspecified location, which looks like this in both music notation and bass guitar tablature:

🔘 *17.18*

Depending on when your next note starts, you could conceivably slide all the way down to the first fret of the D string! Usually the best idea is to slide while relaxing your finger more and more, letting the sound of the slide fade away as it descends. This is another technique that can make a simple riff sound a lot more interesting.

But it's important to be alert. Suppose the above example was more like this:

🔘 *17.19*

Here you can slide down from the D at the 12th fret of the D string for one beat and you can get pretty far on one beat! But you also want to be ready for the D note (on the fifth fret of the A string) following it. So choose your fingering and timing with a little care. If you use your middle finger to slide and then time your slide to the rhythm of the song, you will be at the fifth fret at the right moment and can simply use your ring finger to "catch your fall." Don't get so caught up in a slide that you lose track of the timing or where you are in a song!

Watching the Note Values

Indeed, paying attention to note values is a lot of what slurring is all about. If you're reading from music notation, look to see whether you're dealing with a grace note or notes of actual time values. It can mean all the difference in how to play a particular bit of music.

In the following illustration, you can hear quite a change between the grace note examples and those that use either straight eighth notes or quarter notes. Getting the timing right is an important part of being the bass player, so make time to learn the distinctions between grace notes and regular ones.

🔊 *17.20*

Hitting the Mute Button

You don't always have to be playing notes as a bass player. Rests, as we've seen in Chapter 5 and in various jam-along songs, can make bass lines more interesting. So, too, can various muting techniques. You can mute a string with either your left hand or right hand. Let's examine the two techniques.

Dead Note Walking

Dead notes, also known as ghost notes, are not truly notes, because they have no particular pitch. They are created by letting a finger of the left hand press a string lightly enough to stop it from sounding but not hard enough for it to sound a proper note. Dead notes, in both bass guitar tablature and music notation, are indicated as notes with an "X" in place of the regular ellipse of the note head. Here is an example of a riff using dead notes:

🔊 *17.21*

In the Palm of Your Right Hand

In punk rock and various genres of metal, *palm muting* is quite often used to create a hushed effect on the bass guitar's sound. Bass players rarely use palm muting, mostly because it's impossible to do if you play with only your fingers. But if you're a bassist who uses a pick or strikes the strings with your thumb quite often, palm muting can provide you with a bit of variety in your sound.

To play a passage of palm muting, lay the heel of your palm, shown in the following illustration, lightly upon the strings of your bass guitar.

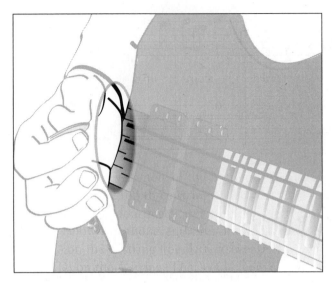

Palm muting.

Now strike the desired string with either your thumb or a pick. Unlike dead notes, you will hear a slight, muffled tone of the note you want. How much tone and how much muting you get is a matter of how much pressure you put on the strings. You can get quite a range of tonal effects by varying the amount of pressure you apply.

Here is an example of a riff that incorporates palm muting:

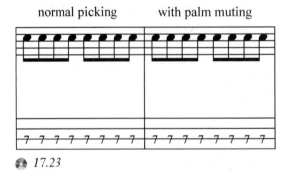

17.23

Both techniques emphasize the bass guitar's role as a rhythm instrument. Dead notes are distinctly percussive, while palm muting allows your instrument to play a bit of tonality.

Double Stops

If you prefer to focus on the bass guitar's harmonic and melodic capabilities, using double stops might be right up your alley. A *double stop* refers to playing two notes at a time instead of the usual single note a bassist tends to play. You can choose to play any two notes you want to, but it's best to find notes that sound good together, not to mention also sound good with the accompanying chordal background. Then there's the little matter of finding notes close enough on the neck to make playing them at the same time possible.

Perhaps one of the most memorable bass lines using the double-stop method is Lou Reed's "Walk on the Wild Side." It's instantly recognizable. There's an arresting quality about double stops in the bass. They can add beauty of harmony to a reflective piece of music or bring a bit of thunder to a blues or rock trio.

Octaves and Fifths

You're already well versed in the intervals of octaves and fifths from your work with alternate bass lines. Fifths you also recognize from our discussion of power chords back in Chapter 8.

In a trio setting, you can use both of these kinds of double stops to give support to a lead guitarist. Fifths can be especially strong reminders of tonal centers. And both fifths and octaves are excellent choices for drones. Here are a few examples of both these types of double stops:

🎵 *17.24*

Tenths

Thirds, as you also learned in Chapter 8, are the best interval for defining harmony. But played on a bass, thirds can sound very muddy. Even pianists, with all the notes they have at their disposal, shy away from using thirds in the bass. The closeness of the root and third generate many overtones which, instead of defining harmony, befuddle the ears.

So even though the third is a very easily fingered interval on the bass, it's unwise to use. Instead, bump the third up an octave, creating the interval of a tenth. Tenths are easy to play and sound wonderfully crisp and clear. An added bonus is that they slide very well as in this example:

🎵 *17.25*

Covering the Basses

Playing double stops usually means using your thumb to strike the strings. For double stops with notes on adjacent strings, you could use both your middle and index fingers to strike the strings at the same time, or "rake" your index finger to quickly strum both strings. But playing double stops where the notes are not on adjacent strings requires a little thought. Most people will use a "pinch" technique, striking the lower note (the one usually on the E or A string) downward with the thumb while playing the higher note (usually on the D or G string) with the index finger. Experiment a bit and see which technique gives you the most comfortable feel and the cleanest sound.

Covering the Basses

As mentioned, you can pick any two notes to serve as a double stop, but it's best to go with something that makes sense harmonically. Fourths, major sixths, and flatted sevenths can be used on certain occasions. Seconds, like thirds, tend to muddy up the sound a lot and should be avoided.

As you can see, you will always find the major tenth of any root note on the E string on the next higher fret on the G string. The minor tenth occupies the same fret as the root note.

Anticipation Participation

Anticipating means to come in slightly ahead of a beat. For instance, say you're playing a song in 4/4 timing in which the chords change every measure—that is, every four beats. While the drummer is creating a steady tempo, you (and other members of the band) might change the chord a half beat ahead of the upcoming measure like this:

17.26

This pull against the rhythm creates an interesting dissonance—it's as if the band were pushing the song faster than the beat. Anticipations give a lot of songs, especially in rock music, a feeling of immediacy.

Sometimes the bassist has to hold things steady while the rhythm guitar plays anticipations, paying close attention to the beat and not following the guitar.

The Least You Need to Know

- Slurs are notes that are usually articulated by the left hand, as opposed to the right hand striking a string.
- Hammer-ons, pull-offs, and slides are the three most common types of slurs used by the bass guitarist.
- Double stops (playing two notes at a time instead of one) can add a lot to many bass lines.
- Octaves, fifths, and tenths are commonly used double stops.
- Anticipations are great ways of creating rhythmic tension—they also require special attention to keeping the beat.

Chapter 18

Further On Up the Neck

In This Chapter

- ◆ Discovering position playing
- ◆ Using slides to expand scales and arpeggios up the neck
- ◆ Combining patterns and note knowledge
- ◆ All about transposing
- ◆ Exercising all over the fingerboard
- ◆ Using open strings as switching points

When you first picked up your bass guitar, you probably noticed that it had a very long neck. Yet, for most of the initial stages of learning, the fingers of your left hand have mostly been hanging around the first five frets. It's time to change that!

In this chapter you'll learn about the notes further up the neck and how knowing the various scale and chord arpeggio patterns you've been using can make playing in these uncharted territories a breeze.

Which Note Do You Want?

The bass guitar, like all members of the guitar family, has an interesting trait. Unlike almost all other instruments, it's possible to play the same note in many different ways. If you wanted to play the A note indicated on the top line of the bass clef on a piano, for instance, there's only one key that will allow you to do that. But on the bass guitar, you have many options. You could play it at the second fret of the G string, the seventh fret of the D string, the twelfth fret of the A string, or even at the seventeenth fret of the E string. They are all the same note.

As you learned way back in Chapter 4, while musical notation will tell you what note to play, it won't tell you where to play it on your bass guitar. Quite often that decision is left up to you. So how do you decide where to play a particular note?

Developing Economy

Ideally, you want to minimize the area on the fingerboard that your fingers need to cover when playing a bass line. The fewer awkward "jumps" you need to make, the less chance of you hitting a clunker note or two. Playing complicated bass lines with minimal flying around the neck of the bass is called an economy of movement.

Developing an economy of movement on your bass lines can help you in all sorts of ways. It can lead you to develop short yet elegant bass lines. It will also allow you to interact with your bandmates as well as the audience. You can't look around much at your surroundings when you're so concerned about playing a wrong note that your eyes never leave your fingers.

Playing a Position

Think back to our discussions on the basic major scale. You can play the A major scale, for instance, in any one of the following ways:

Here you have the A major scale played first in open position, then played again, starting with the root note on the fifth fret of the E string and then finally played once more beginning with the root note at the twelfth fret of the A string. In essence, you are playing the major scale in different positions on the neck.

Most teachers and tutorial books use the term *position* in a specific way—it refers to the fret on which your index finger should be placed for a particular pattern. Playing in position also assumes you're using the "one finger, one fret" method of finger placement and that you aren't using any open strings. The second A major scale in the preceding figure, for instance, would be considered playing in

Position IV. The third A major scale in that illustration is played in Position XI, since you use your index finger for the notes played on the 11th fret.

Some people like to think of the bass as having three specific target areas, which correspond with low, middle, and high ranges of notes. You might like to look at the neck of your bass guitar in this manner:

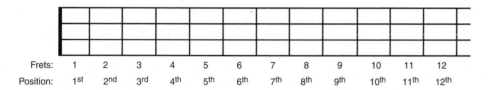

Frets:	1	2	3	4	5	6	7	8	9	10	11	12
Position:	1st	2nd	3rd	4th	5th	6th	7th	8th	9th	10th	11th	12th

"Position playing" can help you decide when on the fingerboard to play certain notes, riffs, or bass lines.

Connecting the Positions Step by Step

You can get from one position on the fingerboard to another in many ways, but sliding is probably the easiest. You've undoubtedly been practicing your slide technique a lot since learning about it in our last chapter. It's time to put it to use. Shall we start out with our old friend, the major scale?

Let's make this as painless as possible by outlining the steps involved in playing each note:

1. A—Begin with your index finger, instead of your middle finger, on the A note at the fifth fret of the E string.

2. B—After playing the A, slide your index finger up two frets to the seventh fret of the E string to play the B note.

3. C#—Use your ring finger to fret the C# at the ninth fret of the E string.

4. D—Your pinky frets the tenth fret of the E string to play the D note.

5. E—Move your index finger up a string to the seventh fret of the A string. This is your E note.

6. F#—After playing the E, slide your index finger up two frets to the ninth fret of the A string to play the F#.

7. G#—Use your ring finger to fret the G# note at the eleventh fret of the A string.

8. A—Your pinky frets the twelfth fret of the A string to play the A note.

You have just completed a major scale, going from the root A to the next A. Time to move on …

9. B—Move your index finger up a string to the ninth fret of the D string. This is your B note.

10. C#—After playing the B, slide your index finger up two frets to the eleventh fret of the D string to play the C#.

11. D—Use your middle finger to fret the D note at the twelfth fret of the D string.

12. E—Your pinky frets the fourteenth fret of the D string to play the E note.

13. F#—Move your index finger up a string to the 11th fret of the G string. This is your G# note.

14. G#—Use your ring finger to fret the G# at the 13th fret of the G string.

15. A—Your pinky frets the 14th fret of the G string to play the A note.

There are, of course, lots of ways to accomplish this two-octave scale technique. Here are two more suggestions—the first one also involves slides using only the

index finger:

In this first variation, you don't slide at all on the D string. Follow the earlier instructions up through step 9, and then continue like this:

10. C#—Use your ring finger to fret the C# at the 11th fret of the D string.

11. D—Your pinky frets the 12th fret of the D string to play the D note.

12. E—Move your index finger up a string to the ninth fret of the G string. This is your E note.

13. F#—After playing the E, slide your index finger up two frets to the

11th fret of the D string to play the F#.

14. G#—Use your ring finger to fret the G# note at the 13th fret of the G string.

15. A—Your pinky frets the 14th fret of the G string to play the A.

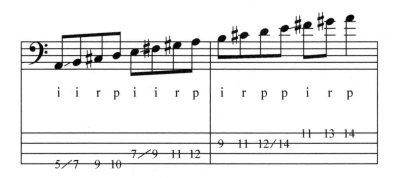

And just to prove that you don't have to slide with only your index finger, here's a method that involves sliding with your pinky:

In this variation, follow the first set of instructions once again up through Step 9 and then continue like this:

10. C#—Use your ring finger to fret the C# at the 11th fret of the D string.

11. D—Your pinky frets the 12th fret of the D string to play the D.

12. E—After playing the D, slide your pinky up two frets to the 14th fret of the D string to play the E note. The rest of your fingers will slide along, too, which lines up your index finger at the 11th fret for the next step.

13. F#—Move your index finger up a string to the 11th fret of the G string. This is your F#.

14. G#—Use your ring finger to fret the G# note at the 13th fret of the G string.

15. A—Your pinky frets the 14th fret of the G string to play the A note.

Be sure to practice whichever pattern you like (or all of them!) in both directions! To descend, simply reverse the steps. Your slides will now be going down two frets instead of up.

Remember that this closed pattern will work anywhere on the fingerboard of your bass guitar, provided your root note is on the E string.

Covering the Basses

Muscle memory comes from repeated practice of patterns, so it's a good idea to pick one scale pattern that fits your hands and work on it until you can do it with your eyes closed. That may seem a ways off right now, but with some concentrated practice you'll be able to play two-octave scales without thinking twice about it.

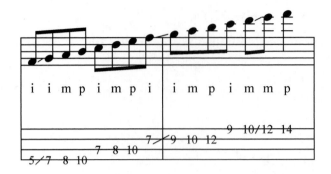

You will, of course, want to be able to come up with two-octave patterns for your minor scales as well. The following shows a closed two-octave pattern for the A natural minor scale.

1. A—Begin with your index finger, instead of your middle finger, on the A note at the fifth fret of the E string.

2. B—After playing the A, slide your index finger up two frets to the seventh fret of the E string to play the B note.

3. C—Use your middle finger to fret the C note at the eighth fret of the E string.

4. D—Your pinky frets the tenth fret of the E string to play the D.

5. E—Move your index finger up a string to the seventh fret of the A string. This is your E note.

6. F—Use your middle finger to fret the F note at the eighth fret of the A string.

7. G—Your pinky frets the tenth fret of the A string to play the G.

8. A—Move your index finger up a string to the seventh fret of the D string. This is your A note.

You have just completed the first octave of the A natural minor scale, going from the root A to the next A. Time to move on …

9. B—After playing the A, slide your index finger up two frets to the ninth fret of the D string to play the B note.

10. C—Use your middle finger to fret the C note at the tenth fret of the D string.

11. D—Your pinky frets the twelfth fret of the D string to play the D.

12. E—Move your index finger up a string to the ninth fret of the G string. This is your E note.

13. F—Use your middle finger to fret the F at the tenth fret of the G string.

14. G—After playing the F, slide your middle finger up two frets to the twelfth fret of the G string to play the G.

15. A—Your pinky frets the fourteenth fret of the G string to play the A.

Again, there are many other ways to play this two-octave minor-scale pattern. Take some time to figure out which patterns come easily to your fingers. You may find sliding easier with the index finger. You might favor sliding with your middle, ring, or pinky for that matter. The point is to get comfortable playing these patterns, and you're the best judge of that.

Here's the real beauty of it all: these positions never change. The A note that you get by playing the open A string of your bass, for example, always occupies the same place on the staff. Once you know where it is, you will always know where it is. But do try out different ways of playing. Something that may seem hard for you at first will only get easier with practice, patience, and persistence.

Arpeggios Across Two Octaves

You can also play chord arpeggios across two octaves. It takes a little more work and care, but it's worth it.

Begin with your ring finger on the A note (fifth fret of the E string) and, after playing the A note, slide your finger to the C# on the ninth fret of the E string. Use your index finger to play the E (seventh fret of the A string) and A (seventh

fret of the D). Then, slide the index finger up to the eleventh fret of the D string for the next C# note. Finally, use either your pinky or ring finger to play the E note (fourteenth fret of the D string) and A note (fourteenth fret of the G).

Minor chord arpeggios are slightly trickier:

Start with your middle finger on the A note (fifth fret of the E string) and, after playing the A note, slide your finger to the C on the eighth fret of the E string. Use your index finger to play the E (seventh fret of the A string) and A (seventh fret of the D). Then, slide the index finger up to the tenth fret of the D string for the next C note.

Here's the tricky part. Place your ring finger on the 12th fret of the D string and slide it up two frets to the fourteenth fret. That's your E note. Play the string only after sliding your ring finger up to the target fret. Finally, use your ring finger to play the A note at the fourteenth fret of the G string.

Practice all the chord arpeggios you know in this manner, finding ways to extend each one at least two octaves. You can expand most arpeggios slightly farther—a few notes up the G string or down the E string. Feeling comfortable with sliding your fingers around and playing both scales and chord arpeggios will open up the fingerboard for you. No longer will you simply hang around the first five frets of your bass guitar!

Patterns, Patterns Everywhere!

You can look at playing bass guitar as simply playing patterns that you move all about the neck. You can play any riff you come up with almost anywhere on the fingerboard, depending of course on how many strings it involves. A pattern that begins on the E string and uses only the E, A, and D strings can also be played starting with a note on the A string. This means the pattern would be played on the A, D, and G strings.

When you create or practice bass lines, notice what note begins the line, what note it ends on, and how many strings (and which ones) are used in the bass line.

Do You Really Learn All the Notes?

A bassist capable of playing some complicated riff that involves flying around the fingerboard at top speed isn't thinking, "Okay, that's an E, next is G followed by C#, then down to B," or something like that. The bassist is letting her fingers play a pattern that's been practiced for quite some time.

But that doesn't mean that knowing the notes isn't important. Patterns begin and end on particular notes, and usually involve notes that are important to the key of the song or the chord being played by the band. At the very least you need to know not only the note you want to start and end on, but also where on

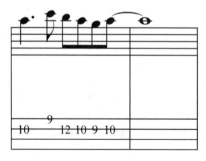

the fingerboard you want to play that first note.

Without being aware of the notes or the relationship of the notes to the key of

Covering the Basses

I know it's been said before, but many people find that saying (or even singing!) the notes as they play them helps them to better learn the location of notes on the fingerboard. And it's certainly easy enough to do while practicing scales in different positions on the neck.

a song, how would you know where to start a particular pattern? Say, for example, you learned the following bass line in the key of C:

Now let's say that you were called on to play this song, but in the key of F#. What would you do?

Transposing

Taking a song that is originally in one key and then playing it in a different key is called *transposing* the song. You might remember doing it back at the start of Chapter 13. People transpose music for all sorts of reasons, but luckily you

don't usually have to worry about them. You just play your patterns, but at different places on the fingerboard.

In our previous example, this bass line in C starts on the C note located at the tenth fret of the D string. To transpose this riff into the key of F#, you need to find the F# note on the D string and start your pattern from there, like this:

You see that the pattern, the relationship of each note on the bass to the next one, holds steady. In the original riff, you began by going from the C up to E (ninth fret of the G) and then to the D note at the twelfth fret of the D string. In the key of F#, you start with the F# and then play the A#, which, being at the third fret of the G string, uses the same movement as going from C to E. Likewise, the G# shares the same relationship to F#, as the D does to the C—the G# is located two frets higher than the F# on the D string, just as the D note is two frets higher than the C.

Secret Decoder Ring

Being able to transpose is simple, but it can require you to know a few things about both music theory and about your bass guitar. It's very much like the secret codes you might have written when you were much younger—where one letter was substituted for another. Going back to our examples, let's take a quick look at the notes of the C major scale:

> C–D–E–F–G–A–B

And now let's compare them to those of the F# major scale:

C–D–E–F–G–A–B
F#–G#–A#–B–C#–D#–E#

When you change where you start your pattern on the fingerboard, you are simply substituting a note from the F scale for its corresponding note in the C major scale. C becomes F#, E becomes A#, and so on.

You can do the same thing in order to transpose chords. Say that the first riff was played under the chord progression of C to Am to Dm to G. If you write out the triads of both keys, they would line up like this:

C–Dm–Em–F–G–Am–Bdim
F#–G#m–A#m–B–C#–D#m–E#dim

So you could easily figure out that, in the new key of F#, the chord progression is now F# to D#m to G#m to B. The root note of any given chord is the most important part of transposing. Any other aspect of the chord, whether it's minor, augmented, or diminished, whether it's a seventh or a ninth or flat thirteen— that's all secondary. If our original progression had been C to A9 to Dm7 to Gaug, then in the key of F# it would be F# to D#9 to G#m7 to Baug.

Doing It in Your Head

It's important to understand the steps of transposing, even if you're simply moving patterns from one place on the fingerboard to another. Write out chord transpositions—take a song that you're playing and figure out what the chords would be if you were to transpose it to another key. Try several different keys!

At first you'll find yourself going through the "secret decoder ring" process. But, with time, you will find that you just "know" what the transposed chord will be. You'll intuit that you're moving from the root to the fifth, for instance, in one key. That means moving from the root to the fifth in your new key.

With a little practice, you'll find transposing to be no big mystery. You may even be able to help out the other members of your band as they try to sort out which key to play a song in.

Covering the Basses

Like note reading, transposing gets easier with practice and you don't have to use your bass to practice this particular skill. Simply take any piece of music, whether it's a lead sheet or a fake sheet or just some chord progression scribbled on a piece of paper, and pick a new key to transpose the old song into. It won't be long before you find that you can do most transposing in your head.

Going Back Full Circle

You've seen both how easy it is to move about the fingerboard and how important transposing can be. One way to combine both of these skills in a single exercise is to return to the Circle of Fifths, which you read about in Chapter 11. Take a simple chord arpeggio, in the key of C, and move it around the circle, changing keys and position with each repetition, like this:

Do the same thing with short riffs or scale runs, like this:

Remember that the Circle of Fifths goes through all 12 possible major or minor keys. If you add this cycling of a pattern to your practice routine, you will quickly feel very comfortable and confident about playing any bass line anyplace on your fingerboard.

Keeping an Open Mind

Another thing to keep in mind, especially when you're playing a bass line that involves a lot of shifting of positions up and down the fingerboard, is that you've got four "open notes." You can use the notes of the open strings to give you some breathing room to move your left hand around the neck. Here's a short bass line to illustrate this:

Use the open G string to allow you to shift your index finger from the E note at the seventh fret of the A string to the C note at the tenth fret of the D string. Similarly, in the descending part of this riff, playing the open D string gives you plenty of time to place your middle or ring finger on the G note at the third fret of the E string for the final walk up to C.

Being aware of the availability of open notes can make some bass lines more like a game of Chutes and Ladders! People will think your fingers are flying all over the place, but the truth is that you're in complete control of where you want them to be.

People learn to be creative in different ways. Some can simply pick up an instrument and start playing original music. Most of us progress in a slightly more methodical manner.

The Least You Need to Know

◆ You can use slides to help you expand your scales and arpeggios up and

Riffs to Clip and Save

In This Chapter

♦ The purpose of riffing
♦ Riffs for single chords
♦ Simple bass lines for basic progressions
♦ Creating something new from something old

People learn to be creative in different ways. Some can just pick up an instrument and start playing original music. Most of us progress in a slightly more methodical manner. We like to understand the "whys" and "hows" of things. Getting started on the bass guitar, you just want to play and have it sound like music. Good music, preferably!

Because bassists play songs, an ideal first step is to listen to the bass in a song you like and learn it note for note. With all the books and Internet bass guitar tablature sites available, there are many sources open to you. But at some point you will realize that, while playing someone else's bass lines is fun and rewarding (people will know what you're playing!), you also don't want to be a "carbon copy" musician. You want to be original and create your own bass lines as well.

Just Riffing

In a lot of ways, creating bass lines is like cooking. Given a basic recipe, a little confidence, and some time to experiment, most of us can come up with interesting and often unique variations on a standard dish.

You can also think of bass playing in terms of speaking. Each new riff you learn becomes a part of your vocabulary. You want to know, for example, how to go from C to F in as many ways as possible. And the more interesting the better!

And that's precisely what you're going to do in this chapter. Here you will find many sample bass lines to try out. Some will be simple, some will be fast, some will be slow, and some will be somewhat tricky. Some will be good for playing with single chords, others will work with different chord progressions. There will be bass lines for different styles and moods of music—some rock, some jazz, some R&B and funk, and all sorts of other genres.

You have a number of tasks here. Listen and play each riff. Think about exactly what's going on in each musical phrase. How was it created? Is it strictly a chord arpeggio or a run up and down the scale, perhaps a combination of both? Does it use any interesting fingerings or techniques? Does it convey a particular mood or emotion to you? What type of song would you play it in?

I'm going to walk you through each riff, pointing out some interesting ideas about them and about playing them. When we're done with this part of the chapter, then we'll talk about how to go about putting what we've learned to practical use.

Hanging On to a Single Chord

Sometimes staying on one single chord is the hardest thing for a bass player to do. Many songs, particularly in funk and hip-hop genres, simply sit on one chord and let the rhythm section do its thing.

But just because the chord progression doesn't move, it doesn't mean the bass player is staying still. Quite often, this is exactly the place for a bassist to shine.

The following illustration contains some examples, in different musical styles, of bass lines that can be played under a single chord.

"Riff 1" is relatively simple, both in style and rhythm, and playing it in closed position (as indicated in the tablature) allows you to transpose it up and down the neck as you see fit.

The tempo can make or break this particular riff. At a moderate tempo, it sounds like a pop song. At a faster speed it has more of a Latin feel (you'll be reading about Latin rhythms in Chapter 25). Slowing it down a lot makes the riff seem sluggish and forced.

Once you have a particular riff down cold, playing around with the speed of it can often help you figure out how you want to use it. Changing the timing of even two notes is a good way to start being creative.

And speaking of faster timings, "Riff 2" certainly moves along! You might use a riff like this one in a fast, horn-fueled R&B song or underneath some distorted guitars in a fast rocker. What helps drive this particular riff is not just the speed, but also the use of the "blue note"—the minor third (more on that in Chapter 23). By changing quickly from the minor third (the Eb in this riff) to the major third (E), you give some added tension that you would miss if this riff stayed strictly diatonic (using only the notes of the C major scale). The Bb in the fourth measure adds to this as well.

I wrote this riff in "open" position (making use of the open strings) in order to make it easier to play. Once you're comfortable with it, try working it out in closed position. You'll need to start very slowly! But once you have it, you'll be able to use it anywhere you'd like on the neck.

Riff 1

Riff 2

Riff 3

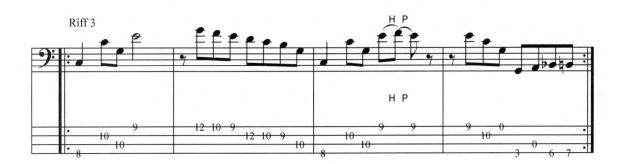

Riff 4

🔘 *19.1*

You get to combine diatonic and chromatic movement in "Riff 3." It starts with a C major arpeggio played at the eighth, ninth, and tenth frets of the fingerboard and then uses the notes of the C major scale in a descending cascade in the second measure. If you use your index finger to get the E note at the end of measure one, you should find the fingering easy going.

The third measure is an echo of the fourth, but it uses a combination hammer-on and pull-off to spice things up a bit. In the fourth measure, note the use of the open G and A strings, both to help get down to the low G (third fret of the E string) and to get back up the neck so that you're ready to repeat the riff.

Compared to these first three riffs, "Riff 4" seems very laid back. It's the sort of bass line you might find in a reggae song (and you'll be learning about those in Chapter 26). Using double stops (from Chapter 17, tenths in this case) in the fourth measure makes this riff stand out a lot more than it otherwise would. This is a great example of how throwing in one little technique can make a simple riff much more interesting without being flashy.

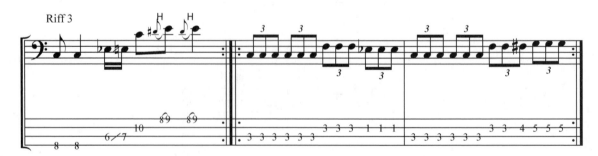

19.2

The first riff of the previous illustration is very busy and full of chromatic movement. It's also an excellent exercise for your fingers! As tempted as you might be to anchor your index finger on the third fret, try to use your middle finger, just as you would to play the C major scale. This will get your pinky into the action—and you definitely want to give the littlest digit some work!

"Riff 2" is a little quirky, the sort of thing you might run into in a funk or R&B song. You'll note that it uses the minor-to-major third movement you played in Example 1's "Riff 2." In this riff, you will find sliding from one note to the other (from the sixth fret of the A string to the seventh fret) with the index finger should make the fingering a snap. The two grace notes at the close of the riff can be played either as hammer-ons or slides. On the CD, they are hammers.

While most of the riffs we've played so far would be played beneath a major chord (C major, since we've been playing them all in the key of C), "Riff 3" works better with a minor chord or even a power chord. The riff itself sounds minor, owing to the use of the Eb—it sounds darker and moodier than most of the previous riffs. If you want to have even more fun with it, try using a pick to play it and add some palm muting.

The last riff in this example is a variation of the chromatic descending bass line you studied in Chapter 13. This one incorporates the use of open strings to make it a little more interesting. It's the sort of bass line you might use in a jazz piece or a ballad.

The timing of this last riff ("swing eighths") may be strange at the moment, but you can skip ahead to the start of Chapters 23 and 25 to learn more about it. We'll be right here when you get back!

Progressing Along

In Chapters 13 and 14, as well as in the jam along songs you've played thus far, you've learned about the importance of moving from chord to chord. After all, songs are full of chord changes.

Let's combine our earlier work with chord progressions with both the new techniques learned in Chapter 17 as well as with the ability to move about of the fingerboard from Chapter 18. We'll start with the simplest, and most common, progressions, moving from I to IV and V (C, F and G in the key of C). Ready?

In the following example, our first riff involves the use of both leading tones (from Chapter 11) and anticipations (from Chapter 17). It also manages to throw in a little of the minor third/major third movement from this chapter's earlier examples. It's got a definite swing to it, the sort you might hear on some pop and R&B styled songs.

Be careful with the timing on this one! You want to hit that first F on the second half of the fourth beat of the first measure and let it carry over into measure two. Likewise, the G at the end of the second measure is played on the last half of the fourth beat. This riff is a great example of the use of syncopation. Even though the timing may seem a bit forced right now, you'll be surprised at how natural it will sound with a bit of practice.

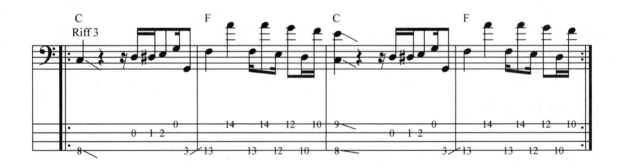

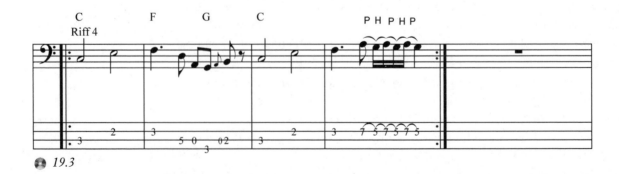

🔵 *19.3*

"Riff 2" has a percolating African feel to it. It's strictly diatonic, not to mention very simple to play. The use of various rhythms, changing from quarter notes to sixteenth notes with the occasional eighth note tossed in, gives it character and style. In the third measure, you might want to try sliding your index finger up from the E (second fret of the D string) to the G (fifth fret of the same string) in order to make the fingering of the final measure a little easier. You'll be exploring African and other exotic styles of music in Chapter 26.

Slides play a big role in "Riff 3," which has a lot going on even though it uses the simplest of progressions (I to IV). Play the C note (eighth fret of the E string) and hold it for a beat before sliding down the neck. This will put your left hand in good position for the chromatic run at the end of the first measure. Be sure to land the last note (the G on the third fret of the E string) with your index finger so you can easily slide it all the way up to the F at the thirteenth fret of the same string.

Thinking of the second measure in terms of double stops may help make it easier to play. Even though you're sounding the notes individually, having your left hand set in position for double stops should assist you in smoothly moving from note to note.

Another example of simplicity can be found in "Riff 4," which is built on the I—IV—V progression. Taking advantage of the open A string and a well-placed grace note in the second measure, and throwing in a trill at the end of measure four, help make this basic progression fun to listen to.

19.4

Even though "Riff 1" in the previous illustration is diatonic, it jumps around the neck a lot! The last measure is full of descending octaves, which is used a lot in disco and dance music, two of the genres we'll touch upon in Chapter 26. You might want to notice how the last two sets of octaves, D and B, help create the sound of the G chord without using the root note (G). This is a great example of how the bass player doesn't always need a root note to establish harmony in a song.

You definitely might want to return to this riff (not to mention others!) after working on your slapping and popping in the next chapter.

Another jazzy descending bass line awaits you in "Riff 2." Sometimes it's easy to forget the versatility of descending bass lines. This one seems tailor-made for the I—IV—V progression, doesn't it?

"Riff 3" might be the funky cousin of "Riff 3" from Example 1. While it uses notes from arpeggios to accent the I—vi—IV—V progression (C to Am to F to G), it gets a bit of freshness from a number of chromatic tones, particularly in the third measure. It also makes great use of the open A string at the third beat of the second measure to allow for repositioning the left hand further up the neck.

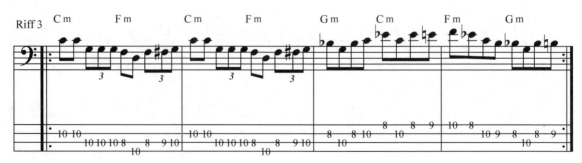

🔘 *19.5*

And Five to Grow On

Let's wrap up this section with a potpourri of different styles and rhythms.

"Riff 1" in the preceding illustration is a light, unassuming Latin style rhythm (which you'll learn in Chapter 25 is the bossa nova). Notice the switch to the open G string in the second measure to accommodate the move from G to G# to A.

Things go from light to dark in a hurry with "Riff 2." You might find this bass line in a hard rock or metal song. Because this minor sounding riff is played entirely on the A string, you might be lulled into thinking it will be a snap, but it will be important to make certain you play cleanly and don't allow the other three strings to create unwanted sympathetic noise. You may find that playing "Riff 2" with a pick adds more of a sharp edge to each note.

"Riff 3" is a nice example of playing in a minor key. This particular chord progression still uses C, F and G, but they are all minor chords. F# and B natural get used as leading tones to G and C respectively, and the open D string can easily be used in place of the D at the tenth fret of the E string if you'd like to do so. This riff is played in swing eighths with a laid-back, lazy feel.

And speaking of swing eighths, use them in the last two riffs as well:

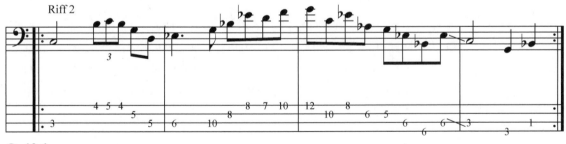

🎵 *19.6*

As noted on many occasions in this book, sometimes not playing is an important part of playing. The eighth rests at the beginning of measures one and three of "Riff 1" play an important part in the overall groove. They give the bass line the same kind of organic feeling you may have noticed on Example 1's "Riff 4" and Example 3's "Riff 3." You can create powerful bass lines by giving them spaces, even if the rest is only as long as a heartbeat.

Almost all of "Riff 1" involves a C9 arpeggio. If you'd like to give it a little more character, you could try starting with the C note at the third fret of the A string and then sliding up to the E at the seventh fret, as shown in the third measure.

Our final riff is decidedly minor in nature, but it's a good reminder that there are three minor scales to be aware of. In the first measure, the C harmonic minor scale should be used in order to play the B notes. In the three remaining measures, you can stay safely with the C natural minor scale.

After the Analysis

Now that you've played these riffs, think about the ones you like and why you like them. Was it the sound or the style? Was it because it was easy to play?

Take the ones you like and get very comfortable playing them. Cycle them through the Circle of Fifths, as you learned how to do in our last chapter. Make certain you can play them in any key.

Once you feel confident in your ability to play any (or all) of these riffs, start tinkering with them. Add some hammer-ons or pull-offs or a slide or two. Start playing around with the timing. Make one note shorter and another longer than their original counterparts. Or add some rests or dead notes to liven things up. You might take the first two measures of one riff and splice them onto the last two measures of a different one. In other words, have fun!

Remember, too, that the more riffs you have at hand, the quicker you can come up with a bass line on the spur of the moment. For instance, if you're playing with some friends and a song comes up with a progression of E to F#m to A and then back to E, you'll be able to recognize it as a I—ii—IV—I progression and be able to play a passable bass line on the first try.

The Least You Need to Know

♦ Learning new riffs helps you build up your "bass vocabulary."

♦ Understanding how a riff is constructed can help you play it easier.

♦ You can create your own riffs using ideas from other riffs you've learned.

♦ The more riffs you know, the easier it will be to improvise or create a bass line at a moment's notice.

20

Going Solo at the Improv

In This Chapter

- ◆ Elements of improvising and soloing
- ◆ Combining knowledge and technique
- ◆ Listening for inspiration
- ◆ Three jam-along songs for improvising
- ◆ Fine-tuning your solos

As you well know, the bass player usually doesn't go seeking the limelight. He or she has more than enough to do holding the band together, keeping the rhythm moving along at a steady pace, and providing the tonal and harmonic textures needed for each song being performed.

But that doesn't mean that the bassist won't shy away from the opportunity to solo or improvise! It's always fun to get a chance to show off your skills and be appreciated, but don't forget that the song still has to be the primary concern. Bass solos, like regular bass lines, should compliment a song and not be a separate part of it.

In this chapter you'll be given your own chance to shine, to improvise and to create a solo or two. But first let's examine the elements that go into soloing and improvisation and explore why all the theory and techniques that you've learned up to this point will help you through the first jitters of creating a cool bass line on demand.

Taking Center Stage

Bass playing, by its very nature, is highly improvisational. More often than not the bassist is given a simple chord chart and expected to create a bass line on the spot. Quite often, as you've seen in past chapters, any given bass line provides an opportunity for a fill or a bit of flashy playing. A bass solo is sort of a formal chance to show an audience what you're already doing in each song.

Solos, like songs, come in all sorts of styles. They can be fast and full of notes tumbling over each other or slow and airy. Solos can be melodic or rhythmic or a combination of the two. A melodic solo is like that of other lead instruments, such as a guitar, saxophone, or piano. Rhythmic solos are percussive and driving, like having a drum solo with specifically pitched notes.

Myths About Solos

Unless you're listening to a jazz band, when you hear a bass player perform a solo, it's not an improvised solo, something made up totally on the spot. Solos are usually the result of planning and practicing. If you know that you're going to be given a solo in a particular song, it makes sense to try to work out what you're going to play ahead of time.

Even when a bassist improvises, he or she tends to have an idea of what to play. Improvising becomes a rapid translation of the musical ideas in the bass player's head to the notes that he or she produces on the bass guitar.

To be good at both soloing and improvising, a bass player needs to have musical ideas. These ideas come from the knowledge and technical skill the bassist already possesses, and from listening and being in tune with the song.

Starting With What You Know

The best way to approach a solo is similar to the way you first approached playing regular bass lines—begin with what you know. Start out with something very simple and then work your way up from there. It doesn't have to be very flashy; it could even be one note played in a very deliberate rhythm.

Let's use the following chord chart as an example. And, since most generic group lead sheets are in treble clef, let's start getting used to seeing it:

You recognize this as a I–vi–IV–V pattern, in the key of D. If you were suddenly told you had a solo and the rest of the band went dead quiet, you'd have to fill in something! Start with something easy:

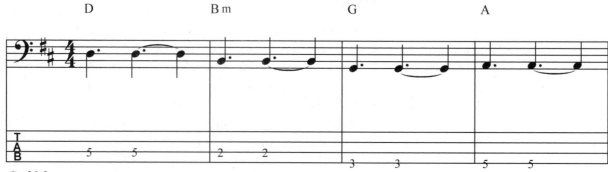

20.2

From there, it's not hard to start filling in a few of the gaps with notes from either the D major scale or the appropriate chord arpeggio:

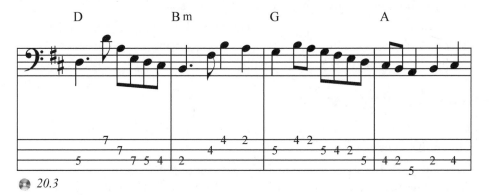

🔊 *20.3*

Finally, try moving around up and down the fingerboard. Remember that in the key of D, you've got a lot of open-string opportunities (the D, G, and A strings are all root notes of chords in this particular progression). Keep being more concerned with keeping things clean rather than playing a lot of notes:

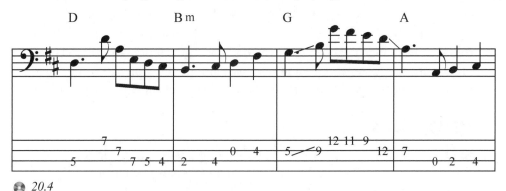

🔊 *20.4*

You can hear how, in four relatively easy steps, you've gone from the simplest idea for a solo, which sounded pretty good, to something that sounds *really* good. Sometimes putting a solo together can be that easy.

Playing to Your Strengths

It also helps to remember two important things: first, play to your strengths. Every bass player has good qualities and things that need work. If you're good at keeping rhythm and playing solid fills, do the same with your solos. If you can create rich melodic bass lines, but have trouble playing very fast, don't try to jam your solos full of sixteenth notes! Play a bass line that sounds like someone singing. If you're a bassist who can churn out rapid notes cleanly and clearly, then go ahead and do so, but only if it is appropriate to the song in question.

The second thing to remember is that, as a bass player, you are a work in progress. Every day you are picking up new skills and techniques. Just because

Covering the Basses

Recording your playing is a great way to work out a solo, as well as a terrific way to measure how you're progressing. You don't need fancy recording equipment; a simple portable cassette player will do fine. When you record ideas for a solo, be sure to state the key you're playing in and the tempo. You can have your metronome playing along in the recording if it helps! Anytime that you think you haven't been making much progress on your bass, play an early recording of yourself and you'll know differently.

you avoid fast notes now doesn't mean that, in a month or so, you won't be playing like a string of firecrackers. As you gain more confidence in your abilities, work those new skills into your bass lines and solos.

Just as you've evolved as a bass player, starting with the very basics and developing new skills and the confidence that goes along with it, you will also evolve as a soloist. Every new thing you learn will be added to the style you've developed.

Calling for a Response

One way to get started on soloing is to take very short solos! Or, you could think of the solos as long fills.

Call and response is a style of lead playing that you might recognize as it shows up a lot in blues music. One member of the band, or possibly even the whole band, will play a short phrase (the "call") and then the designated soloist will play a short lead (the "response"), or vice versa. Because it is used so much in blues songs, people tend to think of "call and response" as being guitar-oriented, but any instrument, even a vocalist, can perform the solo response. Think of the beginning of Elvis Presley's "Jailhouse Rock," when the band plays a few notes and then the snare drum plays all by itself. That's a call and response.

Participating in a call and response arrangement is an easy way to get over the solo jitters. You don't play long, so you don't have much time to worry about playing any wrong notes. Call and responses also tend to pop up several times in the arrangement of a given song, so you have lots of chances to try out new ideas.

Trading Spaces

Another similarly painless way to take the plunge as a soloist is known as *trading fours*. This usually involves the whole band, but can also be between selected players. Instead of one member getting a long solo, band members take turns soloing for short periods, usually no more than one to four measures. The lead guitarist may start, play his lick, then the keyboardist or second guitar player gets his or her shot. The bassist is usually along for the ride. The band can get back to the song after one set of trading, or pass the solos from one member to the next.

Again, because the time to solo is relatively short, there tends to be little to worry about for the fledgling soloist. Just being able to toss the leads around like hot potatoes can be a lot of fun.

Listening for Inspiration

Listening is an important part of soloing. Many ideas for solos can come from just listening to what's going on around you in a song. Does it have a memorable melody line? Using the melody as a starting point is a tried-and-true method for professionals. You can also concentrate on being rhythmic rather than melodic. Is the drummer playing a catchy, funky rhythm? Echo it in your solo.

Listen also to the spaces in the song. Having a good feel for how a song breathes will help you come up with solos that feel like a natural complement to the music. Above all, you want your listeners to feel that the solo is a part of the song and not something that's been surgically attached.

Three Jam-Along Songs for Improvising and Soloing

The ultimate goal of this chapter's jam-along songs is different than ones in our previous chapters. Here you want to focus on improvising and soloing. But it's still good to use the same steps we covered in past jam-along songs. Before you even think about your solo, be more concerned about simply playing along with the band. Be the bassist first. Listen to the songs and get a feeling for them. Come up with some bass lines that you like and that you can play easily. Use those first bass lines as a starting point for your soloing.

Key into the rhythms of the songs. Then focus on the chord progressions. Once you feel comfortable with the songs, start working out an improvisation. Begin very slowly. When you're done, try to write down the ideas you liked so that you won't forget them. Build off of those the next time around.

Eventually, you may come up with a completely worked-out arrangement for a solo. But don't stop there. The next step would be to come up with an entirely different one, or at least something slightly different!

And don't forget to keep coming back to these songs, as you get better as a bass player. Each time you learn something new, try to incorporate it into a new solo, or even use it to spice up an old one. Learning should be an ongoing process.

> **Covering the Basses**
>
> As you explore the art of soloing, you might want to remember the three Ss: short, simple, and singable. The "short" and "simple" are obvious. And if you can sing, whistle, or hum your solo, then chances are you can play it, too. If you're ever stuck for ideas, put your bass down and simply try to sing along with a song. Start with the melody if you'd like, but also try to come up with a harmony or counterpoint (a melody line that plays against the original melody). Once you've gotten your part set in your mind, then work on transferring it to your bass guitar. This takes time and practice, but like all your other skills, it's easy to develop.

Song #1

Song #1 is more of a loop than the jam-along songs in our previous chapters. It's a mood piece, meant to give you a huge canvas on which to paint your first solo. It consists of four chords played over and over again:

20.5

This song definitely leans toward creating some very melodic lines. And be sure to play around with some Am(add9) chord arpeggios (you might remember "add9" chords from Chapter 9), using the C natural note to lead you to the B of the following Emaj7 chord. Experiment with chromatic tones as well, as in the following example.

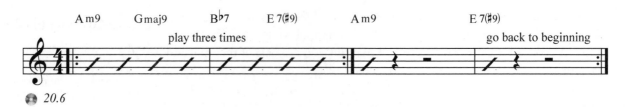

🔘 *20.6*

Here you have a short phrase that repeats with variations according to the chord at hand. As you can see and hear, you don't need a bushel of sixteenth notes to create a moving bass line. Work your way up to more complicated ideas after getting a solid start.

Song #2

Song #2 is slightly more complicated and has a built-in place for a bass fill in the last two measures:

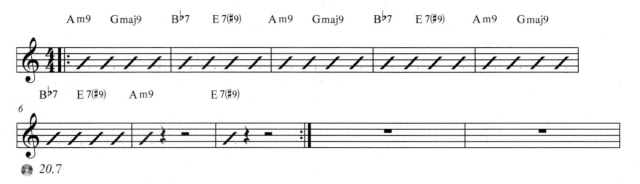

🔘 *20.7*

If you're lost for an easy way to get started on this song, try a descending bass line like this:

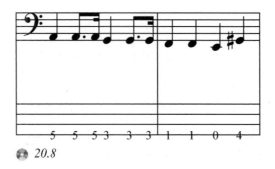

🔘 *20.8*

And don't be afraid to leave spaces! Here is one possible turnaround:

🎵 *20.9*

Song #3

Your third jam-along song is a bit of a rocker, but it also has a tricky minor chord progression:

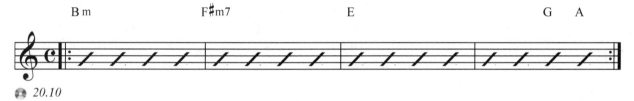

🎵 *20.10*

The trick here will be keeping things moving while also keeping the Bm tonal center in place. Don't settle for one scale, or you'll have problems with the switch from E to G and back at the end of this one!

Fine-Tuning Your Solos

Solos, like bass players, are often works in progress. One musical brainstorm usually leads to another and before you know it, you're trying to cram a 16-measure solo with 237 ideas.

Generally, the best way to approach a bass solo is in four steps. First be sure you have the song down cold, knowing all the chord changes and keeping the beat steady. Having a sense of the mood of the song and a general idea of how you'd like to approach it helps as well.

Your first attempt at a solo will usually be more workmanlike than inspired, but inspiration will come, often when you're away from the song and the band and your bass guitar. This is why it's important to work on solos on your own, which is the second step. In this step you can come up with a melodic phrase to repeat at various points of the solo, or a rhythmic pattern that holds it all together. You may also start to add all sorts of little frills and ornamentation to your basic solo, things like slides, dead notes, and the like.

Step three involves getting back with the band and trying out your ideas in a "real" setting. You may find that some of your musical thoughts work out wonderfully in a group while others may still require rethinking or even discarding. Don't be disheartened if a phrase or two needs to go back to the drawing board. That's part of the growing process.

> ### Covering the Basses
>
> Don't be afraid to leave spaces in a solo! Just as regular bass lines will often give you room for a fill (a short flurry of notes), solos should provide you with spaces. Not every space needs to be chock full of notes. Pauses and rests give a solo dynamic tension and get the attention of the listener. You can even do a call and response with yourself!

Basso Profondo

Q: *If improvising is spontaneous, how does one prepare for doing an improvisation?*

A: Improvisation seems spontaneous, but it's really the result of a lot of practicing and listening. One good way to practice is to take a recording of a song you know the chords for (but don't usually play) and play along with it. Be sure to turn the bass down on the stereo so that you're free to come up with your own ideas. There are also many jam-along tracks, such as the ones that come with this book, available for purchase at music stores or for download on the Internet. Try to go through the same steps outlined earlier in this chapter: start off easy and then work your way into more complicated improvisations and solos. The more you do it, the more ready you'll be when it's your turn in the spotlight.

During your second pass at fine-tuning your solo, start to think about dynamics. Will you play it as loudly as possible from beginning to end or will you add in changes of volume? Usually the drummer plays along with the bass solo, so thinking about how to play off of each other is also something to take into account.

Calling It a Day

At some point you have to be able to say, "That's it. I'm done!" It's easy to keep working on a solo and then refining it over and over again, and yet never play it in a practice or a show. Do yourself a favor and don't try to put every musical idea you have into your first solo! You'll surely have more than one in your life as a bassist.

When performing, it's important for a soloist to have something musically to say. But it's just as important to not be a musical "rambler," going on and on and adding little to the song. Unless you're covering for a guitarist changing a broken string or some other happy accident on stage, try to keep your solos relatively short. Usually a verse or two of a song, or a verse and a chorus, is more than enough for both you and your audience. Always leave them wanting more—don't give them reasons to want less.

The Least You Need to Know

- Soloing and improvising are skills that need to be practiced.
- When working out a solo, start out with simple musical ideas and then build up to more complicated ones.
- As a beginner, it's good to keep your solos short, simple, and singable.
- Be sure to take time to fine-tune your solos to make them as clean and memorable as possible.

Part

Playing for Life

Every song is an adventure, a chance for the bass player to explore various musical possibilities while still holding the band together both rhythmically and harmonically.

There are more musical styles in the world than can ever be included in any one book, but we've done our best to give you the rundown on most of the popular musical genres you're likely to encounter while playing bass.

And since you're going to be playing bass guitar for the rest of your life, we also talk about taking good care of your instrument so that the two of you will continue to create beautiful music for a long, long time.

Chapter 21

Slap, Crackle, Pop–Some More Fun Techniques

In This Chapter

- ◆ Creating vibrato
- ◆ The slap/pop style of bass guitar playing
- ◆ Discovering harmonics
- ◆ How to tap
- ◆ Combining various techniques

In Chapter 17 you learned techniques, such as hammer-ons, pull-offs, and slides, which add a lot of style to your playing. In this chapter you'll find some more techniques that you can incorporate into your bass playing.

Good Vibrato

While the electric bass guitar is a relatively new instrument, the technique of vibrato is older than the hills. Essentially, vibrato is a way to provide a little more interest in notes that are held for two or more beats. The technique gives a note more of a quavering effect, which in turn gives the note slightly more sustain.

You can create vibrato in a number of ways. First place your finger on the fret of the note to which you want to add vibrato. Strike the string with your right hand and immediately begin moving the finger of your left hand (the one fretting the note), sliding it rapidly along the string, but keeping your finger within the fret.

In classical vibrato, you slide your finger *along* the string. This creates a very subtle sustain. Rock vibrato goes *against* the string, vibrating the string in a perpendicular motion. This gives the vibrato much more of a wavelike sound, almost like when a guitarist "bends" his strings. You, of course, control the amount of vibrato the string gets, as well as the speed of the vibrato. Both of these factors can give your vibrato all sorts of different characters.

In both music notation and bass guitar tablature, vibrato is signaled by a wavy line (~), placed above the note in question:

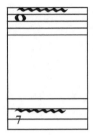

🔘 *21.1*

In the above example, the audio CD demonstrated different types of vibrato attack and speeds for the same riff. First you'll hear a classical style and then two different rock-style vibratos.

Slap/Pop Happy

All of the slurring techniques in Chapter 17 (the hammer-ons, pull-offs, and slides), as well as the vibrato techniques, are considered left-hand techniques for an obvious reason—the left hand does the work. But there are right-hand techniques as well, such as the slap/pop style of playing.

While most bassists use either the index or middle fingers of their right hand to strike the strings, a "slapper" relies on his thumb, using the small bone on its side (just by the joint) to strike the string and sound the note. The following illustration shows you what part of your thumb to use:

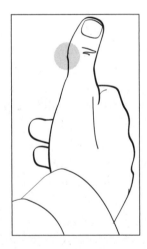

The "pop" part of slap/pop is usually produced by the index finger plucking a string in an upward motion. This technique is a mainstay of funk bassists, but can also be heard in many other types of music, especially dance-oriented genres.

Of all the techniques that we've covered so far, the slap/pop is probably the one most likely to frustrate beginners. It's truly not hard to do, but it can take a while to get the hang of it. Be patient and persistent, and you'll be slapping and popping before long!

Slapping

Most bass players slap close to the base of the neck of the bass guitar. You can also strike the strings close to the bridge and saddle of your instrument. The following illustration shows you where:

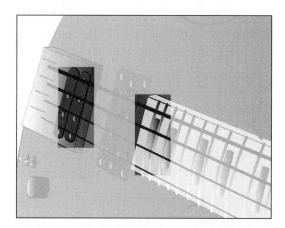

The actual "slap" is a simple flick of the wrist, like this:

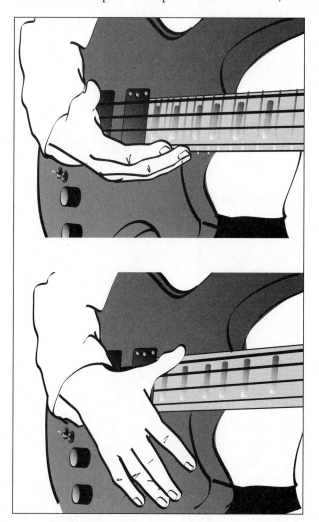

To get a better idea of the motion, lay your right hand flat on a tabletop. Now, keeping your thumb straight, use your wrist to raise the thumb and then to drum it on the tabletop. It's important to keep your hand relaxed and comfortable.

Again, it may take time and practice to get the feel of this technique on the strings. Also, different basses have different sweet spots, places at the base of the neck where you get the best tone from your slap. You may find it easier to perform a slap close to the bridge or between the lower pickup and the bridge of your bass.

Pop Art

To pop a string, hook the index finger of your right hand under the string. Pull on the string, tugging it away from the body of the bass, then release it. It will snap back against the neck and the frets of the bass guitar, causing it to pop.

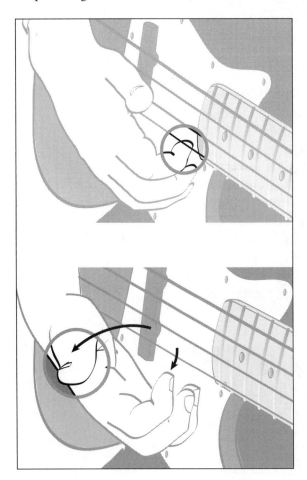

To make things easier while starting out, fret a note on the G string with your left hand before popping the string with the index finger of your right hand. Try to get a good, clean tone along with your pop!

A Winning Combination

It's time to put both techniques together. First, fret the E note at the ninth fret of the G string with any finger of your left hand. Now slap the open E string and then immediately do a pop of the G string:

With practice, you will find yourself doing the slap/pop in one fluid motion. It will almost feel like your thumb is simply falling on the strings of its own accord. Remember to stay relaxed and let your wrist do the work.

The slap/pop technique is an especially popular way to play octaves on the bass guitar, like this:

🔘 *21.7*

> **Covering the Basses**
>
> Generally, beginning bass players find popping easier than slapping. It helps to try, initially, to do your slapping on the E and A strings while popping on the G and D strings.

The spacing of octaves on the fingerboard of the bass guitar gives you a lot of room to ply the slap/pop technique. This can be a great substitute for a simple, single-note walking bass line.

Harmonics

Harmonics is a technique that can involve both the left and right hands. A harmonic is a clear, bell-like tone that you are able to produce either at certain places on the fingerboard of your bass guitar, or by playing a string in a certain manner with the right hand.

Natural Harmonics

You can find *natural harmonics* at particular spots on the neck of your instrument. The easiest place to produce them is at the 12th fret. Just follow these steps:

Place the index finger of your left hand lightly on the 12th fret of the G string. "On the fret," in this case, means literally on the metal of the fret and not on the fingerboard between the two metal frets. If you're not sure which metal fret to place your finger on, choose the one closer to the body of the guitar.

Position your index finger very lightly on the metal of the fret. You should barely feel yourself touching the metal.

Strike the G string with either the index finger or middle finger as you normally would strike a note. You will hear a clear, ringing tone.

Strike the G string again with a finger of your right hand. This time, lift the index finger of your left hand from the G string as soon after you make the strike with your right hand as possible. The clear, ringing tone should sound stronger and last a while longer than on your first attempt.

You can create natural harmonics on each string. They occur at the twelfth, seventh, and fifth frets as well as many other places, some not on specific frets but rather at specific points along the strings.

Natural harmonics are note-specific. The ones found at the 12th fret are the same notes you would get by fretting the string at the same spot. The ones located at the seventh fret are the interval of a fifth higher.

Knowing what notes can be produced by means of harmonics, natural or artificial, gives you another cool technique to use in your bass playing. Here is a bass line using natural harmonics:

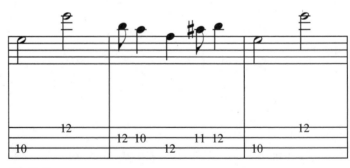

🔊 *21.8*

Just as with all the other techniques you've learned, take time to experiment and use harmonics in some of your bass lines. You may decide that they're not your style, or you may make them a big part of your repertoire.

Artificial Harmonics

Artificial harmonics are trickier to play, but allow you to make a harmonic for just about any note you can play on your bass guitar. To create an artificial harmonic, follow these steps:

Fret any note on any string with a finger of your left hand. Let's use the F note at the third fret of the D string.

Place the tip of your right index finger lightly on the same string, but 12 frets higher. In this example, since you're fingering the F note (third fret of the D string) with your left hand, that means placing it at the 15th fret of the D string. As you did with the natural harmonics, be sure that your finger is on the metal of the fret, but so lightly you can hardly feel it.

Use your right thumb to strike the string. As you do, quickly lift your right index finger from the string. You will get a clean, ringing tone, sounding one octave higher in tone than the note you're fingering with your left hand.

Unlike natural harmonics, artificial ones give you a chance to create a harmonic for almost any note you can find on your fingerboard. You can create riffs like this one with artificial harmonics:

🔊 *21.9*

Tap Dancing

Tapping is another technique that, while it can be performed solely with the right hand, is more commonly performed with both the left and right hand. The sound of a tapped note is created by striking the fingertips of either hand firmly onto a string, pressing it firmly onto the fingerboard, as in this illustration:

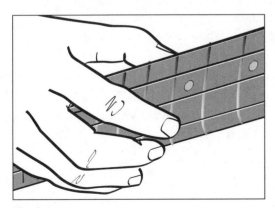

Tapping

You can think of this as a hammer-on, only without a preceding note. Tapping can be done with either the left or right hand. The note produced will be the same note that you would get by fretting the string normally.

Combination Tapping

Using tapping in combination with hammer-ons and pull-offs can assist you in creating some flashy riffs, once you get more comfortable and confident with the technique. Start out slowly with some simple exercises, like this one:

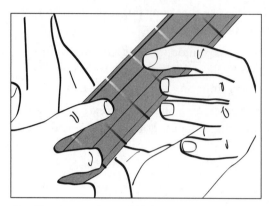

Combination tapping positioning.

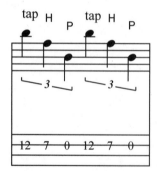

🔘 *21.12*

First, position your right index finger over the 12th fret of the D string. Have your left middle finger ready to strike the D string at the seventh fret.

Tap your right index finger solidly onto the 12th fret of the D string, sounding the note. Take your right index finger away while tapping the seventh fret of the D string solidly with your right middle finger.

Perform a pull-off with your left hand, sounding the note of the open D string.

Tapping allows you to create lightning-fast barrages of notes. You have to be careful though, because it's easy for tapping to become muddy sounding. It's a technique you might want to save for a special occasion.

Talking Scales

And speaking of special occasions, let's take a moment to return to the subject of scales. When you last saw a scale, way back in Chapter 15, you learned about modes as well as the pentatonic scale. There are many more scales that you can learn—for now, though, I'd like to introduce you to two that you might find a lot of fun, since each has a distinctly different feel to it.

The Whole Tone

The first scale, called the *whole tone* scale, is easy to remember because each note is one whole step from another. This makes for a total of six different notes. In the key of C, this would mean using the notes C, D, E, F#, G#, Bb, and C.

You'll find this scale used a lot in jazz and classical pieces, but it's also a good one to pull out occasionally when soloing or improvising.

The Dimished Stroke

As you learned in Chapter 15, scales don't have to have only seven notes. Sometimes they can even have more! This next scale, *the diminished scale*, has eight. Besides being quirky in that way, it also has two different forms:

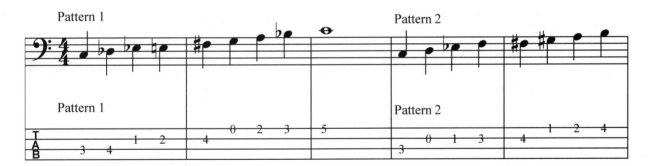

These may seem weird at first, but look carefully at the intervals. In "Pattern 1," you start with the root and then alternate between a half step and a whole step the rest of the way. "Pattern 2" is the opposite, switching between whole steps and half steps. As with the whole tone scale, you're likely to find a use for the diminished scale in jazz pieces as well as some Latin and other ethnic music.

The Least You Need to Know

- ◆ Vibrato is a left-hand technique used generally on long notes.
- ◆ The slap/pop technique is done with the right hand and is often heard in funk and other dance-oriented music.

- Harmonics, clear ringing bell-like tones, can be produced naturally or artificially.

- Tapping techniques can be performed in combination with hammer-ons and pull-offs.

- The whole-tone and diminished scales are examples of the many types of exotic scales you might encounter.

Chapter 22

The Loud Stuff: Rock 'n' Roll

In This Chapter

- ◆ The role of the rock bass player
- ◆ Basic rock 'n' roll bass lines
- ◆ Giving a harder edge to rock music
- ◆ Dealing with different rock styles
- ◆ Two jam-along rock songs

Some people say that the invention of the electric guitar set the stage for rock music. But a very good argument can be made for the bass guitar being responsible for rock's rise to the forefront of the music scene. As more and more bass players switched from the typical stand-up to the electric bass guitar, an intriguing thing happened—suddenly the bass was *felt* as well as heard. Here was an instrument that gave you the melodic abilities of the guitar and the stand-up bass, while delivering the physical punch of a drum.

Leo Fender introduced the first electric bass guitar to the public in 1951, but it took the better part of the decade to gain widespread use among musicians. As bass players got better acquainted with the new instrument, they became more innovative. The technology of bass guitars and amplifiers improved, and the bass guitar got louder and louder, eventually dominating the rhythm section of a band. Quite often a good bass player could lead a drummer around instead of simply following along in the drummer's footsteps. A good bass player could also fill in enough sound harmonically to allow the guitarist to play more leads instead of chords and rhythm fills.

The driving, pulsating rhythm dominates and defines rock music. Even though the electric guitar had been around for quite a while, it needed the big kick of electric bass guitar to truly get it rocking.

I Love Rock 'n' Roll

Today's rock bassist still attends to these two primary functions—driving the music along rhythmically and providing a tonal center for the song. Most rock bass lines, regardless of which subgenre we're talking about, center around the root of a chord, providing the most basic feel of tonality possible. If a song were in C, for example, and switched from C to F and then back to C, a standard rock bass line would be like this:

🔘 *22.1*

There's no subtlety here! Your first concern as a rock bassist is giving the song a driving beat that, along with the drums, propels the music forward.

Steady eighth notes are usually the heart of any rock bass line. Depending upon the style of rock you play, you may liven the beat up even more with sixteenth and thirty-second notes, but the eighth note will still hold everything together.

These days it seems there are more types of rock music than there are characters in *War And Peace*. You've got rockabilly, rock 'n' roll, classic rock, alternative, punk rock, progressive rock, art rock, and several different genres that most people just call metal. Some folks even subdivide their rock by decade or country of origin, such as '60s American rock or '80s British new wave. It can all get pretty confusing (and downright silly) at times.

To the rock bassist, the major concern is still the rhythm and the tonality. Some rock styles lend themselves very nicely to powerful melodic fills while others seem to sound better when the bass player just concentrates on the rhythm and the root of a chord. Most rock music is a combination of the two.

That Old Time Rock 'n' Roll

Old rock 'n' roll, the sort that started in the mid- to late 1950s, developed out of blues music. Many early rock songs were simply blues songs given more of a rock beat. And a lot of early rock bands had stand-up basses instead of bass guitars. When the bass player picked up a bass guitar, he often would still play the same bass lines he played on the big acoustic bass.

Just as in blues music (which we'll cover in the next chapter), rock music tends to play around a lot with the sound of the dominant seventh. Even when the rest of the band is playing a straight major chord, you will often hear the flatted seventh being used in the bass. Let's go back to our earlier example and give it more of an old time rock 'n' roll feel by using dominant seventh arpeggios as shown in the following example.

You can hear that this really moves without being very busy. In order to be able to play a steady yet up-tempo bass line, you don't want to worry a lot about your fingering. That's why patterns are so important. In the second example you take the same pattern of fingering you use for the C chord and simply shift it up to the A string in order to play the same pattern for the F chord.

🔘 *22.2*

Let's expand on this idea of repeated patterns in the following example. We'll also use the A note from the C major scale to flesh out our bass line a little:

🔘 *22.3*

Even though it's a simple line, it perfectly suits the song, moving it along and establishing the tonal centers of each chord.

Less Melody, a Little More Drive

Sometimes a little accenting with the right hand is all it takes to change the feel of a song. A lot of modern rock styles rely on a good right-hand attack to create a sense of urgency. Listen to this variation of our first example:

🔘 *22.4*

The only difference between this example and the first one are the accented notes. On the first and third beat of each measure, the right hand strikes the string noticeably harder, stressing these particular beats.

While this last example was played with only the root notes of the chords, you can certainly add more to the mix. But how much is enough? You could simply throw in the flatted seventh of each root and come up with an arresting bass line.

● 22.5

Covering the Basses

Rock's pounding beat is usually driven home by the bass drum thumping out the first and third beats and the snare drum smacking on the second and fourth. The bass player can key into the drummer, focusing on the first beat and adding some thunder to the bass drum, which leaves the snare drum some space to stand out. The bassist can also choose to key on the snare, playing lightly on the first beat and then strongly accenting the second and fourth beats. Dynamics of this sort bring a lot of interest to the rhythm section and also give the rest of the band space in which to play fills.

Playing accented notes, combined in this example with hammer-ons, gives the bass line a harder, edgier feel, made all the more immediate by the use of the flatted seventh notes (Bb for the C and Eb for the F). Hard-rock bass players use the minor pentatonic scale a lot for simple chord progressions because it contains the flatted seventh of the three principal chords, the I, IV, and V chords. Even though the song in this example is in the key of C major, you would want the C minor pentatonic (C, Eb, F, G, and Bb), because each of the major chord's flatted sevenths (Bb for the C, Eb for the F, and F for the G) are present.

Rock songs often contain a flatted seventh major chord, using progressions like I–bVII–IV–I, which you saw in Chapter 14. The Dorian and Mixolydian scales, in addition to the minor pentatonic, are good choices for progressions of this sort.

Between a Rock and a Hard-Rock Place

Just as accenting a note will give a harder edge to your sound, so too will more speed. Triplets and sixteenth notes sometimes show up in hard-rock songs, from alternative to punk to metal, in order to give it more urgency. A typical I–IV progression might have this kind of feel to it:

● 22.6

The addition of sixteenth notes provides a greater rush to the music. Even at slower tempos, there's so much going on that it's hard not to get carried away by the rhythm.

But the bass player isn't limited to pure speed. Smart combinations of longer notes, combined with a short burst of fast ones, can produce the same edgy feel.

🔘 22.7

Spunky Punk

Punk rock tends to be even faster, and the bass lines, for the most part, are pure root-note rhythmic lines. A lot of the dynamic in a punk bass line comes from the attack on the string itself. Bass players do a lot of palm muting, as well as sharply striking the string with a pick. The following illustration demonstrates some of the nuances you can achieve by paying attention to your right-hand technique:

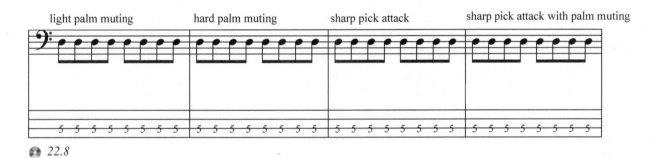

🔘 22.8

Another trademark of punk, metal, and other harder styles of rock music, is *unison* playing. When the guitar (or guitars) and bass play the same line, they are playing in unison. It may not be truly the same line—the guitar part is usually an octave higher than the bass—but depending on how low the notes are on the guitar and how high they are on the bass, they certainly might be playing the exact same notes.

Another musical characteristic of today's more mainstream pop bands is to have the guitar play a chord with a lot of distortion and let it sustain for several measures while the bass plays a stream of eighth notes beneath it, as in the following example.

Remember that none of these techniques is limited to one particular musical genre. You will hear arrangements like this last example in pop, metal, alternative, and other rock styles. As you listen to more music, you will hear bass parts from all types of music. It's up to the bassist to come up with a bass line that is appropriate to the song in question—and "borrowing" from other genres is a great way to give a new spin to an old song.

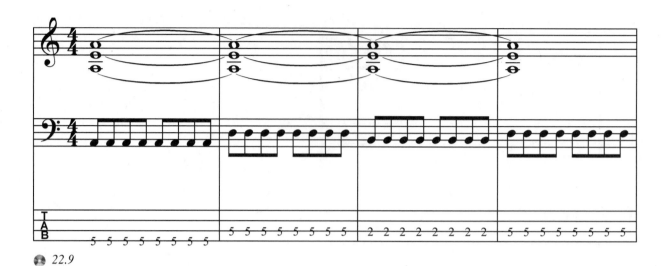

● 22.9

def•i•ni•tion

Standard tuning—having your strings tuned (from low to high) to E, A, D, and G—is just that; it's how most bass guitars are tuned. But there are certainly other ways to tune your bass guitar. Many metal bands use **lowered tunings**, tuning each string down anywhere from a half step (Eb, Ab, Db, Gb), to a whole step (D, G, C, F), to two whole steps (C, F, Bb, Eb). Another tuning favored by many metal bass players is **Drop D** tuning, when only the E string is tuned down, or "dropped," one full step to D, making the strings, from low to high, D, A, D, and G.

Full Metal Jacket

The various types of metal share a love of low notes. Often the bass players tune their basses down from standard tuning, using lowered tunings (also called "alternate tunings"). Some use five-string basses with a low B or A string.

Metal bassists can be surprisingly melodic. You will often find elegant and enchanting chord arpeggios played high up on the neck of the bass while the guitar player is scratching out the lowest power chords possible from her guitar. This switching of roles gives the bass player lots of space for fills and leads.

Metal also involves a lot of unison playing, with much more complicated timing than in punk rock.

Progressively Arty

Whether you call it art rock, progressive rock, or prog rock, this subgenre of rock music often involves complicated timings and complex chord changes. You will often find unusual time signatures and changes of keys occurring in progressive rock songs. And you'll come across a lot of sixteenth notes and sixteenth-note triplets, or three evenly spaced notes played in the space of half a beat!

The bassist, understandably, has a little more on her hands in progressive rock. A typical bass line might be something like the following.

Here you can see and hear the abrupt changes of rhythm and how the bass player holds it all together, propelling the song along in the first two measures and then strictly keeping the beat, albeit by use of some fast notes, when the time signature changes in measure three, before bounding off again in the fourth measure.

🔘 *22.10*

Two Rock-Style Jam-Along Songs

To cap off our look at the many styles of rock music, here are two jam-along songs.

Rock Song #1

We'll start out with an old-style rock jam-along song, something along the lines of "Jailhouse Rock" or "Blue Suede Shoes":

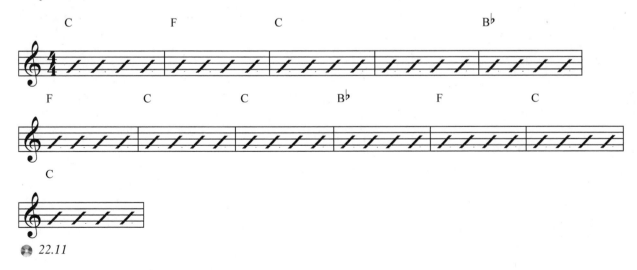

🔘 *22.11*

Listen to how the band holds off at the very beginning, playing on the very first beat of the first four measures and giving the rhythm chores for the rest of the measure to the drummer. You can choose to side with either the drummer or the rest of the band here. Or play it one way the first time and another the second time through!

Remember that dominant seventh arpeggios are fair game in this style of playing.

Rock Song #2

Our second rock song is a little edgier. Here's the chord chart:

22.12

On this one, definitely start out with just the roots and then try an occasional fill as you gain more confidence. Remember that keeping the beat is your number one priority!

The Least You Need to Know

◆ The rock bassist must both drive the song and provide harmonic support.

◆ Playing a solid rhythm line, even if it's only root notes, is more important than being flashy.

◆ Good right-hand technique can create interesting dynamics for punk rock and other types of music.

◆ Many metal bass players use "dropped" or alternate tunings.

◆ Progressive rock can involve complicated changes of both time and key signatures.

Chapter **23**

The Blues

In This Chapter

- ◆ Learning how to shuffle
- ◆ Basic blues song formats
- ◆ Discovering the blues scale
- ◆ Blues bass lines for you to play
- ◆ Two jam-along blues songs

You might remember that your very first jam-along song, all the way back in Chapter 3, was a blues song. And you played that on your bass guitar before learning any notes on the fingerboard! While the blues, in its simplest forms, might be easy to play, playing it well takes some practice. Being good at playing the blues will open all kinds of doors for you as a bass player. Many songs in other genres, notably rock, country, and bluegrass, have chord progressions that come straight from the blues. Other forms of music, such as many types of jazz and pop, use rhythmic patterns based on the blues shuffle.

Blues has many moods. It can be hard and edgy like rock or slow and melancholy like a ballad. It can be jaunty like an old folk song, uplifting like a gospel piece, or swinging like a jazz number.

Bass players might initially find playing the blues a little boring since there aren't that many chord changes, but you can always find a challenge coming up with ways to make fresh bass parts for a blues song. Because blues is often played in small groups, the bass gets plenty of chances to fill in the spaces.

Shuffling Along

The key to playing a blues rhythm is the "shuffle." You can't hear a shuffle without your head telling you, "That's the blues!" Essentially, the shuffle comes from the triplet, but you want to only play the first and third notes.

Blues shuffles can be notated in different ways. Usually a sort of shorthand is used so that the person doing the notation of the music doesn't have to write out each triplet. It's a lot easier to write eighth notes than triplets. If you see the words "swing eighths" written at the start of a piece of music, it means to play the eighth notes, even though they are written normally, in a blues shuffle style.

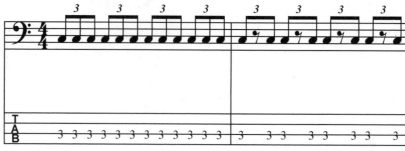

23.1

You can hear a steady stream of triplets in the first measure. In measure two, the bass switches to a blues shuffle rhythm. Notice the sense of the rhythm—it's almost like listening to a heartbeat. And it's certainly a different feel from the straight eighth-note pulse of rock.

Quite often, it's up to the bass player to carry this heartbeat throughout an entire blues song. Fortunately, the shuffle rhythm works well on arpeggios and riffs taken from scales, such as this example:

23.2

Rock Bottom

As you read in Chapter 22, many old rock 'n' roll song progressions are derived from blues music, and most are 12-bar blues. Elvis Presley's "Hound Dog," for instance, is a 12-bar blues, and many other rock songs are slight variations of the 12-bar blues. One of the more common variations uses two measures of V for measures nine and ten, instead of the single measures of V and IV. Chuck Berry's "Johnny B. Goode" and "Respectable" by the Rolling Stones are good examples of this variation on the 12-bar blues.

This riff uses the same notes as Example 22.3 from our last chapter, but you can hear there's more "swing" than "drive" to it. The shuffle, no matter what tempo you play it at, tends to amble along. You can't propel it the way you can a rock bass line.

Something in a Basic Blue

When you have the shuffle rhythm safely locked in your fingers, you can concentrate on the structure of the blues song. The 12-bar blues is far and away the most typical type of blues played today, but there are other variations worth knowing.

Most blues songs are in major keys and will use only the I, IV, and V chords of their given key. As in many rock songs, the dominant seventh chord is the prevailing tonality. You should feel free to include a flatted seventh in any arpeggios you might want to try.

Twelve-Bar Blues

"Twelve-bar blues" gets its name from being 12 measures (bars) long. Songs in 12-bar blues usually adhere to a specific chord progression:

Measures 1 through 4 use the I chord

Measures 5 and 6 use the IV chord

Measures 7 and 8 use the I chord again

Measure 9 uses the V chord

Measure 10 uses the IV chord

Measure 11 uses the I chord

Measure 12 is either the I chord or a turnaround, which will start on the I chord and end on the V chord, typically by the third beat. Often the turnaround will also include the IV chord as a passing tone from the I chord to the V chord.

Here is a lead sheet for a 12-bar blues song in the key of C, which means that C is the I chord, F is the IV, and G is the V:

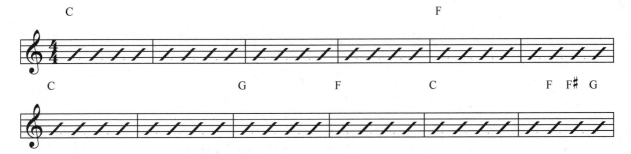

This example uses a chromatic turnaround, similar to the ones you encountered in Chapter 14. The last measure begins with one beat of C. F is played on the first half of the second beat, immediately followed by F# on the second half of the beat. G rounds things out for the final two beats of the measure.

You should be able to see why the blues can be fun for a beginning bass player. If you've got a riff you like, all you have to do is play it in three different places on the fingerboard, like this:

🔊 23.4

In this example, the riff in C begins on the C located at the eighth fret of the E string. To play the same riff in F, it's simply a matter of starting it on the eighth fret of the A string, which is the F note. Beginning the riff on G means sliding two frets up the fingerboard and starting on the tenth fret of the A string.

A Quick Change to the Standard Blues

One variation to the 12-bar blues that occurs quite often is known as the "quick change." In this variation, you go immediately from playing the I chord in the first measure to playing the IV chord in the second. Then you return to the I chord for measures 3 and 4. A lead sheet for a quick-change blues song in the key of C would look like this:

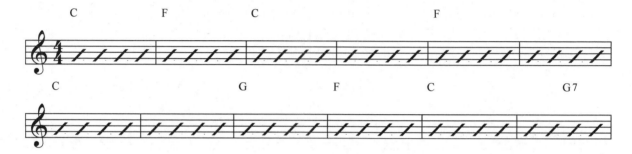

Blues classics like "Before You Accuse Me" or the first verse of "Sweet Home Chicago" are songs using the quick-change blues format.

Minor Blues, Slow Blues, and Other Oddities

Blues songs can be in minor keys, like B. B. King's "The Thrill Is Gone." Usually blues songs in minor keys use the harmonic minor scale, so they can have a major V chord. But the V tends to be used directly before the I chord, so you often end up getting a progression like this one:

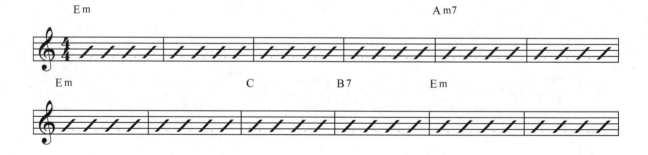

Here, measure 9 gets a C chord, which would be VI in the key of Em. This changes to B7, the V chord, in measure 10, which leads very nicely back to the Em.

As you might remember from Chapter 12, the major VII chord is another way to resolve back to a minor root. Blues songs that stay in the natural minor scale will often use a VII–VI–i progression in the final measures, as shown in the following example:

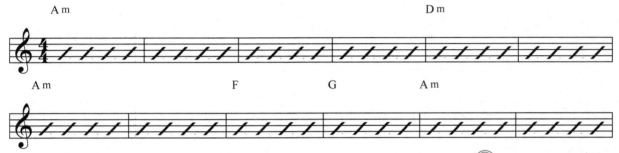

This may seem a little strange, but remember the relation of relative majors and minors. In this example, G is the relative major of Em and F is the relative major of Dm. So going from G to F to Am (VII–VI–i) is not that far off from playing Em to Dm to Am, which is v–iv–i.

Blues songs in slow tempos tend to be a little more creative in their chord progressions. While the basic I–IV–V framework remains the same, they will often incorporate chromatic chords from outside the key in order to move more dramatically to these changes. Here's a good example of a slow blues progression.

These chord changes are very deliberate. You're meant to take your time getting from the I to the IV chord, for example. Another typical blues change is demonstrated here in measures 9 and 10, when the G9 changes to F9 by way of the chromatic step F#9.

> **Covering the Basses**
>
> Ninth chords can be used as substitutes for dominant seventh chords, and often are in slow-paced blues songs. Using ninth chord arpeggios on the bass opens up the neck a little more, allowing you to expand your range during a slow blues song. A classic blues technique is to approach the target ninth chord chromatically from above.

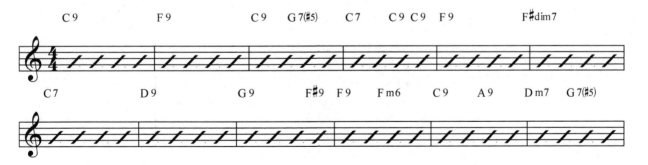

If you play more traditional blues, and we're talking about *very* old blues, you may occasionally run into an odd timing or two. Something along these lines:

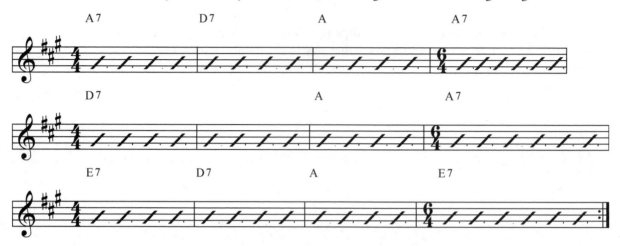

Note that measures 4, 8, and 12 are in 6/4 timing. This sort of quirk occurs in many blues songs dating before 1950. It will certainly keep you on your toes!

Blues Note Special

The blues has a feeling all its own, quite unlike other music. You're more apt to say that a country song (or pop or rock, etc.) has a "blues feel" rather than say that a blues song sounds like another genre. Part of what gives the blues its special characteristic is its sound. Even though most blues songs are in major keys, they sound a little sad.

This feeling of sadness comes, in part, from the use of "blue notes." A blue note is a note that is slightly flat. The most common blue notes are the minor (flat) third and flatted seventh. In a blues song, the vocalist or lead instrument may be singing or playing the minor third, while the rest of the band is playing a major chord. This creates a lot of musical tension and this interplay between the minor blue notes and the major chord gives the blues a lot of its signature sound.

This is why bassists often will choose to use the *minor* pentatonic scale of whichever major key the blues song happens to be in. For instance, if you were playing a blues song in C, the C minor pentatonic scale (whose notes are C, Eb, F, G, and Bb) should be the first scale you think of using to create a bass line. If you look at each note and think of that note's relationship to each of the chords being used (here the I chord is C, the IV chord is F, and the V chord is G), you can see why:

Note	C Chord	F Chord	G Chord
C	root	5th	—
Eb	minor 3rd	flat 7th	diminished 5th
F	—	root	flat 7th
G	5th	—	root
Bb	flat 7th	—	minor 3rd

As you can see, every note of the minor pentatonic is part of at least two of the three chords used in a typical blues song. Not only that, but the note also often serves as a "blue note" for at least one of the three chords.

If you use the minor pentatonic scale to solo over a blues progression, it's close to impossible to ever hit a wrong note. This scale was made for playing the blues!

The Blues Scale

Another scale that is seemingly tailor-made for the blues is the appropriately named "blues scale." In essence, the blues scale is just the minor pentatonic scale with one additional note, which is the diminished fifth. The C blues scale, in closed position, looks like this:

Some people will quibble about whether the blues scale has a "flat five" or a "sharp four," but it really doesn't matter what you call it. This extra note readily serves as a leading tone between the IV chord and the V chord (or vice versa).

Because the blues scale only has the one additional note, it's a pretty easy scale to pick up, especially since you've already got the minor pentatonic down cold. That simple extra note can spice things up a lot. Try incorporating it with some of the older jam-along songs where you found yourself favoring the minor pentatonic.

I Woke Up This Morning ...

There are all sorts of "standard" blues bass lines. As I've mentioned, learning one in root position and then transposing it to the IV and V positions can get you through any blues song. Here in the following illustration are a number of them for you to play and experiment with. Do remember to take the time to try out the ones you like in every key by cycling them through the Circle of Fifths.

Example #1

Example #2

Example #3

Example #4

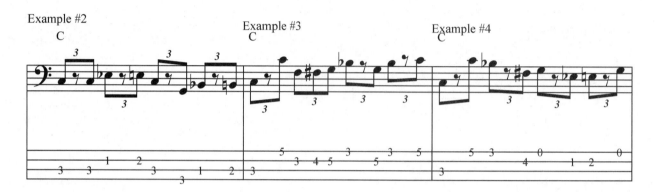

Example #5

Example #6

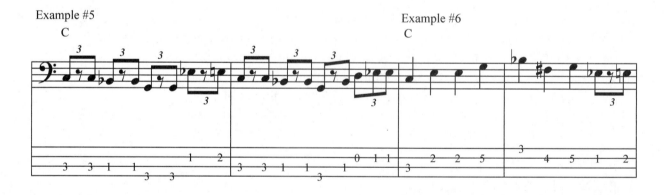

Example #7

Example #8

23.11

Two Blues Jam-Along Songs

Now it's time to put some of these blues lines to good use! Here are two new blues jam-along songs for you to play.

Blues Song #1

The first song is a hopping blues number, using the quick-change style format:

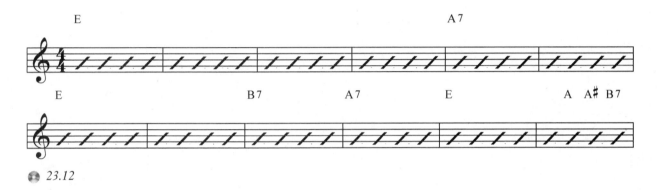

23.12

Blues Song #2

Blues Song #2 is slower and moodier. Besides using the minor pentatonic scale and the blues scale, you might also experiment with various chromatic tones, particularly in measures four through six.

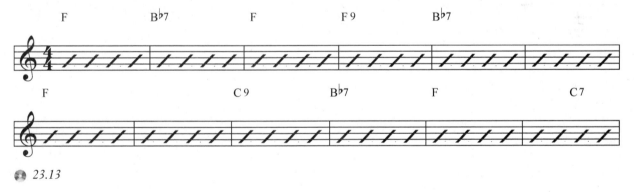

23.13

The Least You Need to Know

- Most blues songs follow the 12-bar blues format.
- In a quick-change blues song, the second measure is the IV chord, while all the other measures are the same as in 12-bar blues.
- Even though most blues songs are of the 12-bar blues variety, there are many that have different chord progressions and occasionally even different timings.
- Bass players tend to use either the minor pentatonic scale or the blues scale of the key of the song, even for blues songs in major keys.

Chapter 24

The Not-So-Loud Stuff

In This Chapter

- ◆ The role of the country bassist
- ◆ Staying out of the folk guitarist's way
- ◆ Giving pop music and ballads a solid bass line
- ◆ Learning from the best—James Jamerson and Motown
- ◆ Two jam-along songs

The electric bass guitar is a loud instrument, or it certainly can be! A lot of people are drawn to the bass by its brashness. It's not an instrument one can ignore.

But the best bass players are also masters of subtlety. They know that *not* playing, inserting a rest or two into a bass line, can be as powerful a statement as a measure of thirty-second notes played at an ear-shattering volume.

While you will find great examples of subtle bass playing in rock music, particularly in many rock ballads, the beginning bass player might find it easier to study this technique in the genres of pop, folk, and especially country music. Here the emphasis of the song is usually on the vocals and the story of the lyrics, and it's up to the bass player to provide solid support with a minimum of fanfare.

"A minimum of fanfare" doesn't mean that you don't have to work hard and be creative. It's easy to think that all you have to do on a country song is to simply show up and play an alternating bass line, but nothing could be further from the truth.

Country Cooking

If you ever doubt whether or not a bassist is important, ask yourself this question: are you more likely to notice a good bass player or a bad one?

Almost every song you hear has a bassist playing on it. There are usually some shining moments that make you sit up and think, "Wow! That's an awesome bass line!" or "I wish I could play like that!" But all the moments that you don't notice are just as important. Without the bass, most songs lack both tone and rhythm. When the bass player is doing her job, all is right in the world.

But when a bass player is off, *everyone* knows it! The rest of the band might be holding its own, but it will still sound harmonically wrong and rhythmically challenged. You'd be hard pressed to find a recording of a bad bass player because no record producer in her right mind would release a song with a truly awful bass part.

In country music, simplicity of bass lines is valued, but so are tastefulness and imagination. You've read time and time again in this book that the song has to be the bass player's primary concern. If possible, it's even more important to the country bass player.

The root and the fifth of any chord is the staple of a country bass line, but country songs will often surprise you with interesting and sometimes complex chord progressions. The change from one chord to another gives the bassist many opportunities to be creative. The use of chromatic leading tones is a good example of this.

Note also the use of half notes to create space. As a country bass player you have to remember that "wide open spaces" are good things! You should never worry about filling all the gaps.

24.1

Another good thing to remember when playing a country song is that you've got a lot of fingerboard to play with. If you play a verse of a country song along the first five frets of your bass, try moving up an octave on the chorus. In the above example, you'll notice that the open D string is used to make the shift in position during the first chord change.

Slides can be a tasteful, graceful way to make a country bass line more fun for both you and your listener. The use of slides and half notes serves to create space for the other instruments as well as the vocalist. As a country bassist you definitely want to leave room for the lead guitar or pedal steel guitar (or both), as well as the pianist and acoustic guitar player. Listening for ways to enhance your band mates' parts is also a way to improve your own playing, as well as to demonstrate your appreciation for the song in question.

Plain, Simple Folks

As much as you need to find ways to create space in country songs, you'll often have to find even more space when playing with folk musicians. There are two reasons for this: first, folk music tends to be played on acoustic instruments, and you don't want to overpower your band mates with your electric bass guitar. The use of longer notes and slow, melodic walking bass lines will help to enhance both the song you're playing as well as your own part.

Secondly, most folk guitarists tend to play a lot of bass lines on their guitars. These are usually simple walking bass lines involving I–IV and V–I progressions such as those you studied back in Chapter 13. Doubling the guitar part or even adding a harmony to it can be just the ticket for a folk song:

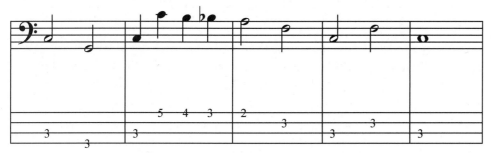

🔘 *24.2*

In this example you can hear the bass player first following along with the guitar part. Then, in the following switch from C to F, the bassist uses a chromatic descending line, which provides lovely harmony to the guitar's ascending walk up from the C to the F chord. Little touches like this one add a lot to a song.

And again, it's important to stress that you should try to make your bass part as appropriate for the song as it can be. In a folk setting, the chances are very likely that your bass guitar is going to be the loudest instrument of the group, so anything you play is going to be noticed! Make every note count, no matter how few there may be.

Top of the Pops

"Pop" is short for "popular," and labeling a piece of music as "pop" often leads to all sorts of interesting (and usually ridiculous) arguments. While no musical genre wants to claim pop as one of its own, you will often find elements of many different musical styles in pop music.

Consequently, a bass player truly needs to be tuned in to the nuances of any pop song that she plays. Is the song influenced by any one particular style? As in country and folk music, the melody or the vocal line is often the crux of the song, but there is usually a lot of room for a creative bass line.

Covering the Basses

Many of the same ideas regarding space apply to playing with bluegrass musicians. Because the focus of bluegrass is often on the lightning-fast lines of the guitar, mandolin, or fiddle, you'll want to counterbalance things with your bass by playing simply and leaving a lot of room for your bandmates.

The dotted quarter and eighth note rhythm that you first encountered in Chapter 5 gets a lot of play in pop music, with the eighth note usually setting up the first and third beats of a measure. Quite often both the bassist and the drummer will lock onto this rhythmic pattern:

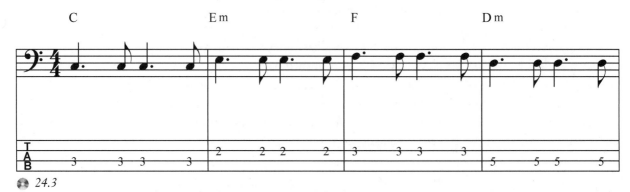

24.3

Pop songs will also often play into a call-and-response type of pattern for the bassist. For example, you might find yourself holding the rhythm steady for three measures and then be given the green light for a short fill during the fourth measure.

Chord progressions of pop music can run from being very simple to very complicated. Often this is a matter of style—some songwriters like to make it a point to use interesting chord changes—but it can also be a matter of when a song was written. Pop music from before 1950 often has chord progressions as complicated as some jazz songs! You will often find augmented chords, not to mention diminished sevenths and half-diminished seventh chords. Songs of this nature will obviously put your knowledge of chord arpeggios to good use.

On the whole, though, pop music tends to be light and airy, centering on the major tonality of a given key. Keeping your bass lines relatively diatonic (depending, of course, on the chord progression) and focusing on the roots and major thirds of your major chords will usually give your bass lines an appropriate feel for the typical pop song.

The Ballad of the Bassist

Ballads, like pop songs, tend to transcend musical genres. Many bands that might not normally find themselves on the radio often have a hit record with a ballad. Here the bass player has almost the opposite task as in playing a pop song. Instead of using different styles to add interest to the piece of pop music, she wants to incorporate enough touches of a particular genre to differentiate this ballad from another. A metal band's ballad, for instance, should have a slightly different sound to it than a country band's ballad.

Be that as it may, the same dotted quarter note and eighth note rhythm that propels many a pop song can usually be found at the heart of any ballad, regardless of its genre.

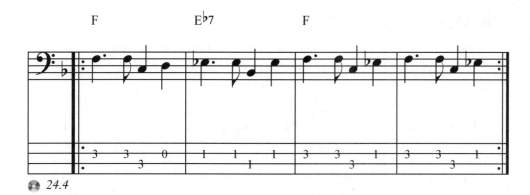

24.4

As in pop songs, chord progressions in ballads can be slightly more complex, often incorporating brief modulations of keys. In this last example, the use of the C# (the third of the A7 chord) in the second measure demonstrates the power of a simple, slow-moving bass line in a ballad.

A Little R&B

The electric bass guitar probably owes more to rhythm and blues, known as R&B, than to any other style of music. From the R&B of the '50s, to the hit machines of Motown and Stax/Volt of the '60s, to the hard funk of the '70s that continues to accent all styles of music these days, the electric bass occupied center stage. That heavy bottom made the music.

Although the vocal and the lyric might not be the focal point of an R&B song, as it is in a country song or piece of pop music, the *feel* of the song should still be the bassist's top priority. Is it a happy song or a sad one? Does it make you want to dance or cry? Is the song romantic in a coy way or downright sexy? The bassist has to tune in to the feel and bring it front and center.

Bass lines in R&B are busy—sixteenth notes pop up often and scales and arpeggios are both a big part of R&B bass riffs:

24.5

In addition to the sixteenth notes, you can also hear the use of syncopation, the accenting of the off beat, throughout the second measure. Syncopation and anticipations (from Chapter 17) are typical characteristics of R&B bass lines, as are dead notes and the use of chromatic tones.

Motown

Detroit's Motown Records produced some of the finest music of the 1960s and '70s. One reason was that they had a man named James Jamerson playing bass for their house band, the now-famous Funk Brothers.

Jamerson studied bass in high school and, after joining Motown in 1959, switched from the upright to the electric bass guitar around 1961. His musical sensibilities and technical skill on his instrument inspired the likes of Paul McCartney, John Entwistle, Jack Bruce, and many, many more of the bass players who came to prominence later in the decade. At a time when the bass guitar was a relatively new instrument, James Jamerson became the first true "born" bass guitar virtuoso.

While his style could be busy and exciting, he could also create simple, driving bass lines that worked well on many levels:

24.6

You can play riffs such as this one under a number of chord changes, because it contains notes common to many chords in its key. You could even play it with many minor chords and it would still sound perfectly fine.

Jamerson frequently used open strings in his playing, not only to shift positions, but also as passing tones in a descending direction, such as in the following example:

24.7

Here the open A string is a chromatic passing tone leading to the Ab note at the fourth fret of the E string. Try to play both of these notes using the same finger in one striking motion across both the A and E strings. This technique is called *raking* the strings.

While most bass lines involve a lot of repetition of a riff or phrase, Jamerson managed to inject his with any number of slight variations. In other words, he could play the same "basic" bass line over and over again in a song and almost never play it the exact same way twice:

🔘 *24.8*

To a casual listener, the overall feeling of the bass line stays the same. But for the bass player and for anyone else listening for it, there was no end to the little ornamentations he could dream up for a basic bass line.

This style of bass playing has become something of a lost art. Advances in digital recording have led to a lot of cut-and-paste performances where a single bass line gets sampled and looped endlessly for a song.

Jamerson's role as a Funk Brother was strictly support. But while he didn't get the spotlight or the lengthy solos, he made the bass guitar the defining sound of each record on which he played. If you ever need a bit of inspiration, or ideas of how to integrate your bass playing in a band, or if you simply want a chance to listen to some of the best bass playing ever done, put on some old Motown tunes and listen to James Jamerson, the first virtuoso of the electric bass guitar.

Two Jam-Along Songs

Here are two jam-along songs to help you solidify some of the ideas we discussed in this chapter.

A simple country song will start you out:

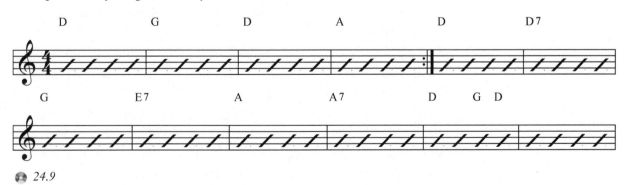

🔘 *24.9*

Remember to lock in with the drummer and to give lots of space to the other instruments of the band. Be interesting, but be sparse.

Your second song is a pop song with a little bit of a Motown feel, and it's simply waiting for you to give it even more of the Jamerson magic:

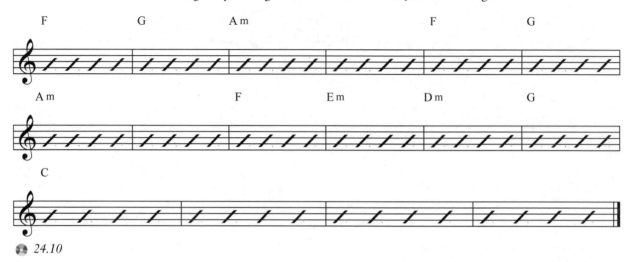

24.10

Even though you have two very contrasting jam-along songs in this section, your goal as a bassist should be the same with both songs: to come up with the best bass line you can that fits each particular song. Just because your bass line for the second song may have more notes and a more complicated rhythm, that doesn't mean that your first bass line has to be less interesting to either you or your listeners.

Remember that no matter what style a song may be, the bass playing is an important part of the sound. A bass line that you might find a little less than exciting can be exactly what a particular song needs. As you learn to appreciate being a part of the "big picture," you will undoubtedly also learn to find the joy in smaller bass parts.

The Least You Need to Know

◆ In musical styles such as country, folk, and pop, the bass is meant to support the vocals.

◆ Locking in with the drummer solidifies the band's rhythm section.

◆ Playing fewer notes with more spacing can create just as interesting a bass line as playing a lot of fast notes.

◆ Using rests as part of your bass lines gives you much more variety in your playing.

◆ Whenever you need an inspiration for your bass playing, put on some Motown music and listen to James Jamerson.

25

All That Jazz and Some Extra Spice

In This Chapter

◆ Learning to swing

◆ Playing jazz bass lines

◆ Discovering Latin rhythms

◆ Creating fusion

◆ Two jam-along songs

Every style of music poses different types of challenges to the bass guitar player. Some styles, such as rock music, involve driving rhythms and spaces that need to be filled with both notes and volume. Blues songs challenge a bassist to come up with fresh approaches to standard formats. In country and folk music, the task is to play imaginatively while creating space for your band mates and vocalists. The R&B bass player combines all of these talents while providing soul to the music.

Swing Time!

In Chapter 23 you learned about the blues shuffle rhythm. This particular pattern is the essence of swing. Bringing the triplet feel to any song will give its rhythm a swinging feel.

The blues shuffle, as you'll recall, takes a triplet and eliminates the middle note. This gives a kind of lopsided feel to the music, almost like riding on a flat tire.

It's not unusual to see the term "swing eighths" written on a piece of sheet music or a lead sheet. This means to treat all pairs of eighth notes as if they were a triplet with the middle note missing.

Let's look and listen to an example of a riff played first with straight eighth notes, and then with swing eighths.

straight eighths   swing eighths

🔊 *25.1*

Listen closely to the difference between straight eighth notes and swing eighths. Even at faster tempos, there is a tangible change of feel between swing and straight. It's pretty easy to get the swing feel into your hands once it's in your head.

Walking the Walk

You've played simple walking bass lines before, as far back as Chapter 13. Jazz walking bass lines are often a little more involved than a simple walk from the I chord to the IV chord using only the notes of the major scale.

To play a jazz walking bass line, you have to have a good concept of which key your song is in and of the notes that make up the chords in the song's chord progression. It may seem as if everything plus the kitchen sink goes into a walking bass line, but, as you'll see, there are guidelines that will help you create good ones.

Assuming that you know the key a song is in, and assuming that the song follows a "one chord per measure" chord progression, a typical walking bass line in 4/4 timing will use the following structure:

♦ First beat—The root of the chord, or a different note of the accompanying chord (such as the third or fifth).

♦ Second beat—Usually either another note of the same chord as used in the first beat, or a note from the scale of the same key as the song.

♦ Third beat—Another different note, either from the original chord or the scale of the song's key.

♦ Fourth beat—Another different note, usually a leading tone that takes you to the target note that begins the next measure.

Your target note, the one that starts the next measure, may be the root note of the new chord, but it doesn't have to be. You can also use a different note of your new chord, the third or fifth for example, as your target.

🔑 **Covering the Basses**

The chord progressions of jazz songs don't always break down conveniently into one chord per measure. If you're playing a measure where there are two chords, each one lasting two beats, then you'll need to adjust your thinking on the walk. The second beat can serve as your leading tone to the new target chord of the third beat. Depending on the chords involved, you can often use a note of the new chord as part of the original walk in order to keep to your original game plan.

A leading tone, remember, is often a chromatic step above or below your target note. Again, it doesn't have to be. For instance, if you're in the key of F and you're going from F to Am7, G is a perfectly fine note to use on the third beat.

Instead of all this discussion, let's take a look at an example of a jazz walking bass line, using a fairly typical jazz chord progression:

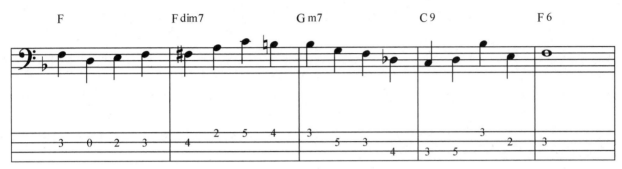

● 25.2

Note the different elements at work in this particular example. The jazz walk starts simply enough, using straight quarter notes and adhering to the guidelines we set forward earlier this section. But then swing eighth notes are added, followed by the appearance of various slurs, such as hammer-ons, pull-offs, and slides. As long as you're keeping the rhythm steady (that's your main priority, remember!) you can jazz up your jazz walk in many different ways.

Two-Note Jazz Bass

Walking jazz bass lines are busy. There's constant motion and resting places are few and far between. The two-note style of jazz bass gives you a little breathing space by concentrating on the first and third beats of any given measure. Usually the second and fourth beats are rests, although you might have a pick-up triplet to carry you on to the upcoming beat.

The following example is a jazz progression done in two-note style. Usually the roots and fifths are the two notes used, but octaves and chromatic leading tones are also good possibilities, especially when combining the two-note style with a Latin rhythm, about which you'll be reading shortly.

You can almost think of the two-note style as practice toward a jazz walking bass line. On jazz tunes played at a fast tempo, you might not hear much difference between the two-note style and the walk, since you'll be playing the two notes rather quickly! The "two-note" style is used a lot in "Gypsy Jazz" music, such as that of Django Reinhardt and Stephane Grappelli.

Both the two-note style and the jazz walking bass line translate well to other genres of music. You'll see the two-note in many of the upcoming examples of Latin rhythms, while the walking bass line shows up in blues, country, rock, and other musical styles.

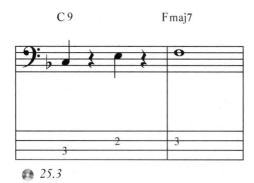

25.3

Latin Rhythms

It's easy to be confused by the term "Latin" music. It's not, as you know, the music of the ancient Roman Empire! Rather, it is the music of Latin America, which covers a lot of territory—Central and South America as well as all the islands of the Caribbean.

Just as confusing, many styles of Latin music have similar rhythms, and, to the beginner, it's hard to work out one from another. Let's try to cover some of the basic rhythms you'll encounter and also give you some ideas for bass lines that will work for most Latin rhythms.

I've Got Your Rumba

Technically, the rumba rhythm is African in origin, but what we think of today as rumba is more a mixing of African- and Caribbean-influenced rhythms. While you can hear rumbas at all tempos, they tend to be in the slow to medium range.

You can see and hear the essential rhythm of the rumba, as well as many other Latin rhythms, in the first four measures of the following example.

🔘 *25.4*

Meet the Bossa Nova

The bossa nova, like many Latin rhythms, comes to us from Brazil. Bossa nova bass lines, at heart, are simply alternating bass lines—that is, they are bass lines using mostly the roots and fifths of the chords. They feature the dotted quarter and eighth note rhythm that you learned back in Chapter 5:

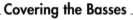 **Covering the Basses**

In a strange way, the best approach to playing bossa nova–styled songs is to adapt the same "bass mentality" of the country bass player. You want to provide a lot of space, giving the song a light and airy feel. Because bossa novas tend to have very colorful chord progressions, often rivaling jazz songs in terms of complexity, you will have all sorts of chances to use chromatic steps to get from one chord to the next.

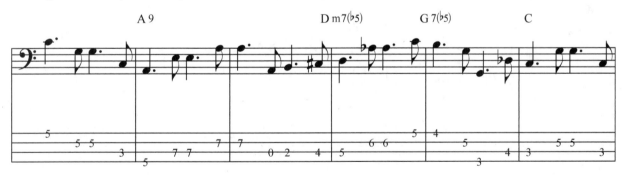

🔘 *25.5*

The first two measures of this example work the root-fifth alternating style. If you don't want to think of it as an alternating bass line, think of it as a two-note style, as in our earlier jazz examples.

The final measures of this example incorporate some short walking bass lines and then some chromatic steps into the mix. You'll also notice the use of diminished fifths when the accompanying chord calls for it. You'll often find diminished chords used in the progressions of bossa nova–styled songs.

25.6

Other Notable Latin Rhythms

Wherever you go in Latin America and the Caribbean, you will find all sorts of variations of Latin rhythms, usually each with its own name. Calypso, which uses the same basic rhythm as the rumba while stressing the notes of the triads, can be found all over the islands. Merengue, on the other hand, is found predominantly in the Dominican Republic.

Many styles, as you've already found out, are the result of blending various influences. The tango, for instance, combines elements of African rhythms and opera-like melodies with chord progressions typically found in Spanish music.

Today's American music has also made its way into the mix. Soca is a blending of R&B, or soul music, with calypso. And, as you'll learn in a moment, many elements of funk style bass playing can be found in Afro-Cuban music.

The preceding example is a small sampling of bass lines that you can use with some of these other Latin rhythms.

Latin rhythms pop up in many songs, from pop and rock to jazz. Flavoring the bass line of a pop song with a Latin rhythm can bring a fresh perspective on it. Many jazz standards get played with Latin rhythms and many Latin songs have become jazz standards.

Afro-Cuban Rhythms

Afro-Cuban music is another blending of styles, taking aspects from various Latin and Caribbean rhythms and mixing them with African influences. As mentioned earlier, some rhythms that have been traditionally thought of as Latin, such as the rumba, are actually Afro-Cuban or Afro-Caribbean combinations. Depending on where you live, all Afro-Cuban rhythms might be lumped under the label of "salsa." Mambo music blends African rhythms with Spanish musical stylings. You might need the assistance of a musical historian to sort it all out!

As with most Latin rhythms, you will often find jazz songs done in Afro-Cuban style. You will also find a lot of funk stylings in the Afro-Cuban bass playing of pros such as Lincoln Goines and Sal Cuevas. Once you have the rhythm established, you can begin to improvise around it, as in the following example.

This riff begins with a simple rumba rhythm, which extends over the first four measures. Then it adds a few fills that keep in line with the basic rhythm. Even when you throw in some slapping and popping, you want to keep the rhythm at the heart of your playing.

🔘 25.7

Fusion

Fusion, as you might guess, involves a mixing, or fusing, of musical styles. For most musicians, fusion means combining the speed and flurry of rock and funk with the harmonic complexities of jazz music.

Bass lines in fusion are frenetic and edgy, full of sixteenth notes and chromatic tones. Often, too, they are liberally laced with dead notes, as in the following example:

🔘 25.8

Strangely enough, you will often find long passages of single chords in fusion music. These can be opportunities for solos, or, if someone else in the band is soloing, for fairly complex rhythmic bass riffs. You don't want to make it so complicated that you overshadow the solo, but you can create interlocking layers of musical ideas that keep the song interesting through these long, single-chord passages.

Two Jam-Along Songs

You get two different jam-along songs with this chapter—a bossa nova and an Afro-Cuban style song.

With each of these jam-along songs, your best bet is to start out simply getting the feel of the rhythms. Don't worry if you find yourself playing only root notes or alternating between octaves and fifths. That will sound absolutely fine with this music.

As you develop more of a sense of a song's rhythm, you will begin to venture farther with your bass lines. Remember that the idea is to learn to play *with* the song, as opposed to being at odds with it! Just as you have with past jam-along songs, try to come up with several bass lines that fit each song.

Bossa Nova Jam-Along Song

Even though the chord progression of our bossa nova is slightly complex, you should get a good feel for it rather quickly by starting with a roots-only bass line:

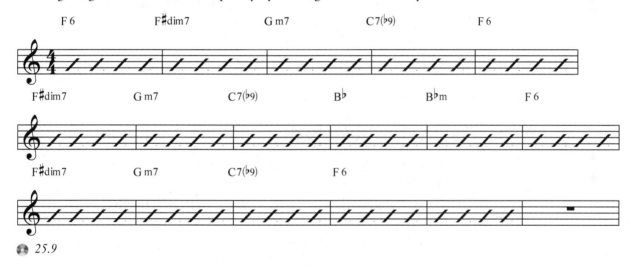

25.9

You can hear how the roots of the first three chords (F to F# to G) are simple chromatic steps from each other. And since Gm7 to C7b9 is, at heart, ii to V in the key of F, you should be able to come up with all sorts of ideas for this jam-along song.

Afro-Cuban Jam-Along Song

Our Afro-Cuban jam is very simple in terms of chord structure in order to allow you a good chance to get into the rhythm. Unlike our other jam-along songs, we'll let the bass kick this one off so you can get a good feel for it:

25.10

A little bit of thought can go a long way toward creating a bass line. Start by examining the notes of the two chords, C and Gm. C is made up of C, E, and G, while Gm is made up of G, Bb, and D. If you put all these notes together, you'd have a C9 chord (C, E, G, Bb, and D). You can come to the conclusion that riffing over a C9 arpeggio would give you a solid place from which to create some cool bass lines:

Start out with a fast but simple (using only roots and fifths if necessary) bossa nova or rumba. Once you feel comfortable, add the two other notes of the C9 chord arpeggio, namely Bb and D. Then work in notes of the C major or G natural minor scales to fill in some riffs.

Grooves like this one are terrific for trying out some improvisations as well. Be sure to come back to this particular jam-along song after reading up on funk in the next chapter. Have a lot of fun with it!

The Least You Need to Know

- Many jazz songs use swing eighths, which are played in the same rhythm style as a blues shuffle.

- The walking jazz bass line will work in almost all jazz songs and is a lot of fun to play.

- Rhumba, bossa nova, merengue, salsa, and tango are all examples of Latin rhythms.

- Afro-Cuban rhythms often involve a lot of syncopation, and you can throw many elements of funk into Afro-Cuban bass lines.

- Fusion music often contains complex, jazz-type chord progressions, but you may also run into long passages of a single chord.

Chapter 26

We Are the World

In This Chapter

- ◆ How to get funky
- ◆ Dance, disco, and hip-hop
- ◆ The art of reggae and ska bass lines
- ◆ Bass lines from Africa and Asia
- ◆ Three jam-along songs

Music makes the world go around. There are more styles of music than you'll ever hear, let alone learn. From a chant in an open-air market in Marrakech to electronic dance music in Berlin, from an Irish folk song to a Broadway show tune, from a French chanson to the latest heavy metal offering of a band from Norway, from raucous rock music out of Australia to the simple strains of a melody played on a Chinese erhu, you will find music everywhere.

As you learned in our last chapter, many musical styles from various parts of the world are interrelated. You will find African rhythms in Latin songs, and you will hear Motown-inspired bass lines in Cuban music.

While we cannot cover every type of music one may hear, you can learn about many of the genres whose influence you will discover in many musical styles around the globe.

Bring on the Funk

Funk music is rhythm-driven. Funk bass lines usually center around the use of sixteenth notes as well as various percussive techniques. Slapping and popping have a big role in funk bass playing, but bassists who favor finger style can certainly be funky, too!

As a funk bassist, you will often find yourself playing long passages under a single chord or, as in the Afro-Cuban jam-along song from the last chapter, a group of chords that share common notes. Finding an extended chord, such as a ninth or eleventh, that contains all or most of the notes of your progression and using that extended chord as a starting point to create your bass line is a smart move.

The following example is typical of a bass line you might play in a funk song:

● 26.1

Notice the use of short rests (usually a beat or half a beat in duration) that give this example a breathing quality. The music seems more alive when it's broken up into small phrases. Also note the use of the slap/pop style of play, not to mention both slapping and popping used on their own.

Funk, like R&B, is all about the feel. You might not be able to explain funk in words, but you certainly know what sounds funky and what doesn't. It's a combination of quickness, spacing, and percussive sound quite unlike other styles.

You can incorporate elements of funk into many other musical styles, particularly dance and various Latin and African types of music. Even rock music can take a healthy injection of funk!

Disco and Dance

Even if you weren't alive in the '70s, you've probably heard the song "YMCA" more than once. Disco is dance music, but it's fairly light in tone and texture compared to today's "dance" dance music.

Typical disco bass lines will involve octaves played in the slap/pop style. Even simple I–IV walking bass lines, such as those from Chapter 13, get this treatment. Be prepared to strongly accent the beat, especially the first one of each measure.

Dance, like disco, stresses the beat but is more driving than disco. Think of it as disco with rock overtones. You will find both syncopations and anticipations more common in dance than in disco.

Bass lines in both disco and dance tend to use the minor pentatonic scale a lot, as the box shape makes for easy fingering of repeated riffs. Having your fingers ready in a box shape also allows you to play octaves at a moment's notice.

Here are examples of each of these styles:

Example of Disco Bass Line

Example of Dance Bass Line

🔘 26.2

Hip-Hop

"Heavy," in music slang, often translates as "low," meaning low notes. The bass player brings the heavy music to any band. Some styles of music, such as hip-hop and reggae, get their trademark sounds from playing as low a note as possible on the neck of the bass guitar. A "heavy" and hypnotic, repetitive bass line is precisely the ticket for most hip-hop songs.

Hip-hop is not as busy as funk, disco, or dance. While you'll get plenty of chances to toss in some slapping and popping, you'll also often find places where a short rest will make a bass line stand out:

🔘 26.3

> ### Covering the Basses
> In hip-hop, the message is the music. That means the bassist has to make supporting the vocals the top priority, just as it is the number-one concern of the country bass player. In hip-hop, though, the vocals are very much an integral part of the song's rhythm. Keying in on the vocals is just as important as keying in on the drums. You will get a lot of ideas for both rhythm and space from listening to the vocalists.

Like rock music, hip-hop favors the use of flatted sevenths of chords. You will also find many opportunities to throw in chromatic notes, especially when changing to a new chord.

Just as with disco and dance, you may find hip-hop extremely repetitive at times. Putting in minor variations on your bass lines, just as you learned in the Motown section in Chapter 24, can make playing a little more interesting to both you and your listeners, but also remember that strict repetition can create a very hypnotic dance beat. Your first concern should be to not distract from the message of the music.

Reggae

If funk is about keeping busy, then reggae is about laying back. The grooves of reggae are just as compelling as those of funk, but in an almost opposite style. The reggae bass line can be slow and melodic or fast and angular but it always yields to space. There are a lot of rests, often on the first beat of a measure.

Reggae stresses the off beats while being played with a triplet feel. You will often find reggae music written with many triplets, or with some indication of "swing eighths." In the following example, be sure to use swing eighths in the second measure:

🔊 *26.4*

Chord arpeggios are frequently used in reggae in order to help establish tonality. This last example combines two notes of an arpeggio with a short scale run leading to a new two-note arpeggio. Reggae tends to be diatonic in nature, but you will find uses for the occasional chromatic tone. Notice the use of the slide at the end of the riff as a kind of turnaround.

In reggae, what you don't play is probably more important than what you do. It's not unusual to have rests of a full measure at a time. It's important to listen to the drummer and your other band mates and to feel comfortable having *totally* empty space.

Keep your notes short and to the point. It's not written in stone, but a good practice habit is to balance every flashy run with an equal amount of rest space.

Ska

Ska is like reggae music that's had too much caffeine. The accent is still on the backbeat but the pace is usually much quicker. As a bassist, you'll get a better feel for it if you think more in terms of R&B bass lines than rock ones.

🎵 *26.5*

Providing your ska bass line with some rests will bring space to the song despite its speed. You will often find rests on the first beat of a measure in both ska and reggae music. And both these styles, while busy, are full of space.

African and Asian Music

The rhythm of African drums can be heard in music styles all around the world. In Chapter 25 you learned of quite a few African rhythms that are considered part of Latin music or Afro-Cuban music, such as rumbas, salsas, and merengues.

Most bass guitar lines in African music come from the beat of the drums. The rhythmic aspect of playing is far more important than being flashy. Still, there is more than enough room for a good bass player to show off her skills.

🎵 *26.6*

Listening to this example, you can hear how other styles of music, especially Latin and fusion styles, borrow a lot from African rhythms. The emphasis on the off beat, the use of chord arpeggios, and even the triplet feel can be found in music across the globe.

African music can be very syncopated, as you just heard. But it can also be pretty straightforward in terms of timing. The following example is more in the style of *mnaqanga*, the electric guitar style of pop music from South Africa.

> ### Covering the Basses
>
> The differences between many of the musical styles covered in the past two chapters may seem small, but people who play these types of music will tell you otherwise. The best way to learn more about the various nuances of any musical genre is to listen to the music. If you can't afford to buy a lot of CDs, then listen to your radio. Better still, check out online radio sites. You can find great directories, such as www.radiofreeworld.com, www.internetradioindex.com, and www.worldmusiccentral.org, that can connect to music from almost everywhere in the world.

🔘 *26.7*

This bass line is infectious—happy, light, and effortlessly moving the song along. You can easily add some slap/pop technique to the first half of any measure to give your bass line a little more of a percussive sound.

Trying to put a single label on Asian music is just as ridiculous as saying African music (or any continent's, for that matter) is all one style. Arabic and Middle Eastern music use different modes, which are based on the minor harmonic scale instead of the major scale. Traditionally, bass lines in Asian music are fairly simple, often serving more as a drone than as a bass line as we think of them today.

But things are changing. Asian music today reflects many Western styles, particularly when it comes to the bass guitar. Most of what you've learned in this book will apply to playing modern Asian music.

Three Jam-Along Songs

You get three different jam-along songs to finish off this chapter—a funk number, a reggae song, and something with a West African flavor. Enjoy!

Funk-Style Jam-Along Song

Playing a bass line for a funk song can scare off a beginning bassist, so I've tried to give you something very easy to get you over any potential jitters:

E m7   (repeat a lot!)

🔘 *26.8*

Hear the bass drum kicking out two eighth notes to start each measure? Key in on that to get you started. Like the Afro-Cuban jam-along song from our last chapter, you can simply sit on a single-chord arpeggio (in this case an Em, Em7, or Em9 will do) to give yourself an anchor for your bass line. As you gain confidence in your ability to hold down the rhythm, experiment with some slapping and popping to spice up your part.

🔑 **Covering the Basses**

Don't forget to revisit jam-along songs from past chapters of the book, even ones from the very first two sections. Try to incorporate new techniques and ideas into earlier exercises. It will improve both your playing and the old songs!

There is a lot of space here, but don't feel obligated to fill it all up! Work instead with short phrases, such as the ones you picked up in Chapter 19 (the section on "single-chord riffs") and try stringing a few together.

Reggae-Style Jam-Along Song

Our reggae jam-along song adds the challenge of being in a minor key:

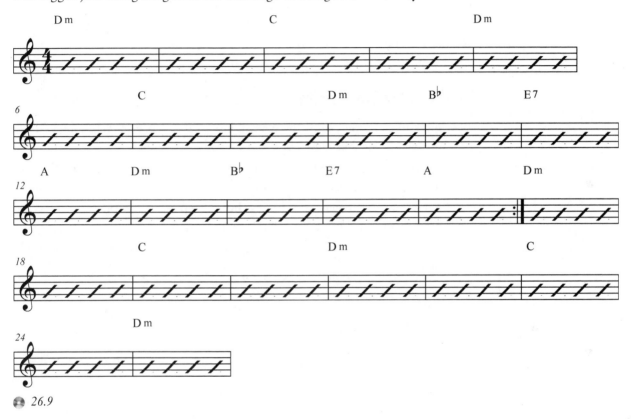

🌐 *26.9*

There are some interesting things to play off of here. Most of the song is in the key of D minor and you can happily come up with bass lines using either chord arpeggios or notes from the D natural minor scale. But when the chord progression switches from Bb to E7, that heralds a short modulation into the key of A major, which is the V chord of the D harmonic or D melodic minor scales.

West African–Style Jam-Along Song

We conclude our jam-along songs with one in the style of West African music:

🌐 *26.10*

Because of the style of the instrumentation, you may not recognize that the chord progression is a simple I–vi–IV–V, just like those you learned back in Chapter 13. There's quite a difference between this song and '50s-style doo-wop, isn't there?

As in reggae, you've got plenty of space for the bass at the beginning of each measure. Listen to the drums and other instruments and try to give each one a little room to groove.

When you get more comfortable playing different styles of music, you will probably notice different aspects of your favorite musical genres creeping into *all* your bass lines. This is a normal part of the evolution of a bassist—you're developing a style that will be your own and no one else's.

The Least You Need to Know

- ◆ Funk music is percussive by nature. Use of the slap/pop technique is prevalent, but there's lots of room for finger style play.
- ◆ Rhythm is the number-one priority when it comes to playing bass lines in the various genres of dance music.
- ◆ When playing reggae and ska bass lines, keeping the chord harmonies prominent is as important as keeping the rhythm.
- ◆ African and Asian music offer both challenges and inspiration to bass players.

Taking Care of Your Best Friend

In This Chapter

- ◆ Keeping your bass clean
- ◆ How to change your strings
- ◆ Making minor adjustments and repairs
- ◆ When to call in help
- ◆ Putting together a gig bag

Playing the bass guitar, as I've mentioned before, is a lifelong relationship. And all relationships require care and attention. Usually the more attention and care you put into a relationship, the better it gets.

Your bass guitar may not seem to need much attention, but simple little things will go a long way toward keeping it at its best. In this chapter we will go over how to give your bass the care it needs for a long life.

Daily Duties

Hopefully, you play your bass every day. Maybe not for long periods of time, but for whatever time you can make free for practicing and playing. You should also set aside a small fraction of that time for some basic maintenance of your bass guitar.

String Cleaning

"Basic" could easily be substituted with the word "obvious." When you think about playing your bass, the first thing that should spring to mind is the state of your hands. After all, your hands are all over your bass guitar. If you've just eaten a handful of potato chips, then you'll soon have salt, oil, and miniscule potato crumbs all over your bass guitar as well!

Washing your hands before picking up and playing your bass guitar is obviously a good start. But remember that your hands have natural oils as well. No matter what, you're going to leave fingerprints, oil, and possibly a little sweat on your guitar before you put it down.

Just as important—you're also leaving a lot of dirt and oil on your strings. Strings get dirty very easily and that dirt will end up on your fingerboard as well, since you're constantly pushing the strings onto the frets and neck of your bass guitar.

Whenever you are finished playing your bass guitar for the day, try to take the following steps before putting it away:

Take a clean, dry cloth (cotton is always good, so are "shimmies," the cloths they use at car washes) and wipe the body of your bass guitar. Try to get rid of any obvious fingerprints and smudges. If you succeed at that, then you've gotten the body pretty clean. Don't forget to also wipe the back and sides!

After dealing with the body of the guitar, wipe the back of the neck down. If your cloth is thin enough, slip it between the strings and the frets so that you can also wipe dirt and oil from the fingerboard.

Lightly clean the headstock. I say "lightly" because you don't want to go knocking the tuning mechanisms all out of whack!

Take a second clean, dry cloth and, using your thumb and finger to pinch it around a string, wipe the string along the entire length of the bass guitar.

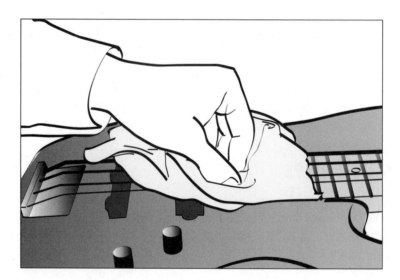

Repeat this with each string of your instrument. You can also use a bit of rubbing alcohol, which you can find in any supermarket or drug store, and put a drop or two onto the cloth before wiping the strings. Be sure to only put it on the cloth! Getting the rubbing alcohol on your fingerboard (or any part of the wood) will dry the wood out. You don't want that!

Keeping Things Cool and Calm

Finally, put your bass guitar away. This may be easier said than done. After all, if you play a lot, you probably don't want to be constantly taking out a case, taking out the bass guitar, putting away the case, playing the bass, and taking out the case again so you can put your instrument back into it before stowing the case a final time.

Most electric bass guitars are solid wood, so you don't have to treat it too differently than you would a houseguest. Whatever you would do to make your guest comfortable will usually work for your bass guitar. Try to keep your instrument out of direct sunlight and away from any significant sources of heat and cold (not directly in front of a heat vent or air conditioner, for example), and also out of any major thoroughfares of your home.

If you have a guitar stand, you can use it for your instrument without worry, provided that you've placed the guitar stand someplace where it's unlikely some family member, guest, or pet will be knocking into it, which usually leads to it falling over on the floor.

If you're not going to be playing for an unusual amount of time, keeping the instrument in its case is the best idea. Again, don't leave the case someplace where it will get overly hot or cold. A cool closet is okay.

The Strings, They Need a-Changin'

Some people think the strings of their bass guitar are immortal. I have met bassists who still have the original strings on their instrument, the ones that came with the bass when they bought it. Compared to guitarists, who often obsess about when to change their guitar strings, bass players seem to *never* think about whether the strings of their instruments need to be changed.

But bass guitar strings get a lot of wear and tear. Each time you play them, they collect a little more dirt. Occasionally, rarely though, they'll even break as guitar strings are wont to do. Having seen this happen on stage during a show, I can tell you that you never want that to happen to you! Trying to finish a song with only three strings is not something that many people practice ahead of time.

Why and When

Old strings sound flat and dull. If your bass doesn't sound like it used to, it may simply need a new set of strings.

Likewise, if your strings feel or look significantly different, then you may benefit from a change. There can be obvious signals, such as discoloration or rust in various spots along the length of the string. There can also be more subtle signs—a lack of smoothness when you slide from one note to another, for instance. You're the one who handles the strings of your bass every day, so you will certainly notice when something just feels wrong.

It's good to set up a string-change schedule. If you play a lot, meaning four or more hours a day consistently, then you probably want to change your strings two or three times a year. Bassists of a more recreational nature, playing an average of four to ten hours a week, can change strings once a year or even once every 18 months.

Covering the Basses

There's a lot of debate as to whether or not it's better to change one string at a time or to change them all at once. Usually it depends on the situation. If you've got a single broken string, then changing just the one seems to make sense. But if you've got a single broken string and the remaining bass strings haven't been changed since gas prices were less than a dollar a gallon, you might as well go and change the whole set. Another thing to remember is that strings tend to wear at the same rate. When one goes, the others may not be far behind. Better to simply change them all and start fresh.

How

Putting new strings on your bass guitar may seem like a daunting task, but it's fairly easy to do. You'll need a good pair of wire cutters (remember that your bass strings are pretty thick!) and a set of new strings.

Before you begin to remove the old strings, take a look at how your old strings attach to the bridge of the bass guitar, how they sit in the saddle, and how each string is wrapped around the tuning pole. Be certain you know which string goes with which tuning pole and also which hole in the bridge each string goes into. Chances are you've never looked this closely at your strings before! Being familiar with how they are attached in the first place will give you ideas if something looks wrong later in the process.

Pay special attention to how the strings are wrapped on the tuning pole. The wrap should start at the top of the pole and wind downward along the pole. Also take note of which way the strings tighten and loosen. Also, if your headstock has a "string guide" for the thinner strings (D and G), make a mental note of how the strings fit onto or under it.

Detune your old strings slightly, giving them more slack. Then take your wire cutters and clip them, one at a time. The easiest place to do this is between the tuning peg and the nut (where the headstock joins the neck of the bass guitar). When you've cut the strings, gently pull them out (again, one at a time!) through the back of the bridge. Unwind and pull the remaining part of the old strings from the tuning pole.

Once you've removed the strings, you might want to make the most of the opportunity and give the fingerboard a thorough cleaning before putting on your new set of strings.

To put on your new strings, begin with the E string. Take it out of its package and uncoil the string. On one end will be a little metal ball. That's the end that gets anchored to the bridge of the bass guitar. The other end will be wrapped, usually in silk. Feed that end through the hole in the bridge and gently pull the string through so that the metal ball is now resting on the bridge.

Pull the string so that the silk end reaches the appropriate tuning pole. You'll see that there's a deep groove in each tuning pole and a hole in the bottom of the groove.

You probably will need to trim the string a little. You'll need between four to five inches of additional string beyond the tuning pole. Use your wire cutters to clip off the excess. Be certain to only cut the wrapped portion of the string. Cut the metal part of the string and it will unravel, and you'll need a new string to replace your new string!

Now, take the tip of the trimmed string and insert it, straight down, into the hole in the groove of the tuning post, as shown in the following figure.

Once inserted, bend the string so that it lies in the groove of the tuning post and pull it slightly toward the inside of the tuning post. Then begin to tighten the string by turning the tuning peg.

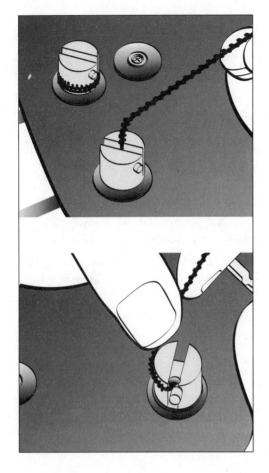

Covering the Basses

One good argument for changing all the strings at once is that doing so offers you a chance to thoroughly clean your fingerboard and even polish your frets. When polishing the frets, use something like the jewelry cloths they sell at grocery stores (the ones with the polish already in the cloth). Your local music store may also have "fret cleaning kits" that you can buy. But be careful! Working with frets requires time and patience. You don't want to get anything on your fingerboard that will either damage it or otherwise hinder your ability to play smoothly. When in doubt, just use a clean, dry cloth!

Be certain that the string is wrapping itself downward on the tuning pole. Each loop around the pole should be lower than the previous one:

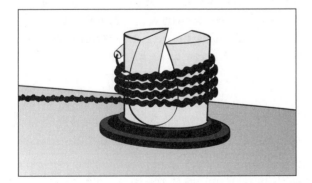

While you're tightening the string, also remember to keep an eye on the other end of your bass guitar. Make sure that the string is sitting properly in the saddle.

Don't worry about tuning the new string just yet. When you've got the string tightened so that there is no appreciable slack, start in on the A string. Only when you have all four strings in place should you get out your tuner and set to work on tuning the strings.

Once you have all four strings on and tuned (see Chapter 3), give each string a gentle tug away from the body of the guitar (like pulling a bow string) and tune all four strings again. It will take a while for the strings to stretch out, so be prepared to repeat the tuning process three to six times before they are ready to play.

Minor Maintenance and Repairs

Your bass guitar doesn't need a lot of attention as much as it needs your common sense. You can do a lot of things to keep it clean and at its best, but there are a number of things that are better left to the professionals. How do you know which is which? Most times your gut will tell you. If you have a degree in electronics or have worked on the insides of electric guitars and other instruments, then you will have a better idea of what to fix than the average person.

It doesn't mean you can't learn how to do a lot of seemingly complicated work on your instrument. But learn under the eye of someone who knows what he is doing!

More Cleaning!

Most maintenance involves keeping things clean. Keeping things clean usually involves using the right tools for the right job. You can find guitar polish and fingerboard oil at your local music store. A dust cloth can keep your tuning pegs and poles shiny and sparkling.

A lot of dust tends to accumulate around the pickups. You don't want to use any kind of liquid or polish on these! Try cotton swabs or your old standby, the clean, dry cloth.

Loose Screws

If you notice that you have a loose screw, one holding a backing plate or a pick guard in place, then find an appropriately sized screwdriver and tighten it. The key here is finding the right-sized screwdriver. Don't use a regular screwdriver on a Phillips-head screw. You don't want to strip a screw while it's still in your bass.

Action and Intonation

Some screws are for special purposes. The screws in the bridge and saddle area of your bass guitar, for example, can be used to adjust the action and the intonation of your instrument.

The *action* is how high the strings sit in relationship to the frets. The screws in the saddle area adjust the height of the saddle, thus changing the action of your guitar.

The screws at the bottom of the saddle (usually found in the same place where you insert the strings of your bass guitar) adjust the intonation of each string.

To check the intonation of your guitar, play the harmonic of the G string at the twelfth fret. Make certain that it's in tune with the tuner. Then play the G note at the twelfth fret of the G string. It should be perfectly in tune with both the tuner and the harmonic. If it's not, then the intonation of your guitar is slightly off.

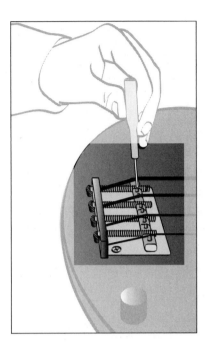

By adjusting the saddle screws, you can shorten or lengthen the string, which adjusts the intonation. This can be a long and involved process and unless you have a lot of patience and a very good ear, might be best left to a professional.

But it is something that you can learn. If you have a friend who's very mechanically minded (or better yet, is a guitar technician), try to see if you can sit in on an intonation or action adjustment. Things of this nature are better learned by watching and asking questions of someone with experience.

This is particularly true of truss-rod adjustments. While anyone can do a truss-rod adjustment, it's a very tricky thing to talk someone through it without being there to demonstrate. It is something you'll want to learn, though, so make friends with your local guitar technician and have him show you the ropes.

Calling In the Experts

Electronics, just like strings and other parts of your bass guitar, need occasional care and attention. It's best to turn these kinds of problems over to your local guitar technician. Many newer basses are coming equipped with all sorts of gadgets and circuitry, and it's best to not mess around with an annoying crackling and make it worse.

Using Your Head

Most maintenance and repair can be dealt with simply. Ultimately you are the one who knows your bass best. You can take courses and get books and read up on more complicated minor repairs. You can get a cheap used bass on which to practice things like soldering or truss rod adjustments. The more you learn about your instrument, physically, the more maintenance and repair work you'll be able to perform.

Being Prepared

If you play at gigs and shows, you never know when you're going to need to use your repair knowledge. Strings can break, screws can fall out. You never know what kind of crisis may occur. But you can be prepared for almost any type of emergency if you take the time to think about it first.

Tool Bag

In addition to your bass guitar case, it's smart to have a small carry bag that can serve two purposes: you'll want it to be a tool bag as well as a gig bag. Obviously, a tool bag will hold all the tools you may need to repair your bass. Keeping your cleaning items along with the tools is a great idea. This should include (but is certainly not limited to):

- Screwdriver (or Allen wrench)—better yet, have one for each size screw on your bass guitar
- Allen wrench for the truss rod
- Spare set of strings and wire cutters
- Rubbing alcohol and clean, dry cloths

Gig Bag

In addition to your tools and cleaning implements, it's a good idea to have all the things you need for performance together in one place. Certain items, such as additional strings and a tuner, may be considered parts of both bags. Here are items that you definitely want to consider making a part of your gig bag:

- Tuner
- Cables (keep one or two spares)
- Extra strap (no one will have a spare if yours breaks)
- Portable guitar stand and music stand
- Extra picks (if you play with picks)
- Spare battery (if you have a bass with active electronics)
- Roll of duct tape

Don't laugh about the last item. If you play out a lot, you will discover that a roll of duct tape can be incredibly useful. It can keep you from tripping over speaker cables and extension cords and it can hold together a case that's decided to fall apart for no apparent reason!

The Least You Need to Know

- Keep your bass clean and help it avoid drastic changes in climate.
- Change your strings on a regular basis—make a schedule that fits your playing time.
- Use common sense when deciding whether or not to seek expert help with repairs to your instrument.
- Put together a tool bag and a gig bag (or a combo bag) that contains all the possible things you might need when playing away from home.

Chapter 28

Afterword

You have reached the last chapter of this book, but you have also come to your new starting point. From here you begin a new level of learning and practicing and playing. That's hardly what I'd call an ending.

It may already seem like another lifetime ago that you first picked up your bass guitar and learned how to tune it, how to fret and sound a note, how to read music and bass tablature, how to play your first major scale. It's easy to forget that you weren't born knowing all that information, especially when you are feeling that you haven't made much improvement as a bassist or a musician.

Playing the bass guitar, or any musical instrument, is a lifetime adventure. For most musicians, learning and improving are everyday activities that never stop. The opportunity to make your own music can make any day special. Playing music makes you happy, and being happy, usually, gives you a better outlook on life.

Following the lessons and exercises of this book, learning some of the fundamentals of music and music theory, creating your own bass lines and trying them out on some of the jam-along songs—all this has hopefully given you a solid foundation to become a good bassist. Before you get on with the next stage of your bass-playing odyssey, I'd like to leave you with some thoughts and ideas to guide you to getting better each day at your instrument.

Being the Best Bassist You Can Be

There are two final pieces of advice that I'd like to give you:

The first is let the song dictate the bass part you play. The bass player's role is to come up with the best possible bass line for a song. Sometimes that could be the simplest thing you can think of. Sometimes you want to play *less* than the simplest thing you can think of!

You can, as I've mentioned often in this book, be the fastest and flashiest bass guitar player that has ever lived. That won't matter to anyone but you if you don't have the ability to play an *appropriate* bass line for a song.

Amongst themselves, most musicians prefer feeling to dazzling technique. And this is not to knock technique and tell you *not* to practice scales, arpeggios, and the like. Good technique gives you the words to express your feelings in music. The better your technique, the more easily you'll be able to express your ideas and creativity. But sometimes, in music as well as in writing, the right single word or sentence can say something better and more articulately than an unwieldy, although well-written, paragraph.

And that brings me to this final thought—be yourself. Don't worry about being the next Jaco Pastorius or James Jamerson or John Entwistle or whomever. Being yourself will bring your ideas into your playing, and will put your emotions into music that others will hear.

Don't forget that you are constantly evolving. Learn as much as you can and from every source you can think of and incorporate what you like into your style. Practice and work on your technique so that you can say exactly what you want to say with your bass.

And above all, have fun and enjoy yourself. Playing brings you joy (and it should always do so!) and nothing communicates itself so quickly to your audience as the happiness you find when playing your bass guitar, even if that audience is only you! Spread the joy of music with each note you play on your bass guitar.

Play well!

Appendix A

Guide to *The Complete Idiot's Guide® to Playing Bass Guitar* CD

26:   14.5 (0:00)
      14.6 (0:15)
      14.7 (0:30)

27:   14.8

28:   14.9 (0:00)
      14.10 (0:11)

29:   14.11 (0:00)
      14.12 (0:23)

30:   15.12

31:   16.1 (jam-along song)

32:   16.2 (0:00)
      16.5 (0:13)
      16.6 (0:36)
      16.7 (0:48)

33:   16.8 (jam-along song)

34:   16.9 (0:00)
      16.11 (0:15)

35:   16.12 (jam-along song)

36:   16.13

37:   17.3 (0:00)
      17.4 (0:09)
      17.5 (0:20)
      17.7 (0:27)
      17.9 (0:34)
      17.10 (0:41)
      17.11 (0:50)
      17.12 (0:57)
      17.14 (1:08)

38:   17.16 (0:00)
      17.17 (0:16)
      17.18 (0:26)
      17.19 (0:32)
      17.20 (0:41)

39:   17.21 (0:00)
      17.23 (0:15)
      17.24 (0:29)
      17.25 (0:40)
      17.26 (0:51)

40:   19.1 (0:00)
      19.2 (0:49)

41:   19.3 (0:00)
      19.4 (1:05)

42:   19.5 (0:00)
      19.6 (0:56)

43:   20.2 (0:00)
      20.3 (0:15)
      20.4 (0:29)

44:   20.5 (jam-along song)

45:   20.6

46:   20.7 (jam-along song)

47:   20.8 (0:00)
      20.9 (0:12)

48:   20.10 (jam-along song)

49:   21.1 (0:00)
      21.7 (0:20)
      21.8 (0:28)
      21.9 (0:41)
      21.12 (0:56)

50:   22.1 (0:00)
      22.2 (0:16)
      22.3 (0:30)

51:   22.4 (0:00)
      22.5 (0:16)
      22.6 (0:30)
      22.7 (0:47)
      22.8 (1:02)

52:   22.9 (0:00)
      22.10 (0:15)

53:   22.11 (old rock style jam-along song)

54:   22.12 (hard rock style jam-along song)

55:   23.1 (0:00)
      23.2 (0:18)
      23.4 (0:29)

56:   23.11

57:   23.12 (Fast blues style jam-along song)

58:   23.13 (Slow blues style jam-along song)

59:   24.1 (0:00)
      24.2 (0:23)
      24.3 (0:47)
      22.4 (1:03)

60:   24.5 (0:00)
      24.6 (0:18)
      24.7 (0:31)
      24.8 (0:51)

61:   24.9 (Country style jam-along song)

62:   24.10 (Motown-inspired pop style jam-along song)

63:   25.1 (0:00)
      25.2 (0:14)
      25.3 (0:31)

64:   25.4 (0:00)
      25.5 (0:29)

65:   25.6

66:   25.7 (0:00)
      25.8 (0:21)

67:   25.9 (Bossa nova style jam-along song)

68:   25.10 (Afro-Cuban style jam-along song)

69:   26.1 (0:00)
      26.2 (0:11)
      26.3 (0:47)

70:   26.4 (0:00)
      26.5 (0:24)

71:   26.6 (0:00)
      26.7 (0:16)

72:   26.8 (Funk style jam-along song)

73:   26.9 (Reggae style jam-along song)

74:   26.10 (West African style jam-along song)

Glossary

accent Applying extra stress to a note, usually by striking it harder with a finger of the right hand.

accidental A sharp sign, flat sign, or natural sign.

anticipation Arriving at your target note or chord before the beat, usually coming in a half a beat earlier.

arpeggio A chord played one note at a time, usually in an ascending or descending order.

articulation How a note is played—crisply, long, short, slurred, etc.

augmented chord One of the four basic chord types, made up of the root, major third, and augmented fifth degrees of the major scale.

bar Also called a measure; a distinct measurement of beats, which is dictated by the time signature; the end of a bar is indicated by a vertical line running through the staff or bass guitar tablature lines.

bass clef Also called an F clef; a symbol at the far left of the music staff, indicating that the F note is on the second line from the top.

chord Three or more different notes played together at the same time.

chord progression A sequence of chords played in a song or in a phrase of a song.

chromatic notes Notes taken from outside of a given major scale; *see* "diatonic."

chromatic scale A scale made up of all 12 possible notes, each one a half step from the other.

Circle of Fifths A pattern that can be used to study the relationship of keys to one another; also an excellent tool for practicing bass lines in all keys.

common time The symbol "C" used as a time signature; another name for 4/4 time.

diatonic The notes used in a given major scale or the chords derived from the triads of that scale.

diminished chord One of the four basic chord types, made up of the root, minor third, and diminished fifth degrees of the major scale.

dotted note   A dot added to a note in order to give it more length; a dotted half note is three beats long; a dotted quarter note is one-and-a-half beats long, etc.

dynamics   Changes in volume or tempo while playing.

eighth note   A note of a half a beat's duration.

eighth-note rest   A rest of a half a beat's duration.

flat   An accidental sign indicating lowering a note a half step.

grace note   A note played and then quickly changed to another note within the shortest time possible.

half note   A note of two beats' duration.

half-note rest   A rest of two beats' duration.

half step   The difference, between two notes, of one fret of the bass guitar.

hammer-on   A left-hand slurring technique in which a second note is sounded by the addition of a finger tap on a string that has already been struck with the right hand.

harmonics   Clear, bell-like tones produced at various points along the fingerboard of the bass guitar.

harmony   Two or more notes played simultaneously.

interval   The distance, in terms of steps and half steps, of one note from another.

inversion   The arrangement of a chord with a note other than the root in the lowest position.

key   The tonal center of a piece of music.

key signature   The number of flats or sharps (if any) used in a song, which indicates the key the song is in.

ledger lines   Lines above or below the staff on which notes may be placed; the E note of the open E string is located on the first ledger line below the staff of the bass clef.

major chord   One of the four basic chord types, made up of the root, major third, and perfect fifth degrees of the major scale.

major scale   The basic building block of music theory, the major scale begins on any note and uses the following sequence:

> root, whole step, whole step, half step, whole step, whole step, whole step, half step (the root again)

measure   Also called a bar; a distinct measurement of beats, which is dictated by the time signature; the end of a measure is indicated by a vertical line running through the staff or bass guitar tablature lines.

metronome   A device used to audibly count out the tempo of music.

minor chord   One of the four basic chord types, made up of the root, minor third, and perfect fifth degrees of the major scale.

modes A scale created by taking a major scale and beginning on a note other than the root and going through the steps of the scale until reaching the starting note again. There are seven modes: Ionian, Dorian, Phrygian, Lydian, Mixolydian, Aeolian, and Locrian.

music notation A system for reading music using a staff and notes placed upon it; the location of the note on the staff determines its name and the type of note indicates its duration.

natural sign An accidental sign indicating a note should be played with neither flats nor sharps.

note A musical tone of a specific pitch.

octave An interval of eight named notes from the root note, always bearing the same name as the root note.

open string A string played without a finger of the left hand fretting it.

pick Also called plectrum; a hard, flat piece of material (usually plastic) used to strike the strings instead of a finger of the right hand.

popping A right-hand technique of sounding the notes by pulling the string away with a finger and then letting it go.

pull-off A left-hand slurring technique in which a second note is sounded by the removal of a finger from a string that has already been struck.

quarter note A note of one beat's duration.

quarter-note rest A rest of one beat's duration.

riff A short musical phrase, often repeated during the course of a song.

root note The note named by a chord; C is the root note of a C major chord.

sharp An accidental sign indicating raising a note a half step.

shuffle A rhythm using the first and third of a set of triplets, commonly used in blues, jazz, and swing styles.

sixteenth note A note of one quarter of a beat's duration.

sixteenth-note rest A rest of one quarter of a beat's duration.

slapping A right-hand technique of sounding notes using the side of the thumb to create the note.

slide A left-hand slurring technique involving sliding a finger from one fret to another.

slur Using a left-hand technique to articulate a note or series of notes.

staff A set of five lines used in music notation to indicate note names.

standard tuning How the strings of a bass guitar are usually tuned; from low to high: E, A, D, G.

step The difference between two notes of two frets of the bass guitar.

syncopation The stressing of the off beat in various types of music.

tablature A system of reading music involving horizontal lines (indicating the strings of the bass guitar) and numbers (indicating which frets to play in order to sound the notes).

tapping   A technique of sounding the strings by solidly tapping the fingertips of either hand directly onto the string on any fret.

tempo   The speed of a song, usually indicated in BPM (beats per measure).

tie   A line connecting two notes of the same pitch, adding the time value of the second note to the first; a whole note tied to a half note will last for six beats.

time signature   Usually indicated by a fraction at the start of a piece of music, the time signature will tell you how many beats each measure receives (the upper number of the fraction) and which type of note is designated as a single beat (the lower number).

transposing   Changing the notes (and chords) of a song from one key to another.

trill   A left-hand technique involving a rapid change from one note to the next higher (or lower) note.

triplet   A note of a third of a beat's duration.

turnaround   A quick chord progression at the end of a song to prepare the listener for a second verse; usually ends on the V chord.

12-bar blues   A standard blues song format involving specific chord changes over the course of 12 measures.

vibrato   A left-hand technique which adds a quavering quality to a note; usually used with notes of longer duration.

whole note   A note of four beats' duration.

whole-note rest   A rest of four beats' duration.

Warm-Ups and Other Exercises

These examples are to help you work out the fingers of your right hand. Try to strike the string with the finger indicated in the exercise: "i" is the index finger of your right hand and "m" is the middle finger.

Here are some exercises to help you warm up your left hand. They will also help you to develop strength and dexterity in the fingers of your left hand. Try to use the fingers that are noted in the examples: "1" is the index finger, "2" is the middle finger, "3" is the ring finger, and "4" is the pinky.

The following examples are to help you as you learn to read rhythms. Count them out loud if it helps. Many pros do!

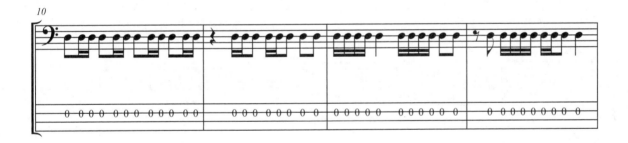

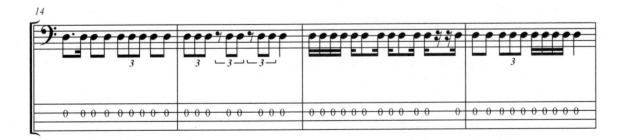

Exercises can help the mind as well as the fingers. The following example is
designed to have you work out the diatonic chord arpeggios of any given major
scale. Cycling this exercise through the Circle of Fifths will walk you through
all possible major and minor arpeggios:

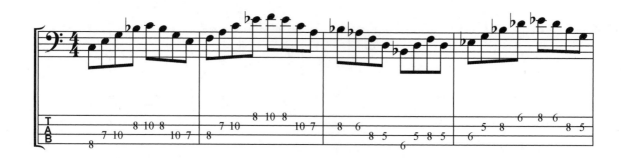

You can create exercises specifically tailored to your needs as a bass player. Be sure to write them down and then to work them through all 12 keys, using the Circle of Fifths as you did in Chapter 18.

Appendix D

For Further Study

There are, literally, hundreds upon hundreds of tutorial books, videos, CDs, DVDs, and more for bass guitarists of all levels. There are also a great number of bass guitar tutorial websites on the Internet. In addition, more and more "note for note" bass guitar transcriptions of all kinds of music are being written.

If you are serious about improving as a bassist, then you should make use of any material you can get your hands on!

And that should also include thinking about getting a teacher for personal instruction.

Don't fall into the trap of preferring one learning source to another. Each one has its strengths and each one has definite shortcomings. But most important of all, each one can teach you something!

And don't forget that many books on general music topics apply directly to the bass guitarist. For example, if you'd like to get better at understanding music theory, you might want to start with *The Complete Idiot's Guide® to Music Theory*, by Michael Miller (Alpha Books, 2002).

If you're more of a scholarly type, then *Harmony*, by Walter Piston (W. W. Norton & Company, Fifth Edition, 1987), might be for you.

Michael Miller has also written a terrific book to help beginners get started on soloing: *The Complete Idiot's Guide® to Solos and Improvisation* (Alpha Books, 2004).

If you'd like to learn more about certain bass players, then you might want to get hold of books such as *Standing in the Shadows of Motown—The Life and Music of Legendary Bassist James Jamerson*, by Dr. Licks (Hal Leonard, 1989), or *Bass Heroes: Styles, Stories & Secrets from 30 Great Bass Players, from the pages of Guitar Player Magazine*, by Tom Mulhern (editor) (Backbeat Books, 1993).

To find out more about the fascinating history of the electric bass guitar, try *How the Fender Bass Changed the World*, by Jim Roberts (Backbeat Books, 2001), and *The Bass Book: A Complete Illustrated History of Bass Guitars*, by Tony Bacon and Barry Moorhouse (Backbeat Books, 1995).

Finally, even though it's not specifically aimed at the bass guitar, Dan Erlewine has written a terrific book that walks step by step through most electric guitar repairs and maintenance: *How to Make Your Electric Guitar Play Great* (Backbeat Books, 2001).

Index

Discover the keys to making great music with these top-selling Idiot's Guides®!

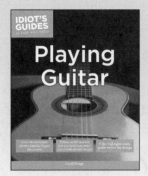

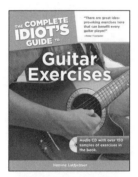
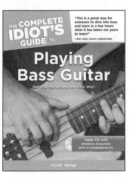

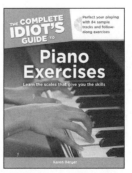
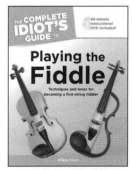